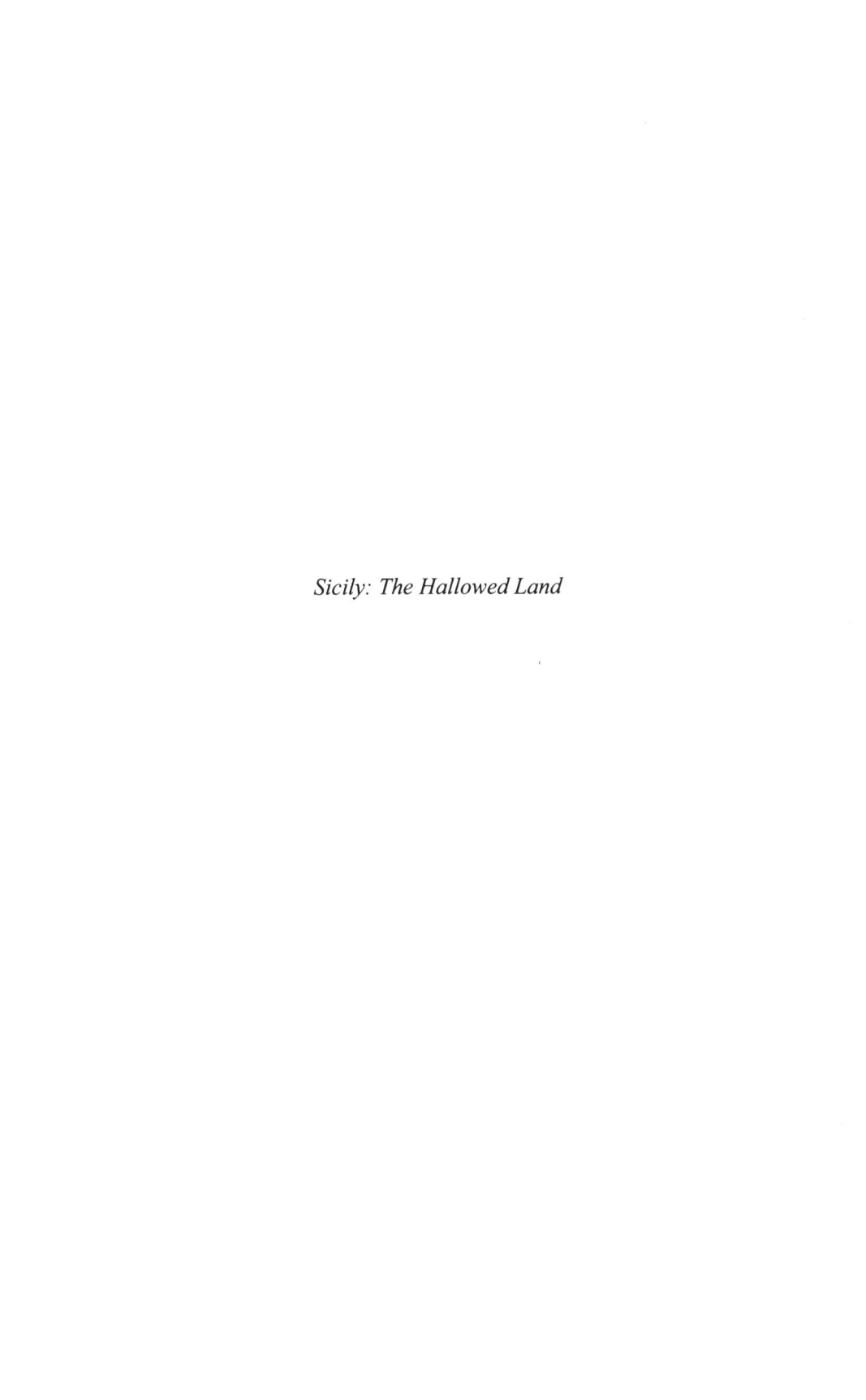

Sicily: The Hallowed Land

Legas

Sicilian Studies

Volume V

Series Editor: Gaetano Cipolla

Printed and bound in Canada

Other volumes in this series:

1. Giuseppe Quatriglio, *A Thousand Years in Sicily: from the Arabs to the Bourbons*, 1992, 1997;
2. Henry Barbera, *Medieval Sicily: the First Absolute State*, 1994;
3. Connie Mandracchia DeCaro, *Sicily, the Trampled Paradise, Revisited*, 1998;
4. Justin Vitiello, *Labyrinths and Volcanoes: Windings Through Sicily*, 1999.

Ben Morreale

SICILY:

The Hallowed Land

A Memoir

LEGAS

© Copyright Legas 2000

No part of this book may be translated or reproduced in any form, by print, photoprint, microfilm, microfiche, or any other means, without the written permission from the copyright holder.

Library of Congress Cataloging-in-Publication Data

Morreale, Ben.

Sicily, the hallowed land: a memoir/ Ben Morreale.

  p. cm.-- (Sicilian studies ; v. 5)

Includes bibliographical references.

ISBN 1-881901-23-8

  1. Sicily (Italy)-- Social life and customs. 2. Morreale, Ben--Homes and haunts--Italy--Sicily. I. Title. II. Series.

DG865.6 .M68 2000

00-023950

Printed and bound in Canada

Acknowledgments

The publisher wishes to gratefully acknowledge the receipt of a generous grant from Arba Sicula that made it possible, in part, to publish this book.

We are also grateful to Carlo Puleo for the use of his painting "Siciliani DOC" for the cover. Carlo Puleo, *La Pittura*, Palermo, Ila Palma, 1999.

For information and for orders, write to:
Legas

P.O. Box 040328	68 Kamloops Ave	2908 Dufferin Ave
Brooklyn, New York	Ottawa, Ontario	Toronto, Ontario
11204, USA	K1N 8T9 Canada	M6B 3S8 Canada

To
My beloved
Carol Wilkerson
Pace e amore

Table of Contents

METHOD AS PROLOGUE · 9

POINT OF DEPARTURE · 17

THE TIME OF THE GREEN MICE · 33

DON BALDASSARE · 55

TIME AS A GENTLEMAN IN THE MIDDLE OF THE HERD · · · · 71

LU RABBI SCHWARTZ · 93

MALANNI · 129

RETURN TO SICILY: THE FASCIST PARENTHESIS · · · · · · · · · · · 141

HARD TIMES · 157

THE WARS · 173

ENDINGS · 189

AVA GARDNER'S BROTHER-IN-LAW · · · · · · · · · · · · · · · · · · · 203

METHOD AS PROLOGUE

I've spent a good part of my life as a participant among Sicilians. I participated in such things as my own birth on Christie Street, where Roosevelt Park now stands on New York's Lower East Side, of a mother and father both born in Racalmuto, Sicily. Although I was not a participant-observer in the meeting between my parents, I was told, in later informal interviews, that they were brought together on Stanton Street, called "Stantoni" by the *Racalmutisi* of that generation. They had not known each other in Racalmuto although their families lived only a few *vaneddri* away; my father in a two-story house (a sign of some wealth) near *La Baruna* (a sign of considerable poverty), and my mother in the Via Cavour, also in a two-story house.

From the beginning I participated in Sicilian church affairs such as baptisms, confirmations, marriages, funerals and Sunday school run by Irish priests. I participated in and observed the social activities on the roof tops of the Lower East Side that smelled of asphalt and coal dust, where I flew kites and later observed the older people of my generation being assimilated through music. They were models for me. I interviewed hundreds of Sicilians and Southern Italians in those tenements, especially the young girls who took care of me while my mother went to work sewing spangles and sequins on the fashionable dresses of those times. These young girls lovingly fondled me as they learned to be mothers. The taught me my first words of English from comic books of the times. In this time too, I was a participant of the role of the older women: Sicilian, Baresi, Calabresi. In the countless interviews by the large black coal stove I learned of the good-natured warmth of those old women. Even as a child I asked, "Don't you think it is immoral to give so much love and affection to the first born male?" They looked at me with eyes suddenly gone dull, like some animal trying hard to understand, but finally giving up the effort. And I knew that in that question there appeared the first spores of change, of a conflict of values, of culture. One old woman whom here I shall call Comare Rosalia, simply threw me up in the air when I asked the question, then hugged me, saying, "My little *Americanu*, my water-washed *Americanu*." I was fair-haired and light skinned then. "When you grow up you'll have a big Cadillac with one of those horns that sounds like the pipes of Pan." I continued interviews in the halls of that tenement everyone called, with a sense of Sicilian irony, *Lu Vaticanu*— The Vatican. I asked Don Cali, a much respected man from Canicattì, "Why do you call it the Vatican?"

"Because it is like that."

"Who called it that first?" I asked.

"Who knows. That's the way it's called. It was always called *Lu Vaticanu*."

I asked the older males of my generation what music they liked and they let me listen when they had their social activities in the front room of the railroad flats to Paul Whiteman, King Oliver, and Lillian Hardin records, records that were like floppy disks.

I made enquiries, even then, to interview criminals, perhaps even to participate in some of their activities, formally or informally. I could not find any, not a mafia fellow, or black-hander or even a Neapolitan *camurrista*, as "wise guys" were called then.

At the age of five I had the opportunity, funded by my maternal grandmother in Racalmuto, to go to Sicily for the first time. If I had known then, I would have gone to interview Charlotte Cower Chapman who was doing field work for her good book on Milocca just few miles from Racalmuto and which we often visited. For all I know she may have interviewed me. Instead I contented myself with being a participant-observer at reunions of returned Sicilians and those who had stayed behind. My informants were priests, old women, men, a grandfather who had stayed behind, *na serva* (a servant), *nu arzuni* (a boy indentured servant), *na criata* (a word which I was to discover in later research came from the Spanish and meant a house maid), and finally a boy with the nickname Bacaredra (Little Bucket) who was to become a good friend.

After a year and half, I returned to America, so immersed in my work that I no longer could speak English. This was to be only a preliminary study, however. My more exciting research did not begin until the age of twelve or so when I returned to Sicily. This trip was sponsored in part by the great depression and again by my grandmother. I was to stay for almost two years. Before leaving, my fifth grade teacher, Miss Borger, was a great help to me. When she heard I was going to Sicily to do research, she counseled me to keep a journal. "Memory is a fragile thing," she said. She was a loving older woman who always wore a hammer and sickle stickpin on her blouse and she reminded be of Comare Rosalia. I took her advice to heart. I kept an accurate and meticulous journal of the Christmas pageants, the festival of the Lady of the Mount, the sexual activity and talk of the *carusi* (boys) in the streets the courts where so many injustices were committed, the theater, the gossip of women in the streets, the talk of men as they took the evening air in the *chiazza* (the *piazza*). I also participated in and observed the Balilla movement. I wore a black shirt and a cap with a tassel and marched with a wooden gun. With the help of my father I continued my interviews with the men in the *chiazza*. I attended the local school where Leonardo Sciascia was only two years ahead of me. I did not have the good sense to interview him then. I participated in and observed the sulphur mines, interviewing miners and owners. I observed the subtle gestures and talk in the Gentlemen's Club.

I was a participant-observer in my own confirmation. My Godfather was a seminarian then from Agrigento who later became one of the most cunning priests in the region.

In all, I spent almost two years in Sicily then and returned when I discovered, through an informal and hurried interview with my father, that he was about to be drafted into the Italian Army. We all returned to America—Brooklyn really—an opportune place to continue my studies of the process of assimilation. Once again I could not speak a word of English. Whenever I shouted up from the streets to my mother, "*Iettami 'nu sordu*" — "Throw me down a penny." I discovered through informal interviews with my colleague-informants in the streets that they did not like my manner of speaking. They responded to my questions with blows or by grabbing my hat and running off with it. This provoked many disturbing confrontations which gave me profound insights to acculturation if not assimilation. I re-learned English very quickly this way. I must add, too, with the help of Miss Cooke, the vice-principal of the Junior High I was enrolled in then. When I arrived for registration, she had the good sense after just one look at my birth certificate which gave my name as Baldassare De Marco Morreale, to say, "We'll call him Benny Moreli." This was a giant step in both acculturation and assimilation and I noted it down. It was a short interview, although formal indeed, but valuable.

The rest of my research was tedious and mundane. High School among ethnics. When the War broke out my acculturation had become so intense I volunteered for the Army Air Force Cadet training. After a month in pilot training I was interviewed by an officer from the Adjutant's office who called me in and asked all sorts of questions. He asked me how my father felt about Mussolini, how I felt about him, how long I had spent in Italy.

"Not long," I said. "Maybe a week in Rome."

"Our records show you were there for two extended stays, both rather long."

"That was not Italy," I said, "that was Sicily." He looked at me sternly as if to let me know he was no fool. The interview was over and within a week, I, and a number of German-American ethnics who had spent time in Germany as boys, were on a boat to New Guinea. My research lapsed for three years, although the stay in the South Pacific did wonders for my understanding of my process of assimilation. I learned folk songs from Mississippi, legends of North Carolina, and the accents and gestures of Texas and Virginia.

It wasn't until some time after the war, while doing research in Paris on other matters, that I returned to Racalmuto and Sicily.

In the seven years I spent in Paris I often returned to Sicily; every year, to be exact, and in all seasons. I picked up my interviews again with informants I had known years ago.

I frequently asked Raffaeli, a man who had Sicily in his bones, "Why do I return to Sicily so often." And he, in that Sicilian mocking way which seemed to mock all authority but his own, said, "Eeh. Because you have spent a good part of your life here." I continued my interviews with men and women now grown older, with priests, and with workers going to Belgium and Germany, and recorded such conversations as this.

"Where are you going, Totò?"

"*Alla Germania.* To Germany."

"Where in Germany?"

"Who knows. There is one from the next street there now, and he says there is work. I'm going to Germany."

Raffaeli bitterly remarked, "We're exporting our greatest commodity—human meat."

Out of these interviews I wrote a short story which appeared in *The Paris Review* and then a number of novels, one of which a reviewer called "more Anthropology than a novel". This gave me a new stature as a participant-observer and put me in touch with the Sicilian opera singer, Luigi Infantino, who also came from Racalmuto, and with Leonardo Sciascia whom I often interviewed informally while walking in the *chiazza*.

It was the opera singer who later made it possible for me to interview the artist Guttuso over a bottle of scotch and listen to him sing Sicilian folk songs.

These men gave me insights to the meaning of being Sicilian that were invaluable. They seemed to be the truth.

I often returned to those streets in Brooklyn and around Stanton Street carrying my old notebooks to interview those once-alert optimistic men and women now grown old, and recorded more than one who told me, "There is nothing in this world and even less in America." In these interviews they talked about their children and their grandchildren, some of Irish-Sicilian descent, or Jewish-Sicilian. Some attended the State University where I've been an observer-participant in other matters for over 15 years. I was often good-humoredly surprised to hear one Kevin Kelly or Mellissa Puma come out with a phrase such as *amuninni a zappari* (let's go to work), learned, they told me, not from their Sicilian mothers but from their Sicilian grandmothers. These were informal interviews which I've filed away over the years. Most of the informants were third generation Sicilian-Americans who indicated an awareness of being Sicilian, perhaps even a little pride, but hardly any of the sense of inferiority so prevalent among second generation Sicilian-Americans who often attempted to excuse their origins by claiming "my mother was Irish." Some now with Irish names admit to Sicilian mothers, not without some good-natured affection.

My participation in Sicilian life and civilization has taught me to mock all authority but my own. My participation in American life has tempered that and has taught me to mock my own authority. For this reason I hesitate using the first person singular, then too the I has distorted most writings on emigration, making them akin in sentimentality to Country Music or bad poetry, which might be another way of saying that it speaks about a personal wound rather than the subject at hand. Yet the first person seems the most direct way of remembering a feeling as intimate as identity change, which after all, is the nature of immigration.

"A civilization cannot simply transplant itself, bag and baggage," wrote Ferdinand Braudel. "By crossing a frontier, the individual becomes a foreigner. He betrays his own civilization by leaving it behind."

Finally, as they say, a word about that part of Sicily where I did my research. Brooklyn needs no introduction.

The province of Agrigento, wedged in the south-central edge of the Island of Sicily has a continuous literary tradition from Empedocles to the present day; more to the point, to the time when families began to think about coming to America. Pirandello was from Agrigento, Leonardo Sciascia from Racalmuto, and Chapman wrote about Milocca. There is this literary tradition and the European success of men such as Sciascia (who is still called "Nardu" in the town of Racalmuto) as well as the great competitive sense (some call it *invidia*) which has turned many others, if not into men of letters, then certainly into writers who have published memoirs and histories of the region.

Racalmuto, just 40 kilometers up in the hills from the sea, is a town of 10,000 or so. It had its own publishing house in the late 19th century and its own men of letters. Pietro Mantia (1870-1933), an anthropologist, member of the Roman Anthropological Society, wrote and published on various subjects. His works were translated into French and German. There were also pioneer Socialists who came from these towns—Racalmuto and Grotte—and left us their impression and records of how people managed to live with one another and why towards the end of the 19th century, a good portion of them decided to take part in a mass migration.

So in time, this work covers a period roughly from 1870 to 1970 and in the lives of a people, three generations, from the province of Agrigento in Sicily which once was so rich and fertile that the ancient Greek geographer Strabo, called it "the hollow land."

POINT OF DEPARTURE

As late as the 1920's the first time I saw the town of Racalmuto in Sicily, Raffaeli, like most of the towns people still had the habit in summer of going out to his *aria*—an airy place in the countryside. His *aria* was a bare stone house surrounded by plum and peach trees, a cluster of almond and walnut trees, a fig tree by a patch of melon vines and all around a sea of wheat fields in which, here and there groups of olive trees rose like grey puffs of smoke in the blazing sun.

Summers were ferociously hot and the earth so dry it would crack wide open and the fields became a danger to the horses, mules and donkeys crossing them. Automobiles were still a great rarity then and when one appeared children would chase after it.

Most everyone left the town in summer, whether as an owner of a small *aria*, as a field worker, as a servant, as a tree surgeon or an invited friend. On those summer nights one would sit in front of the stone house and watch the light fade and the world shrink, as Giovanni Verga so vividly described in *I Malavoglia*, that to see it for oneself is to know he wrote the truth. Now the road to Rocca Russa was gone, then the scarred hillside of the Gibellini sulphur mines disappeared, and when it was totally dark only those strident voices used to living in the open were left. After a while one could see the lights of other towns. The voices would say, "That's Favara."

"Those are the lights of Montedoro."

"And there's Agrigento."

"Canicattì."

"No, it can't be. That's Milocca."

"There are no lights in Milocca."

"It's Grotte."

Raffaeli then pointed to the circle of lights close by and said, "That's our town, there, Racalmuto. You can be sure of that."

Raffaeli who taught me so much about Sicily was a man of average height, with tight curly hair who smoked so much his fingers were stained a caramel brown. He had traveled much, working as a waiter in Tunis and in Rome as a tailor. He had been, for a brief time, a policeman in Venice, but he always returned to Racalmuto where he maintained a tailor shop which was the intellectual center of the town. He spoke French with a marked Italian accent that he was hardly aware he was speaking Italian with a French accent. He was well read and he loved to recite poetry, especially in Roman Dialect to those who gathered in his shop. He was orphaned at an early age and the rest of his family— sisters and brothers, cousins and aunts, all had gone to America by 1914. He remained to take care of the bit of land left to the family— The Don Baldassare family. The hope was that at least some would come back. Often I asked why he had not gone also, he said, "Eeh. Life got in the way. I married, the family began. Things turned sour in America. More people were coming back than going. And I got to like to sit *all'aria* at Rocca Russa and watch the lights of the towns come on."

Whenever I returned to Racalmuto his tailor shop was the first place I visited. And Raffaeli would greet me with, "Hey, at least did you make love in the Forum in Rome?" No matter what I answered he would say, "You should, you know. By moonlight, by the light of the moon."

Those who came to America in the late 19th century and the early 20th identified, not so much with the area encompassed by the sight of the church tower, but with the lights they could see on the horizon on summer nights. These were the towns they were involved with economically and socially.

Agrigento, or Girgenti as it was known then, was the center of power: here were the courts, here too, were the outlets for agricultural produce and sulphur. Raffaeli told me in his mocking professorial tone that seemed to mock all authority but his own, "Agrigento was a peaceful city then to which came peasants and miners from Grotte and Racalmuto with their faces dry and red as clay, eyes like wolves, dressed in their blue cloth of Sunday best and those bonnets that seemed to have come out of the great revolution in France. And they walked in the streets with such names as Via Atenea, Rupe Atenea and Empedocles, ancient names of light that makes even sadder the misery and ugliness of today." And Raffaeli ended with, "These are not my words, but the words of Pirandello."

There were sadder towns. Milocca, just north of Racalmuto, of which Charlotte Chapman wrote so intelligently, is a curious town, a village really. In 1901 there were 39 inhabitants in the center of town, the others lived in scattered settlements. Although a road was built in 1929, in the time of the great emigration every thing was brought to Milocca by mule and if a piano or a diesel engine was needed in Milocca, they were brought across country on sledges drawn by bullocks winding about in their effort to find the most level and least hazardous path.

For some reason the village acquired the reputation of a hick town. A real fool or blunderer was always greeted with, "Eeh, where are you from, Milocca?" Or if one were dressed inelegantly or in an old-fashioned way, he was accused of having just arrived from Milocca.

In 1928 the town had reputation of backwardness, forgotten by God and man.

The railroads in the 1920s never reached this village and in recent times one had to go to Milocca on foot. To those immigrants of the turn of the century who returned, their nostalgia, if they ever had any, quickly disappeared.

There was great traffic between these towns then. Mule-drawn carts, the great legends of Saracen and Norman battles painted on their side boards barely visible under the sulphur dust, went from Racalmuto to Favara and Agrigento. Donkey drivers with leather vests and long poles, at times in groups of two or three, herded long lines of donkeys, each loaded with 225 pounds of sulphur stumbled blindly under the weight and blows of the drivers' poles. The sulphur carts and donkey trains headed for Port Empedocles, Girgenti's port where freighters waited to take Girgentian sulphur all over the world. This was before Texas sulphur sucked out of the earth, (as the local miners said) destroyed the Sicilian sulphur industry.

Of those who came from the Province of Agrigento did not consider themselves Sicilian, let alone Italian; that was to come later when new relationships in a broader world gave them different identities or character— a character bestowed by others, really. For the moment, they were *Racalmutisi*, they were from Girgenti, from Milocca or from Favara. Each town gave a person characteristics.

Not all would agree but Raffaeli often said, In Racalmuto all are either *furbi o pazzi*—cunning or crazy. In Milocca, backward, good natured simpletons.

Favara was a town of *malandrini*—tough guys, but then it was founded as a penal colony. Grotte was a poor small town with a socialist and Protestant tradition where those in Racalmuto who wanted take a long walk would go. In the Socialist upheavals of 1893-4 many took this walk. As Raffaeli said, Pirandello was not Sicilian, he was a man from Agrigento.

But then travel was hazardous and left the towns and villages with an incest of the mind. Only aristocrats could afford to travel for pleasure in their *carrozzi* drawn by high spirited almost frail horses. These same horses of Sicily were winners of Olympic and Pythian crowns for the lords of Syracuse and ancient Akragas (Agrigento) who enjoyed a renown which Athenian dramatists ventured to carry back to the mythic ages of Greece. These horses were remembered by a group of *Racalmutisi* in Hamilton, Ontario, who tried to import them to race in North America. Nothing ever came of it. In the 1950's one could still see these auburn colored horses with large open nostrils, half starved, their ribs showing, stamping the wheat before winnowing— a man, kerchief on his head, gently leading on, round and round and singing to it, "wind, wind, Saint Anthony, for tomorrow we'll be winnowing." The horse lifted its tail to drop a load of manure in the midst of the grain it trampled and the man sang in the plaintive Arabic chant that so often echoes in the hills, "Oh, tell me where you found those beautiful grains of oats."

The mule had always been the great means of transportation, moving across roads which were at best rough, at worst impossible. Mules, until the coming of the automobile, were the trucks and cars of the times. In the evenings they hauled sulphur from the mines, brought wheat from fields in large cane-woven baskets set on either side for balance. In the mornings the mules returned to the fields with children in the empty baskets and women riding behind the men.

The donkey though was the symbol of Sicily. The animal is still intermingled with the island's legends, suffering and humor. Man first appeared in Sicily 20,000 years ago, Raffaeli tells me, contemporaneously with *Equus hydruntinus*, that is, the donkey.

Sceccu, the word for donkey in Sicilian, might be of Turkish origin, some feel. Others explain it by telling this story.

The Saracens, when they first conquered the island, much as the English decreed in Ireland, decreed that Sicilians could neither bear arms or ride horses. In response, the islanders poisoned all the wells and water holes with the cry of neither them nor us. When all the horses had died, the Arabs were forced to bring animals from their own land. But a storm sank all the ships except those carrying a load of donkeys. Up until then Sicilians had always called the animal by its Latin name, *amino*. Now, however, they named it *sceccu* or sheik, after their new rulers.

Children were taught the alphabet in the time of great migration with the rhyme:

"A-E-I-O-U e sceccu ca si tu."

A-E-I-O-U and the donkey that are you. The donkey is present in all the stories told in the towns around Racalmuto. Some are wise, others are fools. One donkey who was wise beyond necessity was once loaded with salt. As he crossed a wide river he noticed that his load became lighter and lighter until it had completely disappeared. The clever donkey tried the same with a load of sponges and drowned. Some said this particular jackass was from Racalmuto.

The donkey is often cunning. If I ever brought a bottle of wine to Raffaeli and drank most of it myself he was sure to remind, "Eeh the jackass brought it and the jackass is drinking it."

Raffaeli, over the years held many political positions in the town of Racalmuto; councilman, assessor of taxes, counselor to mayors. He had good word for every one, the farmer coming home from the fields, to the elected officials whom he mockingly addressed in the old manner, "Kiss your hand my Lord." often told him, Raffaeli, if you had gone to America you have become at least the mayor of Philadelphia." Without looking up from his work he answered, "at least."

Raffaeli though, made his living as a tailor. His shop on a narrow street just behind the *chiazza* was the intellectual center of the town. If, while he was cutting out a pattern, a cigarette dangling from his mouth, someone would mention Jackass, Raffaeli would stop his work and tell you the story of the Donkey of St. Giuseppi. It's the story of a happy Jackass who is passed from one exploiting master to another until he ends up with an impoverished woman with a sick child. On the way to market the donkey drops dead and is sold along with its load for five *tarì*. The buyer sealed the sale and gave a kick to the carcass which sounded like a broken drum.

I often stayed with Raffaeli whenever I visited Racalmuto. One day we went to visit a piece of land which belonged to Raffaeli's family all of whom had gone to America. It was a rich piece of land, watered by underground springs. There pistachio trees, vineyards, almonds and a huge fertile fig tree by a small stone hut which Raffaeli had given to a family whose young son had been crippled in a mine accident. The husband had been out of work for a year. In exchange, the family guarded the land, as Raffaeli said, from people who felt that the fruits belonged to everyone just because a public road passed through it.

The dog, dragging its hind legs along the ground, started barking as soon as we appeared. The young son, sitting on a chair, two clubs by his side as crutches, was about 18 or 19, a broad shouldered, big handsome young man. His legs were paralyzed. A woman who had just arrived with an older man, her father, was crying desperately at the doorless entrance of the stone hut. When she saw us she stopped crying. The dog kept barking and barking. Raffaeli explained to me that the week before the husband had taken a knife and had gone shouting through the *chiazza* that he was going to kill the Virgin Mary. It had taken three carabinieri to subdue him. The wife had just returned from trying to see him at the insane asylum. She had been refused. The dog kept barking; the boy shouted to it to stop.

Raffaeli asked what had happened to the dog. The boy explained over the barking of the dog; he was run over by the car of John T. He's a good dog, a watch dog, he keeps me company and those *figghi di buttana*— those sons of bitches, they didn't even stop. If it weren't for these legs of mine, I'd have pulled him and his partner out of the car and cut their throats.

The dog barked insistently and we had to strain to hear the boy.

"Stop it! Stop it!" The boy shouted. "Come here!" The dog stopped barking and dragged itself toward the boy. As soon as it was within reach, the boy gave it a blow sending it on its back. The dog howled in pain. The boy dropped his clubs, picked the dog up and cradled it in his arms, swaying back and forth saying, *C'ama fari? C'ama fari?* —What are we to do? What are we to do?

We drove back in silence.

In the countryside before the war, there was always the voice of some one singing in that Arabic chant-like lament, or the braying of a jackass.

It took an hour or two to get to one's fields in the Rocca Russa or The Saracen section. The trip, except in the summer months, was made everyday. One left before the sun rose and returned after dark. Trips to the other towns, such as Canicattì or Favara were made to visit relatives and then only on such occasions as deaths, family litigations or marriages. If one moved from one town to another, then all the household affairs would be put on mules and donkeys, the children set in the large *panari*— baskets and the women rode behind the men. These were long trips: five or six hours of riding over bad roads. The province of Agrigento is hilly country, at times mountainous. From Racalmuto, closer towns like Grotte and Castrofilippo and Favara could be made in an hour or two.

Men involved in the sulfur trade could go to Cianciana, Canicattì and to Agrigento, those in wheat to Agrigento and at times to as far as Caltanissetta, a commercial city about fifty kilometers away—almost a days journey. Raffaeli's family involved in mining and agriculture often went to these cities and towns.

The men, of course, traveled more than the women. They knew these cities and towns. At night, sitting in the dark countryside they could point them out.

These towns and cities were small. Racalmuto in 1901 had a population of 16,000, and this was a peak since 1570 when the population was recorded as 5,279.

Milocca had a population of 2,500 in the 1920's: Agrigento, the provincial capital, over 25,000. Racalmuto was the middle town set in one of the many valleys of the undulating barren mountains which rise almost immediately out of the sea near Agrigento and then move one beyond the other as far as the eye can see into the interior.

The ancient Greek geographer, Strabo, as I said earlier, called Sicily "the hollow land" for its apparently bottomless agricultural wealth. All manner of things came from its seemingly inexhaustible insides. The mountains and hills were covered with oak, its plains with corn fields and fruit olive groves and vineyards. But I prefer to call it "the hallowed land". It is understandable then, if the ancient Greeks found their underworld in Selinous, the city they founded which is now called Sciacca. There, large caves let out hot rhythmical puffs of hot air, coming from somewhere beneath the ground. Outside Agrigento there still bubbles up the volcanic mud of Maccluba. And not far from Racalmuto, on the Plain of Terra Pilata, near Caltanissetta, there also pours volcanic mud.

An Englishman who wrote with care and affection of Sicily, had this to say of Ancient Sicily. "In Sicily then the powers of the netherworld held the first place. They ruled over the land and the sea and over the fiery furnace of the burning mountain. It was they who gave even the corn and the wine for which the burning mountain made ready a more fruitful soil. And in the phrase of Strabo, the Hallowed Land also sent forth many rivers as well as much fire."

In Sicily the Greeks found their legend of Demeter and her daughter Persephone. These were Sikel legends, the people who gave their name to Sicily and whom the Greeks conquered.

Demeter and Persephone were the Sikel powers of the earth and the underworld that sent up not fire and water, but this time, "fruits that strengthen man's heart." The cult of Demeter and her daughter were worshiped in the ancient Sikel town of Henna, now Enna. Sicily remained the island of fruitfulness of Demeter where her gifts grew of themselves, almost without the help of man for centuries. It was to become the granary of Rome and all its conquerors centuries to come. In 1890 an Englishman could still write, "not only do the many valleys, the few plains, stand thick with corn, but wherever, on the rocky hillsides a blade of wheat can grow between two stones, there it is seen growing. The good wheat of Sicily is still sold at Naples and the worst wheat of Italy brought back again."

Sicily's vegetation is a history of its conquerors and Sicily's receptiveness. Papyrus was brought by the Phoenicians.

The Ancient Greeks brought the vine and the olive tree, the Arab, the palm tree, the orange and lemon tree. The Saracen brought the cotton plant and sugar cane grown in the 12 century but now no longer cultivated. The Spanish brought the prickly pear and let it run wild.

In the land of Demeter and Persephone, the non-fruit bearing trees are at best tolerated, and in most cases not cared for. Only the useful is cared for. The beautiful and green tree is scorned like the useless beauty of a man, some say. The ornamental tree, in the time of the emigration was associated with the noblemen who planted or had them planted and cared for by the peasants, who looked upon it as another corvee. It became a symbol of the aristocrat who "broke his ass watching his trees bloom". Where shade trees were planted, men peed on them until they died, others were exorcised, and spells were cast on them until they withered.

"The oaks and other trees of which Theokritos speaks so largely," wrote one traveler, "have in most places vanished: the mountain sides are as bare as they are in Greece and Dalmatia... and with this destruction of the statelier trees there is a strange lack of animal life— no deer... a bird of any size is almost as rare... all lived in towns and in winter the countryside had an abandoned look."

Some, in 1890 attributed the barrenness to the introduction of the goat that had eaten every seedling as it appeared. Raffaeli, the last time I saw him in 1969, preferred to think it was the peasant's animosity towards the noblemen's tree and the modern planners', "who wish to cement Sicily from one end to another."

In the magnificent drawings of the Sicilian painter, Bruno Caruso there is a brooding sinister feeling about the useless vegetable world. The novelist Sciascia who is from Racalmuto wrote of that sinister feeling, as of the places where he grew up, where the beautiful and green trees mingle their shade with the smell of burning flesh of the Inquisition. Only the palm tree was cared for and at times adored. The Arab-Sicilian poet, Abu-Haten wrote in the 10 century, "The palm tree is waiting for the true believer in heaven. Beneath it he will caress black-eyed virgins. Palm tree, image and similitude of man, image of the human spirit... is a gift of God to those countries ruled by Islam."

Raffaeli, in his mocking tone, often called a woman he admired—*Parmuzza d'oru*—my little golden palm tree.

There were few palm trees in Agrigento at the turn of the century; there were none in Racalmuto and certainly none in Grotte or Milocca.

The useful tree was another matter: the almond, walnut, fig and carob trees were cared for with affection and the men who cared for them, the *nnistaturi*, were held in high esteem.

In Racalmuto there were no shade trees. The cube-like houses seemed to have been spilled down from the high ground where the railroad passes, down to the oldest part of the town in the hollow below. Those who live in the lower part of the town complained of its dampness and stagnant air. Those who had rheumatism were advised to move up the hill. But most of them were men who worked in the mines and it would be easier for them to go to America than to move up the hill.

If was in the lower part of the town, it was said, that the Saracen conquerors found such a squalid village, infected with plague, that they called it *Rahalmut*, the village of the dead.

In the old part of town where the land drops off suddenly there is the Castello del Malconvent built around 1017 by Robert Il Malconvent. He was given the lands and the barons of *Rahalmut* for his services as captain the conquering forces of Roger the Norman. The twin round towers of the castle rise fortress-like from a broad paved plain called the *chianu casteddru*, where the town festivals came to an end. From the towers one could look out to the undulating hill and in the distance— about an hour's ride by mule— see *lu Castiddruzzu*—the massive Saracen fortress—Al Minsar. Built in the early 10th century, its delicate arabesque arches, even in the time of the great emigration, had been cemented in with so much stone and mortar by peasants who lived in it, for fear the delicate arches could not support the heavy walls. that they seemed to be made of peanut brittle. But then the *Castiddruzzu* over the centuries has been used by brigands as a place to hide, as a place to sleep for migrant workers, a place to store wheat and wine. Of course it has been the source of many legends.

One legend tells of secret passages leading to great treasures. Another tells of Saracen traitors who betrayed their brothers to the Normans. From the towers of the Norman castle the two fortresses still seem like the confrontation of two civilizations. The Saracen fortress has been abandoned for centuries. The Norman castle in town has served many purposes: a jail, administrative offices, a farmhouse, a most recently a vocational school.

From the Castle's plain, three long, worn steps lead up to *La Matrici*—the town's mother church, its twin towers, the shape of hooded nightriders looms over the *chiazza*.

The men would stroll arm in arm, in groups of two or three sometimes four or five, from one end of the *chiazza* where the Mother church stood, stop, chat for a while, glance about at the others, then start for the other end, to the café owned for generations by the same family. As they walked one would nod to others, greet those of one's own station. A passing woman was greeted only if she were accompanied by her husband. A woman walking alone was ignored, for a man could be made cuckold by a glance. At times the young men might even walk the road past cemetery of Santa Maria to the town of Grotte, past the wayside shrine which in the old days always had a candle burning inside the beehive-shaped shrine.

Choosing a partner or partners for the evening stroll was determined by one's rank and status in the community. Carters strolled with carters or miners, priests with priests or members of the bourgeoisie and a retinue of unemployed but educated young men seeking jobs. Peasants walked with peasants. Fascists with Fascists; Socialists with theirs—Anarchists with their companions. Mothers walked their marriageable daughters—dressed in color, to the church, the shops and home again.

These strolls defined class structure: the *Borghesi*, the comfortable *contadini*, one who did not lack the absolute necessities of life, walked with his own kind.

The bourgeoisie was divided into *lu burgiseddu* (the little bourgeois and the upper bourgeois. There was, too, for lack of a better word, a lumpen proletariat; agricultural workers, from which Raffaeli hinted as he pointed to someone in the chiazza in his mocking professorial tone, "From such as these rose the phenomena of mafia."

The climate is tropical in Sicily at times one is reminded of Southern California. The summers are hot and dry, the fall windy with rain. It is the sort of climate that permits, almost forces one to live out of doors. People seem to speak louder, women shout to one another. Everything seems to be out in the open. One often feels on a stage, aware that one is being observed, watched. This is true of the *chiazza*, especially on those summer nights when the light lingers and the *chiazza* takes on the dramatic air of a stage with four entrances. It is understandable then if, in the relationships one is tempted to say negotiated—or developed in the square one finds his identity.

The Gentlemen's Club—known simply as *lu Circulu* in a building facing the *chiazza*. It had intellectual pretensions, although the true intellectuals might be found in the Pharmacist's or in Raffaeli's tailor shop.

Economic conditions could be measured by the crowds in the *chiazza*. In bad times it was as animated as a feast day. In times of prosperity there were less but the *chiazza* was never empty and rarely sparsely populated.

At night it was left to stray dogs, rarely to cats, for cats were valuable animals and not left to roam freely. Dogs were another matter. In a land where one can still see the ancient bas-reliefs depict the dogs of cirnechi of the god Adrano who welcomed the good and attacked the evil—it is understandable that people still say to an evil person—*Chi ti pozzanu manciari li cani*—may you be eaten by the dogs. One night while coming home I saw a tawny colored dog with a short snout, large brown, almost red eyes and long alert ears—a replica of the *cirnechi* dogs. "The animal startled me," I told Raffaeli.

"Eh what do you want? We recycle everything here."

The oldest name for Sicily was Trinakria. The first people to come to the island were Iberians, perhaps Basques, then came the Sikans and Sikels who gave the name to Sikelia in antiquity. These Sikels lived in the hill towns perched on heights. For this reason, no doubt, many towns from a distance seem to have spilled down from a promontory. The main street of Agrigento cuts down its center to a small plain that overlooks the temples of Concordia and Juno and the giant Hercules, fallen on his back some 2,000 years ago, but still hunched over as if holding up the world on his shoulders.

The houses most people lived in the time when Raffaeli's family left for America were cube-like huts of stone. The poor usually lived in a loft above, crude ladder leading to their beds. The ground level was left to the animals: a mule, chickens, and for the more fortunate, a pig. The streets were narrow, cobblestoned and in need of repair, the missing cobblestones usually filled with water and debris. In the summer there was the fetid smell of clay, hot straw and pungent herbs in the air.

In the streets the mules' and donkeys' hooves resounding on the cobblestones were the first sounds of daylight. In the early morning a goatherd carrying a great staff, behind a cluster of goats, their udders swaying and swollen with milk, the leader's bell sounding deep-throated in the streets, appeared. The women, hearing the lead goat's bell, came to their doors with a bowl. The goatherd set the hind legs of the goat on the stone step, filled the bowl, collected his money and, with his staff, directed his herd up the street where another woman waited for the morning milk to be delivered, the morning wore on, the quiet was broken; chickens were let out, women greeted each other from the balconies and up from the street. A kerosene vendor with a large container on his head shouted, "I have oil, I have oil," letting 'oi' trail away in a long vowel. Then a cloth merchant shouted in the same way. A woman could not understand and she shouted to a neighbor, "What's he selling?" "Who knows. I can't make him out." "It's *cumpari* Cali who sells bed sheets." The day was on its way.

The wealthy had a second story, even a third story to their homes. The ground floor opened up much like a garage to let in the animals; again a mule, donkey, chickens, perhaps rabbits. Another door led up steep steps painted blue, in the belief that this color kept flies away, to the second floor. Here there might be a small kitchen, with an oven in which straw and twigs were used as fuel— and a sink with a drain that ran out into the street. Those who didn't have a drain threw the water into the streets. To the right of the stairs there might be a large room with a tile floor usually lined with cane-bottomed chairs and an alcove, a bedroom for the head of the family. A still narrower and steeper set of stairs lead to the upper floor where the men might sleep and to a storeroom where wheat, fruits, and melons were stored over the winter.

The aristocrats, professional men or even the shipping agents at the turn of the century lived in ochre-colored villas and *palazzi*. Some of these *palazzi* had large *porte cochere*, through which carriages could pass into large courts surrounded by a simple, almost austere façade. Only the ochre color indicated the many splendid rooms within. Many of these *palazzi* are in ruin now or have been turned into artisan shops, as in Racalmuto, where one has been converted to a furniture factory. There, 17th century cherubs look down mournfully, their eyes hooded with sawdust, at men, wearing paper hats, working at modern machines.

For both the rich and the poor, plumbing was not existent. Children defecated and urinated in the streets. In Racalmuto there was a great plain in the lower end of town, where Raffaeli's family once lived, known, with some irony, as *La Baruna*. It was used as a public toilet by the children and men. Women or servants brought the accumulation of their own and their masters' waste and dumped it there. Boys played here, too, among the lemon and orange orchards that adjoined the area. In winter, Raffaeli, remembered, he trapped canaries that flocked there and roasted them over straw and herb twigs and ate them hungrily while they talked vulgarly of women.

At times walking in the streets I would kick a mound that suddenly became a thick cloud of buzzing flies I had to walk through. There were no out-houses or running water in the homes and most women spent the day hauling water. Women rolled a rag into a bun, set it on their heads, then lifted an ochre colored jar, shaped as that ancient Greek amphora jars, onto their heads and walked to the nearest fountain. Women carried most things on their heads: baskets filled with figs or cherries, or laundry they took to the spring. Laughingly they often took pride in how easily they could carry great burdens gracefully for long distances. "I tell you," Raffaeli often said pointing to a woman carrying a huge load on her head, "Two women like that with a lever and a place to stand could easily carry the world."

Electricity did not come to Racalmuto until the 1920's. Before then the homes were lit with kerosene lamps, and in the poorer homes one could still find the lamps as ancient as those found in museums today. Most homes had ovens fired with straw and twigs. The very poor cooked outside on makeshift stone piles. Fuel was the straw and faggots gathered in the fall and winter. This was known as to go a "*ristucia*". And the *sfasci* were kept in a corner of the *dammusu* a ground level cellar.

Food for the people of these towns was Spartan, if not simple. The staples were lentils, split peas, or fave beans called *maccu*, which were often made into a soup with escarole or chicory. On special occasions some form of pasta might be added. In late summer, women sat outside their doors splitting the peas or beans with a hammer or a rock to make *maccu* literally mashed beans, for the soups they would make in the coming year.

There was an abundance of fruit. Besides the oranges, plums, apples and lemons, there were the *ficud'innia* or figs of India (West Indies, that is— prickly pears. These were cooling to eat in the summer with their resplendent colors of magenta, purple, rose and various hues of yellow. There were fruit those who left for America would never find again: *zorbi, zalori, scuboli*, and *nespuli*. Nuts were desserts—almonds, walnuts, pistachios, hazelnuts.

In the spring the almonds were eaten green and had a sweet meaty taste. On rare occasions for dessert there were the cannoli, and in Racalmuto a lemon scented cookie, light and fluffy, called *taralli*, named after the man who made them.

Of course there was the sturdy bread which was the mainstay for most people. When taken hot from the oven, Cut open and spread with olive oil, pepper and salt, was an instant good-tasting pizza, dipped, when stale in wine, it made a heady meal in itself.

The most irreligious of men when cutting a new loaf of bread would make the sign of the cross on its level side and kiss the knife before cutting into the bread. And he would never set the bread on its rounded side. Bread was respected. A good man was referred to as "piece of bread".

The wine of the region was heavy, the kind the French call—*le gros rouge qui tache* and it did stain table cloths and teeth a grey purple. It was high in alcohol content as much as 16 percent at times. This was looked upon as a good thing, for much of the wine was sold to cut other foreign wines. But it would be a mistake to think that all Sicilian wines are thick and heavy. There are some from a particular vineyard around Agrigento and Racalmuto that are as light and mouth-puckering as any Bordeaux. For they are wines that come from a special hillside made by men who take care with them. Some, when eaten with walnuts, seem to encompass those light spring days around the sea. Sciascia, the writer from Racalmuto, his wine attests to that.

The modest family— not the poor, for the poor never ate meat; the modest family ate meat twice a year; chicken or a capon for Christmas, roasted kid for Easter. There was fear of eating pork and it was avoided except in sausages, and then it was carefully bought from the right person at the right time. On special occasions, when the hogs were slaughtered, there was *sangunazzu* blood sausage— Cheese was a staple. All the varying stages of cheese-making: curd, ricotta, *cannistrata* with whole black peppers— made from sheep's or goat's milk. Cheese, along with sardines and onions, was the staple for field workers and miners. Mothers in America often warned their children who would not eat the food put before them. "Eat or you'll be given bread and onions and nothing else."

The *Racalmutisi*, of Raffaeli's generation brought simple and Spartan eating habits with them. They came with a great hunger. The Sicilian stores in America, crowded with food stuffs, made to look like an Ali-Baba cavern of food treasures, with the very ceiling hung with cheeses and salamis, reflected this memory of hunger. They were to learn to cook in America from other groups from Italy. They developed a new cuisine in the tenements of the Lower East Side that would be quite different from anything they had known in Sicily.

Raffaeli was the only one of the Don Baldassare family not to go to America; all the others left between 1900 and 1914, a period which saw more Italians come to America than any other group in so short a time. It was a hemorrhaging of people, Raffaeli said, "and our family went in the middle of the herd."

"In all of human history no country or no people have suffered such terrible slavery, conquest and foreign oppression and no country and no people have struggled so strenuously for their emancipation than Sicily and Sicilians."

Karl Marx in *The New York Tribune*
May 1860

THE TIME OF THE GREEN MICE

(Leaving)

Raffaeli remembered Marco, the eldest son of the Don Baldassare family, speak of hunger.

"It was unbearable. My brother Luigi was six then and I was 7. Every morning we'd get up before sunrise and start walking about 4 or 5 miles to the farm of the Patruni—the boss. Many times we went without breakfast. For lunch we ate a piece of bread and plenty of water. If we were lucky, sometimes we would have a small piece of cheese or an onion. We worked in the hot Sicilian sun until the late afternoon, then we had to drag ourselves home. We got there exhausted, just before sunset, so tired we could barely eat and fell asleep with all our clothes on. If we complained that the work was too hard our mother—god rest her soul— would say, 'And who is going to give you something to eat?' And life went on this way day in and day out, until *si vidivamu i surci virdi*—we began to see green mice.

In 1970 I asked the mayor of Racalmuto if there were any archives in town which might give imformation as to why Sicilians left for America at the turn of the century. "You want to know why people left," he said, "Hunger, that's why."

I insisted, "But the archives."

"What archives! They fled here without regrets and most of them clandestinely. What records!" And he held up his fingers in a bunch and shook them before my face, as emphasis.

The reasons for leaving Sicily and coming to America are often given, like the mayor of Racalmuto and some historians in one word: hunger. And with good reason. But if one looks at the period from 1870 to 1914, that time when the young were making up their minds to leave for America, the reasons are not that simple. There had been many periods of hunger before in Sicily and few left. Many in this period stayed behind.

Raffaeli was one of the many young men who did not go to America before World War I, although he saw almost all of his friends and relatives leave. He did other things. He worked as a *carabiniere* in Trieste, as a tailor in Rome and Tunis, as a government employee in Rome and as customs officer in Reggio. After the World War, he returned to Racalmuto. The government positions had been temporary to open his tailor shop. There Raphaeli, smoking one cigarette after another, would sit surrounded by his apprentices, helpers, and men who had come to pass the time of day. In his travels he had learned to read French, Spanish and a number of northern Italian dialects. He could mimic a number of dialects and give commands and assurance,in the American he had picked up from returning relatives and friends. He often would pause, put down his cigarette at the edge of his machine to tell a story in his husky mocking voice.

For the Americans who returned to his shop he read his favorite poet in Roman dialect. Then he would quickly ask, "Eeh, you've been to Rome haven't you? Well, did you at least make love in the forum by moonlight?"

He had learned enough American from his visitors to nod his head in agreement and say, "Sure, sure". He had a good word for everyone in town who deserved it, of the others he said nothing. He spoke to everyone quietly with the grave air of a sympathetic listener. He talked to men of all stations from the arch-priest to a peasant coming home from the fields well after dark, to whom he would call out, *travagghiaturi si, Giuvà*—You're a hard worker, Johnny — with his slight teasing manner, so as not to offend him. He became a well read man, reading everything from a favorite Roman poet to the latest novel of Leonardo Sciascia whom he called 'Nardu' when the writer came into his shop. Raffaeli was a true intellectual, but his failure to make use of it gave him an undertone of bitterness that made him mock all authority but his own. He was a fairly tall man, with tight, thick, curly hair and nicotine stained fingers. Whenever I came to visit, he would walk me to the cemetery of Santa Maria and show me his ancestors' graves. On such occasions he would pause before his mother's grave and weep unabashedly. He did this each time we went. When he was 58 years old he became secretary to the town council. It was he who made this remark about emigration; "I tell you it would have been better for everyone if America had never been invented. All that it did was to transfer the problems. Everyone here always said, 'Why do anything? Why pave a road? Build a school?

Why have a revolution? You know the French had their great revolution and they had no mass emigration. And look at those cuckold aristocrats, like Tulumello, they encouraged it. 'Why do anything—next week, next year, my papers will come and we'll be in America' And nothing was done. No reforms, no revolution. The world is finite, you know. all you're doing is transfering the problems. In a hundred years, five hundred, America will have all our problems—the rich will be ferocious in destroying the earth or anyone who prevents them from becoming richer and the poor will live on wind and smoke. It would have been better to have been forced to work things out here. Instead they all left singing, *maladittu l'America e cu la sprimintà!* (Goddamned America and he who invented it)."

It took decades for scholars to come to the same conclusion. The Sicilian historian, Renda, wrote in 1963, the loss Sicily suffered because of emigration: It deadened the political scene, the parties of left lost their masses, the lack of farm workers forced many small owners out, concentrating land in the hands of the Latifondista; for lack of help olive trees were cut down and sold for wood; wheat land turned into pasture and if any money was sent back from America it found its way to Northern banks to help develop the North—explaining the low rate of emigration there. The South lost its best people and the villages were left with the old, the women and children.

At the turn of the century a dignitary visiting a small town around Agrigento was greeted by the mayor with, "I salute you, sir, in the name of the 8,000 I govern 3,000 of whom have emigrated to America and the 5,000 that are preparing to follow them."

The migration was over a hundred years in the making. It began as an internal migration with the population of those mountain top villages leaving for the lower towns and then, much like mountain water finding its way to streams and rivers, to the town and cities by the sea.

The unification of Italy was not remembered—if remembered at all—with affection by workers or peasants in Racalmuto. Their hope of land reform was crushed when an alliance of their betters with the new rulers of Italy seemed to worsen their condition. There was a short period of prosperity soon after the unification, however. The 1870's saw a quickening of economic activity in the towns around Agrigento. Demand for grains, olive oil, almonds and walnuts, increased. New lands were put into production, agricultural workers found work. A veritable sulphur rush took place. Between 1860 and 1885 sulphur production doubled and became, "the most substantial industrial concentration". The British who had used gun boat diplomacy to force the break up of a French-Sicilian monopoly known as TAIX, took the lead in this development.

Agriculture in general boomed: olive oil production was up by 10 percent, wines up by 72 percent, Citrus fruits by 120 percent. There was good reason for optimism and the young refused to live in the self denying way of their fathers. A way of life in which most men had one suit made, for their marriage, paid for it in wheat, wood or services and worn again for their burial. Doctors were paid in chickens—preferably capons; barbers and cobblers in fava beans or eggs. It was a self contained life in which most people spun and wove their own cloths on *lu tilaru*. The good woman was one who sat by her loom, and image as old as Penelope and Ulysses.

The incident of the Santa Cruci shrine exemplified the conflict between the old and the young.

The young and progressive in Racalmuto took hold of the local government in the late 1870's. And in 1879 the city theater was completed; Rigoletto was the first opera presented. The narrow streets, crowded with cube-like houses were opened up. In a moment of enthusiasm some men donated land and houses for this renovation. Wide streets were constructed. The railroad came to Racalmuto. The first hissing and pounding steam engine prompted a wise peasant to remark, "What a fine boiling cauldron. Fine boiling thing, but it doesn't walk." When he saw it move he said, "No one can take me for a *fissa*—a fool—they have horses hidden beneath all that." Soon after a branch of the Banco di Sicilia opened in town.

To widen one of the streets leading to the railroad station the shrine of Santa Cruci had to be torn down, much to the horror of the older generation. And when a drought hit the area the following year, 1885, the arch-priest preached a sermon in which he said the lord was offended by the destruction of the shrine and no one should expect either grain or fava beans from the good earth. As the peasants saw their crops yellowing in the burning sun, they massed in the *chiazza* chanting:

> Vulemu la Santa Cruci,
> Ma si nno nun chiovi.
> Lu munti cravariu s'avi a rifari,
> Sinno semmu morti di fami.

> We want the Holy Cross
> If not it won't rain.
> The shrine must redone
> Or we're all dead of hunger.

Th demonstrators went to the new road and were about to tear it up when troops from Agrigento arrived and dispersed the crowd. The bitterness remained. It was understandable then, if, when the economic crisis hit the region, the religious blamed it on the desecration of the ancient shrine.

1890 agricultural prices dropped. As a consequence, a commercial war began with France. Prices dropped even further. Climate too turned against those who worked the land. Drought caused grain production to drop from 7,744,000 *ettolitri* in 1891 to 4,363,000 in 1892. Wine production was cut in half. Citrus fruits dropped by 200,000 *quintali*. The next year saw more of the same. Everyone was hurt, workers, small and middle bourgeois. But most of all, it was the agricultural worker who was hurt, the *braccianti*, who was left with a despairing hunger and a hatred of the land.

In these years the proverb—*Dopu Natali veni la fami*—after Christmas there is nothing but hunger, was never more true. The young and hardy turned to stealing and the more organized and determined to banditry. One band, still remembered, operated out of *Lu Castidruzzu*, the Saracen fortress that stood on a high point overlooking the valley known as Sirunni. It was understood that the family who owned the *feudo* of Villanova gave it protection. Yet the connivance of the rich and the bandit so often portrayed as invincibly in Sicily, did not work. The police learned that on the night of June 24, 1902 the band was to meet in a house in the area known as *Gessi*

Caduti. The brigadieri, set out with two of his men and let it be known, "Tonight either I shall be honored or gunned down."

When he and his men arrived, the house was pitch dark. The brigadieri knocked. A woman's voice asked. "Who is it?"

"The Law," answered the *brigadieri.*

The door opened and an old woman appeared holding a lamp up to the brigadieri's face momentarily blinding him. The woman then suddenly dropped the lamp and a volley of gunshots cut down the police. One lawman was not touched, a young man who was known to be a good shot. He fell to the ground, fired and moved to another position. With each of his shots, he moved still to another spot, drew fire, moved and fired again, gathering ammunition from the dead. He killed everyone of the band. The next day the bodies of the bandits were taken away and the *brigadieri* was given a hero's funeral. No one knows what became of the old woman.

The times did not improve, for the honest or the bandits. Those who could, began to leave—some for Tunis to set up shops, others to work in the French mines around Lille. America was still "The other world". Now if a miner was laid off, he sold his household goods, went to talk to the steamship line agent and off he went.

What started the great exodus of people however, was *La piccola favilla che gran fuoco seconda*—The small spark which engenders great fires. And that was the Fasci Siciliani—a rebellion which began among the sulphur miners.

An old man, a neighbor of Raffaeli, often told me stories of old Sicily usually with visual demonstrations appropriate to a child listening intently. One day he gave me a twig and asked me to break it. I did easily, then he asked to put two twigs together and break them. With some effort I did. Then the old man took four twigs, tied them together with a braid of grass and said, "Now break it." No matter how hard I tried I could not break the bundle—the *fasci.*

"That's the way it was with the Fasci Siciliani. If people stick together no one can break them."

Later, a "Youth Leader" could go through the same process only this time he cut a cactus stalk into the shape of an axe, inserted it in the bundle or *fasci* and there was the symbol of Fascism.

It was ironic that just 30 years before Mussolini's March on Rome, the *Fasci* was a symbol of unity of workers and peasants in an early Sicilian Socialist movement. But then too, it was understandable if the *Fasci* became the symbol of working class unity in Sicily. Men, Woman, children and animals were seen everywhere carrying on their shoulders that symbol of Sicilian poverty—the *Fasci*—a bundle of twigs collected in the fields and brought home to cook the evening meal.

The Ancient Greeks in Sicily had Pluto sitting on a throne of sulphur. And the Devil, in legends of Christian Sicily, is still preceded by the odor of sulphur and his home in Hell is a place of sulphur and brimstone—two products of the area around Racalmuto.

The mining of sulphur around Racalmuto in the early 19th century was limited and primitive. Men burrowed in the side of a hill and from a cave-like opening hacked out the mineral. With the rise of the importance of sulfuric acid, attributed to the Napoleonic Wars, came a sulphur rush and deeper mines with all the hazards associated with them.

In 1838 a sulphur combine of French and Bourbon interests from Naples was formed to create a sulphur monopoly—TAIX. The British protested and finally sent the fleet in, landed troops and forced the disbandment of the combine. A British group then bought into many of the mines around Racalmuto. Based in London it was never interested in safety or modern methods of mining. Labor was cheap. It is without bitterness that Raffaeli often spoke of those lazy characters in the novels of Henry James "who sat on the shoulders of our Racalmutisi miners."

As late as the 1930's men walked down to the work area, because it was on their own time and it also saved the expense and insurance of running the elevators. Nor did the government do anything to regulate the conditions of work. Accident statistics began only in 1933. To work in a mine around Racalmuto is to understand why the Greeks discovered their concept of Hell here.

In town the old miners chant; *Cu l' arti 'nfami di lu surfararu ca notti e iornu travagghia a lu scuru.* (In the infamous work of the miner, a man works night and day in dark.)

The miners woke before dawn and started walking 15 kilometers to the mines in the dark. Each man, with a lunch of bread, onions and perhaps a salted sardine, took his own way across the fields. Some were followed by their dogs. They passed the cemetery of Santa Maria where they might meet their carusi, the boys who hauled out the sulphur. The principal worker was the picconiere, the pick man, who did the setting of explosives, and the pick-work of breaking up the sulphur. His *carusi* then took over, filling the flat baskets with sulphur rock in the narrow low sections, dragging them out, to fill sacks which when filled weighed about 30 kilos. The *carusi* then carried them up a corridor cut into the earth, slopping up so narrowly that niches were cut in the sides at regular intervals for other coming down to pass them. It took me once an hour to walk down to the working area.

The *carusi* were contracted to the *picconieri* by their parents. The *picconieri* gave an advance to the father of, flour, grain and other food stuffs, and the boy worked it off, doing about fifty such trips a day. The mines were wet, hot and fetid. The smell of acid hung heavy in the air. Men worked naked. A slight cut could fester for months. In the salt mines one hardly ever survived beyond the age of 40 without some form of crippling arthritis.

The temperature was so high perspiration cut into the slightest wound. At times they came up to the top so exhausted that they would not return to town, but slept in the surrounding caves, covered with tarpaulins. Only on Saturday did they return to their families. In the dark they would tie their oil lamps to their waists, then holding each other's belts they would begin their long walk home. From the town one could see the serpentining lights coming down from the hills. Those who had the strength sang:

Lampiuni lampiuni
mi raccumandu a tia
ca quannu passu lustru m'a fari.

Little lamp, little lamp
I recommend myself to thee,
so when I pass make light for me.

The *picconieri* were paid by the casse of sulphur he and his caruso brought out. A *cassa* measured *due canne siciliane* or "eight palms".

The few who could translate this to known measurements say it was about 2.06 meters in length and 1.03 meters high or approximately three feet by six feet.

These were ancient Sicilian measures and they varied from owner to owner, always in their favor if the workers weren't careful. There were also company stores to which miners were always in debt. Some companies forced the miners to buy there. It is understandable if the *picconieri* pushed himself with curses and obscenities and drove his *carusi* to exhaustion. Fights often broke out.

Only a good *capumastru*—the good foreman could keep the men working. A *carusi's* chant paid homage to a good *capumastru* with:

Piglia la lumera e facci lustru
Ca cala lu bonu capumastru.

Bring out the lamp and light his way
For here comes down the good foreman.

The conditions of work, the poor diet, the early childhood spent in the mines by many, produced a generation of cripples. Between 1881 and 1884, of the 3,870 miners called up for military service, only 202 passed the physical examination. A medical commission in the time of the *Fasci* found that out of 539 *carusi*, 170 were "defective". What was meant by that statistic is hard to say. But in the town of Racalmuto there are many old men with hunchbacks who sit before the Mother Church on sunny days, reminders of those days when they were sent into the crevices no one else could reach and then carry, 30 kilos, a half mile up on backs that were not fully developed. Some still remembered the songs they sang while carrying their loads to the top.

Matri mia, nun mi nannati a la pirrera,
ca notti e iornu mi pigghiu tirrura,
a mala pena scinnu a la pirrera

s'apri lu tettu e cadinu li mura
accussì voli la mala carrera
fammi pigghiari sempri di paura.
Ora c'acchianammu nni lu chianu.
viva Diu e San Gaitanu.
Semmu iunti a la catastedda,
Viva Santa Barbaredda.
Novi nni vaiu a pigghiu ed è d'aura
unnici mi n'arrestanu di pena
chi lustru ca mi fa la mia lumera
chistu è lu signu ca vaiu a livari,
Cci l' haiu a diri a lu ma pirriaturi.
ca chistu è l'ultimu ca si nni po' acchianari

Don' t send me to the mines mother of mine.
As soon as I set foot in that damned gallery
the ceiling opens, the walls cave in.
I'm frightened to death.
Here we are at level one
Long live God and Saint Gaetano
Thank God here's level two
Long live little Saint Barbara.
This the load of pain number nine
eleven more loads and it will be time
What a strange light my little lamp
gives off.
Must be time to quit.
Must tell the *picconieri* this is the last
I have to tell him he can come up.

On the whole the increased sulphur production did not make towns such as Racalmuto better places. Fifty years of mine exploitation based on poorly paid labor which could barely buy adequate diet, divided the population more than ever before.

An old school teacher who frequented Raffaeli's shop wrote, "On one side the rich bought up land, constructed palazzi, sent their children on to study, on the other side the mass of the people was an aggregation of the deformed, the wounded and the mutilated."

And yet the picconieri and the *carusi* were recruited from the peasants who looked upon the miners with envy because working the land, one did not live at all. A farm worker made 0.50 lire a day. Grain cost 0,20 lire a kilo. It took more than a day's wages to supply a family with bread, that is, the cost of the grain, its grinding and the baking. Most families did not have an oven.

Working the land, whether as a share-cropper or a day worker meant primitive work: the basic implement was *na zappa*, a hoe. And there was seeding, weeding, harvesting with a sickle; then a horse or a mule stamping the cut wheat, winnowing, if the wind was favorable and the carting. There was no mutual aid or government assistance. In the best of times life was marginal and in times of crisis, such as 1890, despairing. Such conditions brought about the rise of the *Fasci* in Racalmuto. It did not happen overnight.

In 1873, *La Società Operaia di Mutuo Soccorso* was formed, taking in men from Grotte, Milocca, Agrigento and Racalmuto. Men from Grotte and Racalmuto were among the first to sign the founding constitution of the Communist International of Agrigento. Federico Campanella was sent as a delegate from Racalmuto to Rome. (One of his descendants became the model for the old Communist in Sciascia's short story, "The Death of Stalin"). These early workers' organizations received newspapers such as *The Citizen* from Caltanissetta and *Justice* from Agrigento, and from Rome, *The Emancipation*.

In this sense these were not isolated towns limited in area to the sound of the bell tower. They were towns caught up in the Socialist International movement, not out of sophistication but out of necessity.

In 1870 in Grotte because of a conflict within the clergy, a Protestant church was founded along with a circolo operaio a workers' circle—named after Savanarola, the 15th century religious heretic. The new pastor, a certain Di Mino, preached a return to a primitive Christian society that was not far from Socialism. Many men from Grotte were converted not only to Protestantism but to Socialism as well. In their contacts with the *Racalmutisi* in the mines and the fields, they proselytized, argued, debated—if nothing else Racalmuto was politicized. The poor became aware of "the gentlemen who broke their asses watching their almond trees bloom" as Raphaeli would say.

Among the young intellectual leaders of Racalmuto at the time was a certain Vincenzo Vella. From old photographs he looks out at the world calmly, his high forehead creased; deep-set serious eyes and a broad nose so common to Racalmuto. In another photograph he is older, leaner and his bearded face gives the impression of seriousness the socialists of that period liked to convey. He lacked, totally, that air of pompousness that a leader of the right, such as Tulumello, tried to convey—a look the Fascists later were to call *birbante* with admiration—the look of a determined scoundrel.

In Vella there was a bit of humor in his upturned moustaches, in the manner of King Umberto. Vella came from a wealthy family of sulphur mine owners who had begun, in his father's time, as picconieri. In the great sulphur boom that preceded the Fasci, the Vella family had made its fortune. Vincenzo was trained in law at the University of Palermo where he, like so many of the other young Sicilian Socialists, took part in the early radical movements. He returned to Racalmuto just in time to witness the economic crisis of the 1880's provoked in large measure by American sulphur being dumped on the European market.

The price of sulphur dropped from 115.36 a ton to 65.36 lire. Those mines that weren't shut down were soon operating at reduced capacity. Wages of those still employed were cut drastically. The *chiazza* was filled with unemployed men pacing, talking, while their families were reduced to hunger.

The winter was cold and rainy. The government, to make up for the loss of revenue caused by the abolishment of a tax on mills, chose this time, to raise the real estate tax, which of course was passed on to the burden of the workers and peasants. It seemed like a provocation to disorder. It was not long in coming; there were warning signs. Voices were raised in anger among the men in the *chiazza*, a politician, File, who sat in the city council, was murdered.

National and international events conspired to depress conditions even further. As Italy moved closer to Germany, her commercial affairs with France deteriorated. By 1887 Italy's commercial ties with France were broken, depressing the sulphur market even further. The price of sulphur dropped to 55.65 lire a ton by 1895. Economic crisis became a long-term, persistent depression.

The collapse of the sulphur industry saw, not only the misery of the miners, but of all the small mine owners who often worked along with the *picconieri*. Even some of the larger *gabelloti*—those managers of large estates were ruined.

Vincenzo Vella spoke to the sullen crowds in the *chiazza*, "standing on a chair near the Mother Church, often with a great Red flag above him. Other men joined him: Baeri, Dinaro, Cimino, Cino, Defelice, Gazzara—names which in forty, fifty years, in the streets of Brooklyn would be as common as fire hydrants.

With these men the first *Fascio dei Lavoratori* of Racalmuto was founded. The mine owners chose this moment, also, to reduce the wages of the *picconieri* and the *carusi*, even further. Strikes broke out—spontaneous explosions of anger and hunger. Two hundred miners on March 28, 1892 struck. They attacked the Mine owners Club, stoning its walls and windows. They broke in and set all its furnishings on fire. Their fury increased with the storming of the club and they marched on to the Santo Argento mine and set it on fire.

After a battle with the police who were set out to stop them, in which miraculously no one was killed, a handful of leaders were arrested. The day ended and nothing changed.

In November, 600 miners were out on the streets again, demanding an end to pay cuts. The mine owners, frightened by the ever-growing numbers of strikers and the sullen aspect of the men, gave in. But no sooner had order been restored than they restored the pay cuts. On April 15 and April 22 1893 the miners were out on the streets again. This time there was no violence. The mining towns were being politicized. Men such as Vella who continued to speak standing on his chair in the *chiazza*, with a warm-hearted sincerity still remembered, about justice, brotherhood, equality, liberty, division of land and of the need for revolution, prevented these strikes from turning into uprising. He, like Colajanni, Bosco and others in the rest of Sicily, did much to channel these furies into political action, rather than into useless and extravagant violence. Leaders, such as Vella, in turn, were radicalized by the violence of the miners. Both leaders and followers in and around Racalmuto became part of the Socialist movement in Southern Italy which up until then had more leaders than followers.

The First International had come to the South in 1867. By 1868 there was a group in Sciacca; soon after, one in Agrigento and Caltanisetta. the miners of the Racalmuto-Grotte region were affected by the rebellious tradition of Grotte. It was in Grotte, fostered by the Protestant, Savanarola Club, that the *Fasci de Lavoratori* was founded in December 1892. With the *Fasci* of Racalmuto they were to become the most important *Fasci* of Sicily.

Strikes spread across the land, to the smallest towns in the province: Canicattì, Cianciana, Milocca and Favara. October 4, the miners of Grotte went on strike demanding higher wages, October 27, in Milocca, this town of "simpletons," demanded the release of their leaders. November 1, in Racalmuto mine property was attacked. The first Congress of Miners organized by the *Fasci* was held in Grotte. Fifteen hundred men assembled, mostly miners but also among them were large contingents of small mine owners who were beginning to throw in their lot with the mine workers.

The small mine owners complained of being exploited by large mine owners who were usually managers for English companies. For them the Congress passed a resolution in favor of abolishing the rights of subsoil. This because large owners often bought up the rights below the soil only, which permitted them to march across any land to exploit it. The small owners however, often worked as miners and peasants tilling the top soil. It was their land that was trampled on by the large mine companies. The Congress also called for a ten percent reduction of the product destined to the gabelloti who were the agents of absentee owners. They called for the establishment of a miners bank.

For the workers, the Congress demanded; raising the age of the *carusi* working in the mines to fourteen (there was no age limit at this time); the abolishment of the *anticipo*, or advance given to parents for boys sent to the mines, "to put an end to this infamous instrument that leads to the sale of human flesh;" a minimum wage of 1.50 lira for the *carusi* up to fifteen years of age and two lira for those older; an eight hour day; standard measurements of the cassa by which the *picconieri* were paid; minimum wage of 4 lira for the *picconieri*; abolition of company stores; payment in cash and promptly.

Property owners began to see "the specter of Socialism and Communism" in the movement. Yet the demonstrators and strikers often chanted of the King and Queen, "Viva Umbertu and Margherita who will put us right", or *Cu l'aiutu di Maria finirà la camurria* (with the help of Mary will end the *camurria)*. (The word *camurria* was used in Racalmuto and by the immigrants in America to signify the action of a *camurrista,* an arrogant, corrupt and domineering person. It came from the Neapolitan crime society known as La Camorra).

Karl Kautsky, the German Socialist wrote of the Fasci Siciliani as being "today at the center of the International Socialists's sympathies." The French were astounded that Sicilian peasants, "so resigned, so far from utopianism are in so short a time champions of collectivist theory." The French may not have known that in Palermo workers had paraded slogans in the English manner, as one reporter put it, which read:

WORKERS OF THE WORD UNITE
WORK IN ORDER TO LIVE AND NOT LIVE IN ORDER TO WORK
8 HOURS OF WORK

If the Fasci put Sicilian workers and peasants in the center of the European workers' movement, they also put the "directing class" in the ranks of those who were suddenly frightened by the "specter of Communism".

In the Spring of 1893, in Caltavuturo, a town about the size of Grotte, a demonstration of peasants and miners chanting "Bread and work—no charity" was fired upon. Thirteen demonstrators were killed. This tough policy was a concession to those who wanted to "teach the *Fasci* a lesson". The massacre succeeded in infuriating the workers. More *Fasci* were established. In the first part of August a Workers and Peasants Congress was held in Corleone.

Those in power insisted on force and the leaders, Verro and Luciano, were arrested, chained hand and foot and sent to prison. Another lesson for the *Fasci*, it was thought. The contrary happened. Strikes broke out all over Sicily until some 150,000 were demonstrating. In Corleone there was the first *contadino* strike ever in Italy.

In Milocca the leaders of the local *Fasci* were chained and imprisoned. The local *Fasci* protested, demonstrated and finally attacked the *carabinieri* barracks and liberated their leaders. In Favara and Racalmuto strikes and demonstrations also broke out.

The government began to hesitate. Even the Prime Minister, Crispi, from Agrigento himself, who later was to crush the movement, said that at heart this was not a political upheaval it was a matter of hunger, poor harvests and "the topography of Sicilian landownership and poor orders given to the police."

In November 1893 *La Tribuna* reminded its readers that Sicily was a land where a few grand noblemen ruled over thousands of slaves, worse off than the slaves of ancient Rome who were at least assured of a mouthful of bread. It reminded them also that the Island, 2,000 years before, was at the heart of a slave uprising which took three years of bloody fighting and the defeat of various Roman legions before the revolt could be put down. There were too many good reasons for a revolt in Sicily. Peace was needed. And it warned, "There are too many students and young Socialists who are willing to sacrifice themselves, ready to have carved on their tombstones, *Cum Spartaco navit*—I fought with Spartacus"

For a moment even some of the *gabelloti*, these usually fierce managers, who were being huffy increased rents instituted by their baron-landlords, called for peace. One wrote, "In education, as in politics, the soul should be mastered by love."

There still was the possibility of a peaceful solution. *Corriere*, however, gave a hint of actions to come.

"Corleone. August 12-13 1893."

"The peasants of our country-side are almost all illiterate: in their minds, made brute-like by work under a ferocious sun, there can not be formed those ideas, let us say, that will lead to a revolution of thought. The day is far off when the Sicilian peasant can understand the Socialist bible. It is pure deduction that leads one to the logical conclusion. When an uncultured people in good faith, surprised by miserable instigators, thoughtless fanatics, eager to overthrow ancient institutions, splattering with ferocious actions an entire history of heroism and gentle idealism, then one must set up a dam, without hesitation with a serenity that comes from the accomplishment of a sacred duty."

In Racalmuto and Grotte those militants who shouted for the King's help were hardly aware that King Umberto had also taken fright. He remembered Napoleon, the Paris Commune: his parents remembered the great French Revolution. He took steps to repress the movement. In November he named not only a Sicilian to head the government, but a man from Agrigento, Francesco Crispi. The task of restoring "order" to Sicily was given to General Mara. The General proclaimed a state of siege on the Island; declared the *Fasci* disbanded and began a systematic arrest of all leaders from the urban centers to the smallest villages such as Milocca.

Thousands were arrested and sent to prison. If no evidence could be found that they had taken part in demonstrations or riots many were convicted and sent to jail on what the military courts called "metaphysical evidence." For every participant in demonstrations and riots two soldiers were sent to Sicily— about 500,000 in all.

Vella, in Racalmuto, escaped from his home, just ahead of the police, by jumping out of a window and running across the roof-tops. He managed to get out to the countryside, only to be captured in the small mining community of Montedoro, along with another member of the *Fasci*, Michele Dinaro.

In Grotte the leaders, Baeri and Figliola, were arrested and sent to prison in Caltanissetta. Figliola's wife, in a time of no social services was reduced to gleaning wheat fields to feed her children. Ingrao of Grotte fled to the mainland where he had a long career as a socialist militant.

Vincenzo Vella, after his release from prison, returned to Racalmuto and was given a hero's welcome. He was met at the railroad station and carried on the shoulders of his followers, with a red flag waving "under a shower of crimson flowers" and the music playing as if it were a festival. It was to be the last Sicilian *Fasci* demonstration in Racalmuto.

Vella was to spend the rest of his life in Racalmuto a militant Marxist talking of great theories to his diminished group of followers. His failure, some said, was attributed to "the immaturity of the masses." Some still remembered seeing him one Sundays, a tray in hand, soliciting money in the *chiazza* for a young girl who had eloped with a young man but had no money to be married, for a window who needed a sewing machine or distributing his own writings still filled with hope for a more humanitarian and socialist future.

In face of this the best of the young men were to begin the great migration to America. This migration itself was to be a cause of the *Fasci*'s failure, some of the intellectuals in Racamuto felt. Particularly Raffaeli, who used this as proof for his remark, "The emigration was a blight for this town. All the young left, those who weren't afraid of taking on a policeman in broad daylight. If they had stayed, they would have brought about a change. It was like the revolution of 1905 in Russia with no suite. Everybody was saying then, 'why do anything? Tomorrow we'll be in America.' The capitalists didn't care about this export of *carne umana*. That's what we were exporting, human meat."

Yet, some change did take place, small as they might be. Workers began to dress in a more worldly fashion they let their moustaches grow they no longer took blows from their employers.

In face of this change, one Don Alfonso Scibetta was supposed to have said:

Chi tempu laidu chi vinni, ca un galantomu mancu pò dari chiù na timpulata.(What ugly times are upon us. When a gentleman can no longer slap a peasant's face.)

The town of Racalmuto now fell into the hands of the Baron Tulumello. The small man with upturned moustaches in the manner of King Umberto had waited patiently during the turmoil of the Fasci. He spoke to all who had grievances: to those who were angered by the tearing down of the shrine, to the unemployed, the peasants, the noblemen. He belonged to no party. He was elected mayor late in 1893 and remained in power through his elegant rhetoric and the failure of the opposition which had lost most of its supporters to emigration.

The Baron was a rooster of a man. And those who disliked him said his family came to its title of Baron in a strange way.

His ancestors, who were merchants, one day were playing cards with King Ferdinand of the then Kingdom of the Two Sicilies.

The merchants were winning and the King exclaimed, "I see why you're winning. You're all a bunch of fucked-up Barons."

The men rose, bowed deeply, thanked the King for raising them to the ranks of Barons and left the room never showing their back-sides to the King, as was expected of newly ennobled men. Their children have remained Barons to this day.

Baron Luigi Tulumello ran the town much like a political boss of Boston, New York, St. Louis or Chicago, for that matter. His elections were won with the help of brigands who wined and dined the poor with baccala and wine, if that didn't work, strong arm tactics were used to round up votes at election time. The brigands in turn were given protection in their criminal activities.

If the rise of Socialism was an international phenomenon, so were the tactics of the urban political boss.

The Baron had a gang of men for his protection and use. But he also worked hard at being popular: talking to everyone, doing favors, punishing enemies. His favorite expressions were, "Who makes a mistake pays," and *popolo cornuto*—The People are Cuckolds. This last was his motto which he began using as an opposition member of the municipal council. Whenever he addressed a crowd he always began with *popolo cornuto*. The crowds applauded, laughed and cheered him. As if to prove the people were cuckolds, his brother, known as the little Baron Arcangel Tulumello, one day ran off with the rural bank's funds which he squandered on the mainland in the manner of some legendary Russian prince. He was caught and brought back to Racalmuto where he was welcomed with music and flowers by the *popolo cornuto*.

Tulumello himself attributed his long rule—he wasn't ousted until 1907—to his ability to dominate people. This he did by distracting them with festivals, putting them to "Sleep" as he said, "with flour and frightening them with a fork". His motto could have been Festivals, Flour and the Fork. Feasts became fantastic under his rule. During the festa of the Madonna of the Mount, a child swung down from the steeple of the Mother Church to a cart carrying the Virgin Mary. Fireworks, a tradition in town, became more and more spectacular. The year 1900 was ushered in with new illuminations in the *chiazza*, music and a *te deum* along the streets, coming out of the

Mother Church at exactly the first minute of the first day of the year 1900.

When King Umberto was assassinated, the Baron had all the town mourn and set the bust of the murdered King beside that of Cavour and Machiavelli in the town council hall.

But the anger of the time of the Fasci remained and from time to time exploded. In 1896 Napoleon Colajanni came through Racalmuto and caused the last of the *Fasci* riots. Colajanni was from Castrogiovanni, Enna, as it is known today. He had been one of the Fasci leaders, a moderating influence, a scholar in the 19th century manner, a doctor, an intellectual who devoted his life to Socialism. He was a hero to the *Fasci* in Racalmuto.

In 1894 he had written, "I don't want the stupid cruelty of those in power, but there must be changes so that the revolutionary Sicilian cry of *Morti a li cappedda* does not acquire that sad celebrity of *Les aristocrates a la lanterne*."

Cappedda referred to the hats worn by the bourgeoisie—*Les aristocrats* etc., of course referred to the slogan in the French Revolution of 1789. His followers, expecting his arrival, mobbed the railroad station. The crowd pressed in on the police sent to maintain order. The carabinieri, either frightened or arrogant, drew their swords. One of the Fasci leaders picked up a stone and with a cry of "Brothers! Workers!" led an attack against the police. Overwhelmed, the police were forced to strip naked.

When Colajanni arrived he could not prevent the crowd from leading the naked police through town. The Baron-Mayor Tulumello was appalled that the Sicilian police would allow themselves to be stripped naked "Without at least killing someone."

He responded to the violence by writing poetry to the glory of Crispi who then had put down the Fasci and to the great and "glorious war" being fought in Abyssinia.

It was soon after the defeat of the Fasci that the English-Sicilian Sulphur Company invested in the mines around Racalmuto. As Raffaeli repeated so often, "The genteel world of Henry James was founded on that suffering meat in our mines." Scholarship, decades later came to the same conclusion.

"The masses," one Sicilian historian wrote, "disillusioned by the failure of the *Fasci Siciliani*, crushed by the ferocious repression of Mara, hoped for little by the coming of the English, and looked to new horizons, the lands beyond the sea, America. The hemorrhaging of our people was about to burst." The year 1900 rung in by the bells of Racalmuto was a cold night.

The cynical Baron was at the height of his power. The people were anguished with a hunger for bread and work and fear of going to a new world for a life that was denied them in their own world.

Bosco, Barbato, and Verro, all three leaders of the *Fasci* were on the way to America when they were caught on board the ship, Balnara and brought to prison.

In 1881, in all of Sicily, 1,093 persons had emigrated. The numbers increased up to 1901. Then the hemorrhaging of people began: in 1906, 127,603; in 1919, 146,061.

DON BALDASSARE

LU ZI GIULIANO
(Old Ties Broken)

Don Baldassare, Raffaeli's uncle, who took the decision to leave Sicily for America, was a tall man with a high forehead, an aquiline nose, and a right eye that, from his youth, leaned inward and which, as he grew older moved more and more towards his other eye. He was to give this trait to most Of his eight sons and three daughters, more markedly in his son, Marco. This eye characteristic gave the family the *ingiuria* or nickname of *Occhi Storti*. The nickname did not stick, no doubt because another, *Ciaccaroccia*, or Rock Breaker, did.

Don Baldassare, if he had thought of it, could have traced his ancestry to the poor Spanish nobility of Catalonia in the early 18th century who came to care for the lands of the Grandees of Spain. For generations his family had made its living in the small towns and cities of the province of Agrigento, by renting large tracts of land and then subletting to agricultural workers on a sharecropping basis. Don Baldassare's family then, were *gabelloti*, managers of the lands of the Barons and Princes who preferred to live in Palermo, Rome or Paris.

The family was fortunate in always having large numbers of male children. Don Baldassare himself was one of four brothers who came from Cianciana, a small hill town about an hour's ride to the West of Racalmuto. He loved horses and as boy learned to ride them, break them and care for them.

He did his military service in the Cavalry, fought in the first Abyssinian War and returned quite changed. It was said he had been an open, cheerful youth, kind to everyone he worked with or supervised as an agent of his father Don Marco, who had 1000 acres under his supervision. The young Baldassare returned from the war a taciturn young man, although he had lost none of his kindness and patience, qualities in a man, Sicilians called, "a piece of bread". Qualities rare in the *gabelloti* who had the reputation for tyranny and who were always addressed as Don or Sir.

Because of his horsemanship Don Baldassare was sent to the outer edges of the lands the family managed and, when necessary, to towns such as Caltanissetta, Canicattì, and Racalmuto. People remembered him as a boy of 15 riding bareback those auburn, nervous horses, at a gallop, one hand lightly on the reins, the other on his hat, and a gentle smile on his face.

Soon after his return from the Army, he was sent to Racalmuto by his father to negotiate the rental of mineral rights in the area. Dressed in high leather boots, a dark suit, a cap, a shot gun across his back, he often came across the countryside, thereafter, to Racalmuto, past *lu castidruzzu* down the hills to the road of *la Nuci*— the Walnut and then the long climb up to the Saracen Point to reach Racalmuto.

On these trips he carried a cane with a broad handle in which was imbedded a mosaic of colored glass. In those lonely wind swept valleys, he would stop, dig the cane's point into the ground. The sun reflecting on the colored glass would send flashes of light around the valley attracting whatever bird life there was in the area. He would sit in the shade of an olive tree and wait. Often he would come into Racalmuto in the late morning with a rabbit or bird on the swaying croup of his horse. His love of hunting proved to be his financial ruin, the women of the family said.

The oldest brother, Calogero, known as Don Cali, had heard that there were mineral rights to be bought in the area and since their small mining operation in Cianciana was doing well, he thought it was time to expand. In Cianciana they had taken part in the general sulphur boom or the 1870s.

In the late 1890's Don Baldassare and his two brothers pooled their resources to lease some two thousand acres of land in the Racalmuto area.

In his trips to Racalmuto Don Baldassare stayed with an uncle who was in charge of the smelting operations in one of mines in Gibellina and in the evening they would stroll in the *chiazza*. On one of the streets off the *chiazza* was a small grocery store run by Tanu Lu Buffu whose name was recorded in the town records as Antonio Puma. The young called him uncle Tanu. People his own age called him Tanu Lu Buffu or to make it more congenial to American "Fat Tony." He was given this *ingiuria* as a young man when he was already sturdy and barrel-chested. He seemed to have grown fatter and fatter, as if to fulfil the prophecy of his nickname.

Lu Buffu had one daughter, Calogira or Caroline. She was a bright, talkative young girl who wore her hair in long pigtails or at times, when she helped out in the store, in twin braids around her head like a crown. At home she had a sharp tongue, quick to make observations about others, nor was she the first to back away from a confrontation with a brother or a male cousin. What she wanted in a marriage, she repeated as a young girl, was a man to lean on who could take care of her, "or what other use is there in a man? Otherwise in this world there is nothing for a woman."

When young Don Baldassare came to Racalmuto and showed an interest in Caroline Puma, he was encouraged. He was a young man of good health, he was in no way related and he was from another town. Then too, Caroline was expecting great things of him and saw herself living in one of those ocre-colored *palazzi*, hidden away in the narrow streets of Racalmuto with a *retinue* of servants.

For his part, Don Baldassare was taken by the small, broad-shouldered girl who wore her hair braided which when it was let down, fell thick and full around her shoulders, hiding the small gold earrings she always wore. She could read and she did the accounts in her father's store. He was taken too, by her self assurance in the home, in the store and her demeanor in public. If in the home she was warm, vivacious, quick to smile, out of the home she never walked alone, she walked, her eyes lowered, never making eye contact with any man, no matter how close the relationship with the family.

She did not want to give the impression to anyone that she spoke to men in public, even with her eyes. "One never knows." Don Baldassare's family accepted the alliance easily; young Baldassare was not the oldest son: and he would not be in a position to inherit much. Then too he was developing into a taciturn man, happiest when he was alone, hunting in those desolate valleys where only the falcons seemed at home.

Once it was understood that a marriage could be arranged, Don Baldassare often came to the Puma house. On those winter evenings before the marriage he would arrive with a gift, a scarf or a gold chain—and sit in the large, tiled, room with Caroline and the family. The mother and a servant sat around *u bracieri*—a copper brazier about the size of a large frying pan set in a wooden holder on the tile floor. From time to time the women would ventilate their thick skirts to catch the heat as it came off the hot coals, left from the fire to cook the evening meal. To keep the embers burning, the servant would toss in a handful of almond shells put aside for this purpose during the summer shelling.

Some women carried a *tanginu*—a small copper bucket with curved brass handles, much like a flower pot—which they kept under their skirts or on their laps. The men refused to make use of any of these warmers. Caroline refused to use them either and kept back, an excuse to be with her fiance. So while the women sat around the brazier reciting the evening rosary, the engaged couple talked in the dark corners of the room.

Don Baldassare, aged 29 and Caroline aged 19, were married in Racalmuto. They went to live in Cianciana where the first three children were born: Santa, Marco and Giuseppina.

Santa was born the same year of the Fasci were organized in Cianciana and the year socialism came to that small town, although no one in the family remembered the revolution.

Marco, many years later, in Brooklyn, remembered in this memoir written in an English which reflected his uneasiness in both languages—I leave his spelling:

"From Ciangiana (Cianciana) my family leave to go Racalmuto—my father an' his brothers with my father went to Racalmuto for speculation to bige track of land I think about 2,000 acres land was leasing for about 5 years. My father took all his family to Racalmuto about hours 'ritting with care to—on way two bandit asults us and demand money.

The driver was friend of bantids. Tell to crooks, these people lefter the town ciangiana because goin look worka'—bandit let us go When we arrive they work with biger speculation they about two hundred working people inside the mine liker subway—after a few years 1,000 acres of weets (wheat) farm produce grains —thousand bushel weets. I remember used to be all boys and girls the age of

15-16 year old the used with basked full of sulfire stones to maker a piramid, take one or two weeks to build the mountains of piramids then capomastro light the fire and liquid sulphire come pour out."

The family moved into a house just off *la Baruna* which at that time was a vast open plain at the "bottom of the town." The plain fell off into a ravine down to the slaughter house. The Baldassare house was made of gypsum stone and mortar; lying in the oldest part of town, probably dated back to the 15th century. The mortar dried and flaked off. So that from time to time a stone would fall away at the foundations. Often, in the area, during a heavy rain. when water would come rushing down the narrow streets, a house would collapse.Don Baldassare did not find his house in good condition.

The foundations were damp, here and there the mortar had fallen out exposing the stone. The rooms were covered with dust and drafty from a wind coming from the north. Caroline was disappointed. It was a far cry from the ocre-colored *palazzo* she had imagined she would live in. A foreman from the mine, a favor to Don Baldassare and with the help of two *carusi*, in a month's time had re-mortared all the weak spots in the house and plastered the front.

Don Baldassare, thereafter remembered he owed the foreman and whenever he returned from hunting he always dropped off a rabbit or some game. If he had no game, he would leave a bushel of wheat at the foreman's door. He was careful to judge when he had paid off, "the debt". He watched for a sign from the foreman each time he left a gift. The foreman, of course, each time, refused the rabbit or the wheat.

Don Baldassare insisted until the foreman accepted. This went on through the winter, each testing the other to find out when the debt had been paid off. When Don Baldassare finally said, "Well I won't insist—*senza ceremoni*—and left with his wheat, the debt was considered paid. But he would not be sure until he met the foreman the next day and see in his eyes, the manner in which he was greeted, that the debt was truly and fully paid. Raffaeli remark, "Sicilians are born worried," that is understandable. Racalmuto, because of the influx of such families as Don Baldassare's from the small inland towns, was growing. As it approached the 20th century the town had 16,000 inhabitants.

The family also grew, every year another child, and all survived: Luigi, Tomaso, Angelo, Antonio, Grazia, Giuseppi, and Salvatore.

The older boys went to school and in the afternoons they played around the Baruna or went to the mines to learn about it's workings. The mine, in Gibellina, about an hours walk from town, was a family affair. Don Baldassare owed one third of the mine, his two brothers owned the other two thirds. Each brother had cut his own tunnel. They shared the above ground installations, transport and smelting. The surrounding fields planted in wheat was left to a manager.

Marco, the first-born son, often helped the *carusi* above ground, imitating their gestures, gathering stones for the smelting furnace. One day, fascinated by the smelting of the sulphur, he took a stone from his own pile and held a match to it. "I was a kit, may-be 7 or years older, not knowing what was doing. I walk around dropping the hot burning sulfire around the dry weets fields."

Only the frantic and quick action of the field workers prevented the fire from consuming the next year's harvest. Marco, who had inherited his father's crooked eye, was developing into a tall, lean boy who preferred to explore on his own, and one who was aware of his own stubbornness which he resolved by avoiding other people. But not without a sense of humor.

The house near *la Baruna* of course had no toilets and each morning the children had to take the urinals to *la Baruna*'s open plain. Usually it was the task of the oldest girl.

As she grew older the duty was passed on to the boys. Marco refused to do it one morning, and it was only his mother's anger that made him go. He returned with the urinal half full, however, saying, "I've emptied my part, the others can go empty theirs."

The years of the late 1800's, like those of all the small mine owners, were not easy for the Don Baldassare family. The price of sulphur on the world market dropped. Competition from American sulphur often left the yellow blocks of sulphur sitting unsold near the railroad station. It was difficult to keep everyone fed. In those hard times Don Baldassare took more and more to hunting while his brothers went to Caltanissetta and to Agrigento looking for new markets for their sulphur. Sales lagged, production stopped. It was in this time that Lutanu, the *capomastru*—the foreman who had been with them for ten years, sold all his belongings and left for America. This was in 1906; he left with 127,603 other Sicilians. Calogero, the middle brother took on the job of *capomastro*.

One day in the year of the Messina earthquake —1908— Don Baldassare returned from a hunting trip to find his section of the mine flooded. There had always been the threat of water flooding the depths of the mine. Elaborate systems of sluices and canals were devised to prevent it. No one had been working the day it happened so that little could be done to prevent the water from rising to a level that made work impossible. At first the flooding was attributed to bad luck.

Caroline, who was now thirty and beginning to thicken around the waist, her fair skin turning a sallow grey, cursed Don Baldassare's brothers for letting the disaster happen. Her sharp tongue grew bitter in her accusations that the brothers had purposely flooded Don Baldassare's section of the mine.

It was not a good time for such an accident. The price of sulphur had dropped and there was no money coming in to put Don Baldassare's section of the mine in operating condition. To let the gallery remain flooded was to let the supporting scaffolding rot and collapse. The longer they waited the more expensive it would be. The brothers weren't willing to invest their money in doing so. Island people are born worried Raffaeli often said. Sicilian historians speak of a *paura storica*—a historical fear, and every islander reacts in his or her way. Thoughts began to fester in Don Baldassare's mind. There was no money coming in, the boys Marco and Luigi had to be hired out as day workers in order to have some food on the table. His wife imagined all sorts of conspiracies on the part of his brothers. If he were to believe her stories his brothers' deception, he would have to confront them and in doing so he would have to take drastic action. He did not want to think of it. He went hunting and in the evenings paced in the *chiazza* with his father-in-law who often spoke of America—*nautru munnu,* another world.

They were disturbing nights when Don Baldassare left the *chiazza*, reluctantly, and headed home. He turned into one of the side streets that led to *la Baruna*. It was pitch dark. From the cracks in the shutters, here and there, he could see the yellow light of the oil lamps.

The streets were empty, The air smelled of damp hay and vanilla. As he walked he could hear behind one door the stamping of a mule, a horse breathing, at another door a man whispering and woman answering, some one softly snoring. On many a night he heard the women singing a song that was popular then:

> Amuri, amuri quantu si luntanu
> cu ti lu conza lu liettu stanotti?
> Cu ti lu conza nun ti lu conza bonu
> e malateddu agghiorni lu matinu.
> Cardiddu ca vai libiru e filici
> a lu paesi va, la sai la via.
> Salutami Racalmuto e li ma amici
> Te' cca sta littra pi la mamma mia.
> Racalmuto pi mia l'urtima notti
> Stasira scura, dumani si parti.

> My love, my love how far you are.
> Who will make your bed tonight?
> Whoever will, will not make it well,
> for sickly you will rise at dawn.
> Little bird, free and happy,
> You know the way to my town,
> Go greet my friends and Racalmuto too.
> Take this letter to my mother.
> This is my last night in Racalmuto—my town.
> The evening darkens. Tomorrow I leave.

Giuliano—or *lu zi* Giuliano as every one came to call him was a heavy set man whose work and whose poverty kept him from growing fat. He had a florid complexion, some might have said because he liked his glass of wine. He gave this trait to his 11 children—a fine white rose completion known as *sciacquati*—water washed. His children were also to inherit his barrel chest, strong legs and broad nose so common to the region. To the men in the family he gave a tendency to grow bald in their early years.

Lu zi Giuliano came from peasant people of the interior region of Agrigento. His ancestors had always been from the area, as far as he, or any one else could remember. He was born in Campobello di Licata, a moderately prosperous agricultural region. At the age of two his mother died and the following year, his father and he was given to an uncle—whose name was never mentioned, along with the lands his father had accumulated. This was done in "the ignorance of the times," as his daughter Pina said, by word of honor, faith in the family. Nothing was put down in writing. The boy was sent out to the fields as soon as he was old enough, about the age of 8. He was sent out to work alone, not permitted the company of others. He grew up alone in the company of an odd shepherd or a traveling farm worker. One would have thought this sort of childhood would make him a taciturn and withdrawn man. Instead he grew up to be a most company-loving person, who grieved to see his own children leave for America.

While the boy spent his night with shepherds and agricultural workers, sleeping in those huts made of new cut hay called *pagliara*, the uncle sold off his inheritance bit by bit. When the boy came of age he was penniless. But he had become a skilled agricultural worker—*nnistaturi*, one who worked with trees and vines. Grafting was an art and—people often spoke of *lu zi* Giuliano making his rounds from orchard to orchard and vine to vine, "carrying a black bag filled with his instruments, just like a doctor." It was this skill which gave him the title of uncle when he was a young man in his twenties.

As uncle, who was never mentioned by name thereafter, apparently was not aware of the legendary family loyalties of Sicilians. Giuliano was ill treated and so blatantly robbed of his inheritance that "out of anger" at the age of 20 he married Crocifissa.

Crucidra—little cross—as she was known, was a very young girl with strong twig-like hands, a high forehead, deep set black eyes and thin black hair which she wore in a bun soon after her marriage at 16. She had taken care of a brood of young brothers and sisters and had developed a maturity at 16 that many first-born girls acquire in Sicily.

She had no illusions about marriages all she looked forward to was a release from the poverty of a family that could give her little else but food and demand of her the work of hauling water, washing clothes, caring for a brood of children. It was a marriage of the poor without much ceremony.

Quickly, however, Giuliano acquired a reputation as a *nnistaturi* of high quality and skill. It was the years of prosperity for the fruit and wine producers and Giuliano pushed their vines and trees to maximum production. He grafted limbs from heavy producing trees to weaker ones, he irrigated with methods he had learned from the itinerant workers. His work was so respected that in his early twenties he was already being called *zi Giuliano* (uncle Giuliano). He was able to put enough money aside with the help of his wife who turned out to be a stern and efficient house-keeper.

In the summer when the migratory workers came to help in the harvest, he heard the news of other areas: how the harvests were going around Caltanissetta, around Agrigento, which lands were producing and which were being neglected, who had died, who had inherited and who wanted to sell. His own work too, took him to the fields around Naro and Racalmuto *lu zi* Giuliano was paid in a share of the produce. Those who paid well, he returned to, those who did not pay well, he said hello in the *chiazza*, but never worked for them again.

One of the jobs he enjoyed most of all took place in the spring—fertilizing the fig trees. To do this properly, he would tie too female figs at each end of a string, then toss the string high up on the tree. This he did over and over again until the trees were hung with dozens of figs on strings. These were the first to appear, *bifari* fat swollen figs—which would soon split and burst open, permitting flies to fertilize the new figs. His method produced a huge and healthy crop of figs which were so large and juicy that when they were split open, one could understand why the peasants called a woman's sex *a fica* or why the leaf of this fertile and sensuous tree should have been used for hundreds of years as a symbol of the only cover for naked sensuality. The fig tree is prized in Sicily.

Zi Giuliano also knew when to cut a vine back and when to plant one, which grafts would produce a certain quality of grape, which best for wine, which best for eating. Some of his plum and peach trees became so burdened with fruit their branches had to be supported by forked poles set in the ground. If Giuliano had gone to America at that moment he would have been considered an illiterate, rather dull, kind hearted simpleton and might have ended his days making artificial flowers in New York City. In Racalmuto he was an important member of the community, respected for his knowledge and skill. That even older men were soon calling him *lu zi* Giuliano attested to this.

His work took him more and more toward Naro where he heard there might be land for sale around Racalmuto. He first went to work for the man who owned the land, an old man in character much like himself. The old man told the same story over and over again, a story which seemed the sum up his way of life.

"One day I hired four men to work for me. Those men who come in the spring like swallows, to do some weeding for me. I gave them 10 *soldi* a day. But before starting work I took each one aside and told them, 'look, I'll give you this egg at the end of the day, if you work harder than the others. Be careful though, not to tell the others. They would become envious and not work too well.' So all day long I sat beneath the almond tree and every once in a while I would sing out, 'Oh the one with the egg.' and all the men would work all the harder to out do each other."

Lu zi Giuliano passed on the story to his children over and over again as if he too had found a profound reality about life.

The happiest time for Giuliano was the *vendemmia* when the grapes were gathered and brought to the slopping trough where they were stamped by young boys in hob nailed boots. He supervised the work. Then after he had sampled last year's wine and his mule had munched on the mounds of grapes sitting in the sun waiting to be pressed, they both went home, he singing his bandit's prayer to the Virgin and the mule braying and kicking up its heels.

The land around *lu Sirunni*, Giuliano had his eye on, was about an hour's ride from Racalmuto, on a good road running through a narrow fertile valley. The stone house or *roba*, as it was called, was large with spacious rooms on both floors and surrounded by well cared for almond, walnut and hazel nut trees. The slope running down to the road was covered with vines of both eating and wine grapes. These were the most valued elements of the land its cash crop. Below, along the road, was a wheat field which in meager years could produce enough bread for a large family. On good years the wheat could be bartered for a pair of shoes, cloth or a mass said by Father Cipuddra. Here and there were olive trees, a melon patch, sesame seed plants, a garden planted with lentils and fava beans. There were no ornamental trees and just beyond the house, the mountains were barren and splintered.

It took *lu zi* Giuliano a year to acquire the land. There were negotiations with the old man himself and with Father Cipuddra of Racalmuto who had set up a banking system. No one called it a bank or he a *banchieri*, as some writers were to call the men who performed the same function in the American cities later on. He cared for the money of those prosperous peasants and bourgeois, giving them a small interest, lent it out to those who needed it at a higher rate of course.

Father Cipuddra looked upon his bank which he operated out of his home as a service to the community. Giuliano, with his help, bought the house and land with the stipulation that the old man live there until the end of his days.

In the spring *lu zi* Giuliano piled all his earthly possessions on one mule and on the lead mule with his two children, Rosa and Giuseppina in baskets on either side and his wife Crucifissa riding behind him, he left for Racalmuto.

They came in on the far side of *la Baruna*, across from the home of Don Baldassare, up the cobblestoned rise, then turned right into the narrow *vaneddra*, then called via Cavour.

Halfway up was the two-story house in which *lu zi* Giuliano was to spend the rest of his life and to die at the age of ninety.

The house then had no water or electricity. But there was a large *dammusu* on the ground level—a small barn, more like a modern garage where the two mules could be kept. along with enough hay for them to survive the winter. There was room too, for chickens.

Giuliano left at dawn each morning to reach his lands at day break. Usually he found the two young men helpers waiting for him. He provided them with lunch and food to take home for the evening meal. Their wages would be paid when the cash crops came in. In this way they helped plough two fields on either side of the road, they weeded and harvested.

The nut harvest was left to the women and children of the helpers who came out singing, some walking, carrying baskets on their heads. They would spread out long sheets beneath the almond trees and then, with long bamboo pole, begin to shake down the nuts. The process was called *scutulari*. The almonds with their velvet shells fell like heavy rain. When collected, they were shelled, the outer coverings carefully put away for the next winter's fuel.

Because of his knowledge of other cities, *lu zi* Giuliano would take his harvest and those of others to Agrigento, sometimes as far as Caltanissetta where prices were higher.

He prospered both in his commerce and his family. Each year brought another child: Rosalia, Sebastiano, Salvatore, Giovanna Santa, and Domenico.

Giuliano was a good humored man who loved the company of others and was always heard singing his way to the fields. He was a gentle tease; often when the women said their rosary.

Sitting around the *bracieri* in winter, he would sit beside them, with a serious air and recite:

Hail Mary, full of grace
the shotgun is hidden in the shed
Hail Mary show your face
protect us from the police and spies.

It was the bandits' prayer he had learned from the men he had worked with as a boy. The women could take his teasing because they knew him to be a religious man. He was remembered as the happiness of the family, always laughing and singing.

Toward the end of the 19th century *lu zi* Giullano's family had grown to eight children. with the help of the mother Crucidra, the family had become close-knit, prosperous land owners, "neither rich nor terribly poor."

The memories and letters of those early immigrants showed little interest or awareness of world events, depressions, or the Fasci movements and these events seemed hardly to effect their immediate decisions. There is no mention of the Fasci, the collapse of sulphur prices, the retaliation of France in an economic war. superficial reading of these memories and letters leaves one with the feeling that each immigrant left for personal reasons. In the case of Don Baldassare because of the flooding of the mine. Yet these personal catastrophes were the direct result of the larger economic strains put on the life of the region. The mine damage could not be repaired because of the lack of sales caused by the glut of sulphur on the world markets. In *lu zi* Giuliano's case, bad harvests and depressed prices were behind his fall. At first glance it would seem his crisis came about because of a priest, as the townspeople believed. Father Cipuddra no doubt might have been happier and would have done more good for the community as an entrepreneur. He had entered the seminary as a *parrinotto*, a boy of ten. He returned to Racalmuto as a young priest of 24.

Some said he did not have the true calling, that he had entered the priesthood, like many others, as a way out of poverty and into a more comfortable life. Rumor had it he had made life comfortable indeed for himself. He was an enterprizing young man full of energy: his housekeepers were young women who often were not accompanied by older women. One might have forgiven him this human failing as he forgave it in himself but financial cuckoldry or taking other men for *fissa* in money matters was something else. Most men shrugged their shoulders angrily and found in him another reason to keep away from the churches. The *arcipreti* saw him seting a bad example to other young priests.

At the beginning it seemed as if he were a man of good faith who was trying to bring economic prosperity to the region. The good father had taken it upon himself to organize a savings and loan association in order to lend money at reasonable rates to small landowners in the area, particularly around Milocca. That he had chosen Milocca, this town of simpletons, made the *Racalmutisi* all the more suspicious later. He was in no way was associated with larger banks. The priest simply took it into his head to keep money for prospering landowners, such as *lu zi* Giuliano and lending it out to others who needed it. It seemed so simple: no papers to sign, no bureaucrats, just a handshake to seal an understanding and a few marks in his books.

Lu zi Giuliano, a deeply Christian man, was persuaded to be a guarantor for some of the loans. Within two years the priest's operation failed. *Lu zi* Giuliano had lost 60,000 lire, a small fortune—his well being. His signing as guarantor put him in a financial disastrous position. Father Cipuddra died shortly thereafter of *vergogna* — shame, it was said. *Lu zi* Giuliano was left to face the creditors in the courts alone. He had eight children to feed.

The reasons for the failure of the priest's "bank" no doubt came from the failure of many of the area's small landowners to bring in a good cash crop in the years between 1900 and 1905.

The suggestion came from the three boys aged 17,18, and 19. Some men from Racalmuto and Grotte had gone to America already—to Argentina, to Brooklyn, to Nova Yorka, to New Jerse.

The oldest boy, Domenico at 19, was a young man of "great curiosity". Then too, as he said, to remain in Racalmuto would mean to work for others to pay off an unjust debt. He would go to America to send back enough money to pay off the debt. *Lu zi* Giuliano could work at his craft as *nnistaturi*. When Domenico had accumulated enough money he would return. One evening that winter, the mother Crucifissa listened to the prayers of her daughters and her servant girl, Giovanna and was shocked to see one of the rosaries break and the beads scatter allover the floor. It was not a good omen The proverb and the ancients said,

> Spila la cruna
> Spila la famigghia.
> Break a rosary
> Break a family.

Domenico was never to come back alive to the family which literally was to be broken and split for the rest of their lives. A great tragedy to *lu zi* Giuliano whose solitary childhood had made him love the company of others, especially his own family.

No one slept the night before Domenico left. Early in the morning *lu zi* Giuliano saddled up the two mules, one for himself, the other for his son and his bags, and they rode up to the station. They both wept in saying good-bye. The train left, loaded with "many others who were leaving the families behind to knead their bread in the future with tears."

Domenico at Palermo caught the overnight Ferry to Naples where he boarded a German liner for New York. *Lu zi* Giuliano returned to his house on his mule and leading the riderless mule on which his son had ridden away.

No doubt all those on that train with Domenico went with a great fear and with a great curiosity, but they went with their eyes open to reality.

There is the myth that Europeans felt the pull of a distant magnet to this place America where the streets were lined with gold. For the *Racalmutisi*, they neither heard such myths, nor, if they had heard them, would they have believed them.

The *Racalmutisi* knew from letters read in their homes, the contents of which were also circulated by word of mouth in the *chiazza*, that construction workers or factory workers could make 190 dollars for ten months' work and an agricultural worker would make 155 dollars for 12 months' work. They knew too that working on *na farma*—a farm—was equivalent in isolation, to entering a convent.

TIME AS A GENTLEMAN IN THE MIDDLE OF THE HERD

Time has split Sicilians who came to America before the Great War in two. One part has remained behind to be found in the newspapers, commission reports, articles in monthlies, and in scholarly journals and histories. The other has moved on in time to settle in the memories of the men and women who lived through the experience. The first, curiously enough is more depressing, despairing America, filled with tuberculosis, crime and insanity. The second, to speak to those old Sicilians, the remnants of the Don Baldassare family or *lu zi* Giuliano's children, who seem like so many survivors now, is a happier, tougher, more content America. But then, life is happier and art perhaps blacker, no doubt as Raffaeli often liked to say, "Time is a gentleman and forgives us everything."

Don Baldassare and his father-in-law, Lu Buffu were among the first to leave Racalmuto. Why Lu Buffu decided to leave for America was vaguely remembered by the members of his family who said, "He heard there was money to be made in America."

There were enough real reasons to leave. The arrogant and corrupt rule of the Baron Tulumello was coming to an end. He was accused of having falsified a promissory note and of falsifying a bankruptcy. An order went out for his arrest, the mayor fled and went into hiding. Soon after the city council voted his dismissal and Emanuele Cavallaro was voted in his place. It was the year of Haley's Comet and children ran through the streets shouting, *li stiddi cu la cuda!* — "the stars with tails, the stars with tail!" The comet was not looked upon as a good omen and to avoid calamities, one was advised to rub vinegar on one's lips and not to sleep as long as the comet was in the sky. As if to prove their worse fears, cholera appeared in the summer of 1910. Those who could, fled to their country homes, but death found them there also. No one knows how many died, those who remembered simply said, "deaths were numerous." But life went on. There was a publishing house in Racalmuto which put out books of all sorts, the most erudite being the Polish poems of

Mikeewecy translated by Raffaeli Palazzolo while he was in prison awaiting trial for murder.No one knows whom he had killed or what became of Palazzolo or his translation.

Racalmuto, however, still had *malanni* —evils years— in its future, the coming of the Great War which had great consequences on the migration to America.

For the moment, those years before the war, the marginal shopkeepers, because of the depressed sulphur and agricultural prices, were forced out of business. Some left for Tunisia or Argentina. Although Lu Buffu survived in these times, he more and more often, as he saw the first to leave the town, repeated to his son-in-law, half jokingly,—Shall we go to America? We make a sack of money and live the rest of our lives like aristocrats." He repeated it so often that in 1910 it took hold.

Don Baldassare made arrangements with his brothers; he took a small down payment for his share of the mine, which would pay for the voyage. The rest would be sent as soon as sulphur prices rose. With his son Marco, the oldest daughters Santa and Giuseppina, Don Baldassare and Lu Buffu left for America. The rest of the family—Luigi, Tomaso, Angelo, Antonio, Grazia, Giuseppi and Salvatore—all stayed behind with their mother, Calogira. Don Baldassare was 47 years old when he left, his son Marco was 14, the daughters 15 and 16.

They left literally in the middle of the herd, for the year 1906 saw 127,000 emigrate from Sicily, 50,000 in 1911. The great year,1913 was just ahead with 146,000.

Lu Buffu was an aggressive man. His appearance almost demanded aggressiveness. He was barrel-chested and broad shouldered, with a large head and thick black hair which never turned grey. He had very thin legs. when he became angry in his store, he had the air of a bull behind the counter which seemed like a protective barrier—for others.

Not knowing English in those early days in New York, he would stand before a landlord or fruit dealer, until he got what he wanted. In face of insults, he only understood when shoved, he waited, and swallowed the humiliation as they said, which came out years later in a violent temper.

No one knows or remembered how they found their first place to live, but it must have been through the efforts of Lu Buffu. Both families moved into Extra Place, a small short alley still in existence, just off the Bowery on First street in Manhattan. It was an area preferred by the immigrants from around Agrigento, whereas Sicilians from other parts of the island moved in and around 69th street. Extra Place was a short dead-end street then, cobblestoned, and surrounded by narrow brick buildings. The hallways were illuminated by gas jets. The toilets were made of cast iron and set in the dark corners of the halls. The apartments were crowded with families from the Province of Agrigento: Puma, Franco, Rizzo. "I can still smell the cooking, hear the commotion, the laughter." Al, the youngest of the Don Baldassare family, remembered. "It was really tribal living; it gave strength to the weak and leadership to the strong."

Everyone went to work upon arrival, women, children and the older men. Extra Place had an advantage it was close to work. Factories around Green, Wooster and Bond street were within walking distance. In summer the children constantly carted home the wooden crates in which woolens were shipped which were broken up and stored in the cellar as fire wood for the winter. Often one saw a sturdy woman carrying an enormous crate on her head, as once they had carried *ristuccia* gleaned in the fields in Sicily.

Not knowing English made looking for work difficult and narrowed opportunities to those fields in which relatives or paisanos worked. No one then spoke of the *padrone* system or *prominente* words so often used by historians of the period. What the participants of the experience described was the help some people gave and which was paid for as a courtesy, as was the custom in Sicily, or at least in Racalmuto. One never went to apply for work alone, or to get papers, you were brought by someone who knew the ropes or had some power.

The expression was, "Is there someone who *lu pò purtari*? —who can take him?" In this way relatives were taken to construction jobs or tailor shops. If a stranger "took you," it was understood that you gave him something. The relative was repaid in gifts or meals. No one complained of this "system" which the emigrants if they called it anything would have called the person who had to be paid a *spiccia faccenni*—a sort of expediter. Then too, there was no alternative.

Those who were asked how they felt about paying for such services answered, "Eeh. Was I to give nothing? That would not have been civil."

The first jobs the Baldassare family had were in the factories surrounding the Bowery. The two girls went to work, escorted by Don Baldassare or one of the boys, as C.P.A.s that is as seamstresses in "Coats, Pants and Alterations," as Giuseppina remembered. Even then she had inherited her mother's sharp tongue tempered with a sense of humor touched with irony. She was a raw boned girl then with a strong jaw who often mimicked her mother's plaintive voice. "*Eeh, chi,* well, look at that, he still has egg shell stuck to his ass and he wants to get married". She, along with Santa were the first to find work, brought to a shop on lower Broadway by a woman from Grotte. Marcu soon after found work in a curtain rod factory on Spring Street.

Marco was joyful to be off the boat where he had been cooped up for almost 12 days. He had cried during the two days he had spent in Ellis Island, for fear he would be sent back. On the streets of the Lower East Side he was happy.

He was pleased to be making three dollars a week, including a half a day on Saturday, working in the factory making curtain rods. When he asked for a raise, on the prompting of lu Buffu and he received only 25 cents more a week he quit. He was taken by a friend to a men's suit factory on Bleeker Street where he was given a job as "pulling baste" which was his way of saying pulling basting on men's coats. There he met a Mr. Catalano, gentleman sewing machine operator who taught him little. The foreman, "Mr. Swhatz offer me to teach the skills of the machine for ten dollars."

But once the foreman had pocketed the money he forgot about "Mike," as he was being called now. "I complaina to the supervise, and would you believe, the foreman was suspended and I became operator on a sewing machine!"

The money the children brought in was enough for Don Baldassare to send for the rest of the family. The following year Calogira, herding the seven other children, arrived from Racalmuto.

Calogira, exhausted by the trip and the caring of the seven children, became ill the first weeks of her stay in Extra Place. She could not or would not eat the food in New York and lived on milk and Uneeda Biscuits for a long time.

She grew sallow and complained, regretting the day she ever married Don Baldassare. The flat was small, the odors turned her stomach; her once vibrant voice trailed off into a whinnying, "*Eeh chi*, so this is America." She rarely went out in Extra Place. Yet she marshalled the family, kept the accounts, told what to shop for and saw that everyone was in bed at night. It was to her that the children all brought the pay envelope. It was at her insistence, since she soon was pregnant, that a new place was found. With the help of Lu Buffu they moved into a six room flat on the top floor of 15 East First Street where Alphonso, the last son of the Baldassare family was born. Al, as he was soon called, kept a long and meticulous journal in his later years of the families growth and the changes taking place if not in America than certainly around Second Avenue.

There were eleven children now ranging from 18 years to the new born Al. The older children who were beginning to be called by their American names now—Susie, Mike, Josey formed a group of their own. They spoke Sicilian, had little contact with America and in general leaned towards a Sicilianess in manner and attitude, especially the women. Since they all had gone to work as soon as they arrived, this group never went to school, although Mike taught himself English.

An anarchist friend, Joe Vaccaro, who worked in the shop beside him, gave Mike an education, feeding him books and pamphlets both in Italian and in English. Anarchism appealed to Mike's nature the core of which seemed to be that he didn't like being told what to do. Nonetheless the anarchist movement and later Carlo Tresca fostered an intellectual interest and an enthusiasm for learning in general. In his own manner he taught himself English, went to Washington Irving High School night classes and began to write "poultry" as he said, took an interest in science and painting. He maintained and developed these interests throughout his life.

The middle group—Louis, Thomas and Angelo were bilingual, speaking English with a slight Sicilian accent and Sicilian with many

Anglicisms mixed with words and accents of other Italian dialects. The youngest of this group, Thomas and Angelo, became great ball-room dancers and had hopes of becoming actors. While waiting they became elegant tango dancers in the ballrooms around Second Ave. and Fourteen Street.

In their personal effects they left back-lighted photographs of themselves in tuxedos, their soft young faces smiling out eagerly.It was the youngest group, Tony, Grace, Sal and Al, who embraced American culture with an enthusiasm and exhuberence appropriate to their times. To see and listen to the one or two survivors now literally huddled into small apartments in Brooklyn or Rego Park as if they have returned to those small flats of Extra Place of 60 years ago, now afraid to open the door to callers, peering out at the world from behind plastic curtains, is to be reminded of the *Racalmutisi* expression—*la vicchiaia è na carogna,* (old age sucks).

The young group went to the schools on the East Side —to P.S. 25 on Fifth Street or P.S. 79 on First Street, then to Junior High School off of Thompkins Square Park, which gave Sal, later, the honor of saying he went to school with Lucky Luciano, Meyer Lansky and Bugsy Siegel.

This younger group was bursting with energy and quickly expended it on the violence of the streets which Americanized them. In a curious way they were introduced to politics at an early age.

In preparation for election day celebrations, the younger boys and Grace, who was turning into a tomboy, along with their street friends, stole straw hats off the heads of well dressed men and strung them on a line between two fire escapes This went on all summer; hats were added to the line, until there was a giant necklace of straw hats strung high across the street crowded with carts, wagons and carriages all drawn by horses. The manure piled up along the gutters, dried into a powder, and rose in the air each time a wagon passed, covering the boys' clothes, hair, and faces, stinging their noses each time they breathed. On the corner of First Street and Fifth Avenue there was a small barn housing two young elephants.

No one knew what they were doing there. No one asked. Late at night one could hear their trumpeting echoing through the tenements.

A few weeks before election night the boys began to collect furniture, some found, some stolen from the cellar bins, and hid it away until election eve. By then all was set.

The hats were strung across the second floor fire escape and the furniture was ready to be piled in the street. When it grew dark all the boys "from 16 to 70" brought out all the furniture stored away, piled it below the hats and started a huge bonfire which rose so high the hats caught fire. At times, in order for the flames to reach the hats, which was the object of the game, the fire had to be fed with more wood. More furniture had to be found. And excitement built up. Boys shouted, some cheered from the windows, other shrieked as they saw their own cabinets or chest of drawers go up in flames. If cops came, put it out, a new fire was set immediately down the block provoking frightened trumpeting from the elephants in the barn.

No one could explain why the hats were strung up, or why they had to be burned by a fire that reached up to the second floor, but it was done in many of the streets around the Bowery, up Stanton Street, all the way up to Fourteen Street.

After seeing Fellini's *Amarcord*, in which spring was celebrated by a huge bonfire I felt it was an Italian tradition. It might be preferable to think the fire was as inexplicable as why there were two elephants in a barn on East First Street.

***

Jacob Riis, the reporter of social ills at the turn of the century, reported seeing many bodies of young boys found floating in the river. No one knew how or why they ended up there. The Don Baldassare boys could have told him.

The youngest of the Don Baldassare family. Al, often in summer, trailed after Sal and Joe as they went off towards the East River for a swim. There it seemed as if the tribes of Europe had gathered around the piers: there were Jews, Poles, Ukranians, Neapolitans and Sicilians, all diving into the same water. Al saw a young boy dive into water hiding scrap metal, he surfaced with cuts and slashes the length of his body. Another boy dove and his head stuck in a milk can floating by. They watched while the can and the boy were carried away beneath the docks and among the maze of barges by the strong current. No one was fast enough to catch the boy. Not even Joe who was the wildest and most acrobatic of the boys.

He had a Chaplinesque body—tall, almost frail, with the quick movements of a bird and a mind so quick he could fix anything.

In an explosion of energy one day, he seized the housekeeper's carpenters saw and ran crazily around the backyard, the housekeeper furious chasing him. Joe laughed and ran to the clothesline pole, leaped and scrambled up to the top, the housekeeper climbing after him. As the janitor was about to reach him, Joe began to shake the pole, slowly at first, then faster and faster until it swayed violently making small cracking sounds.

People came to the windows. They shouted in Sicilian, Calabrian, and in English, "What you craze? *Pazzu si*. Carefully the frightened housekeeper climbed down. Joe remained up the pole for a while, swaying gently, until the yard was quiet and empty.

Then he climbed down, leaving the saw on the top spike of the pole. "If he wants it, he can go get it," he told his brother Al. How cruel it was to visit Joe the old man. Now locked in an apartment in Brooklyn, fearful of the night, of traveling on the subway or riding in cars, of leaving his block. Time in his case has not been a gentleman, but more in keeping with the Sicilian saying, *la vicchiaia è na carogna*.

***

Jacob Riis's descriptions of the tenements the Don Baldassare family lived in, leave one with images of unhealthy and nauseating overcrowding. This was true. But the herding instinct was strong. If, in educational pamphlets, the Daughters of the American Revolution advised the immigrants, much like officers telling men not to bunch up in battle, to leave the crowded slums for agricultural work, the Sicilian families paid no head. They crowded around First Street and the Bowery.

To the old, literally dying of loneliness, the herding of the great migration was a comfort. If hundreds died, threw their shoulders upon the ground, as they said, the mass survived. Nor was this herding together a unique trait of the Sicilians.

Riis wrote of a family living in terrible misery on Elizabeth Street. The father died, the mother could not work and the children were near death. Through a social agency they were moved from their dark one room flat to live in New Jersey, in a comfortable sunlit house. Within three weeks they were back, the mother said in her Irish accented English, "We do get so kind 'o downhearted living this way, that we have to be where something is going on, or we just can't stand it."

The Don Baldassare family certainly was in the middle of herd on the eve of the Great War. Lu Buffu was a comfort to them all. He had managed to open a grocery store in Cherry Street in one of those old houses, once so fashionable, now so often remodeled, it seemed gerrymandered. The store was small and sparsely stocked at first. Most of the space was allotted to goods piled behind the counter. Later he built shelves for the Italian produce large cans of olive oil with images of the King of Italy, and the new brand-name Pastene, with its motto *Chi mangia bene mangia Pastene*. The store began to take on the crowded look Italian grocers later loved to create.

There were sacks of lentils, rice, nuts, and barrels of olives and dried fish (baccalà). He kept his pasta in windowed drawers, dozens of varieties. Lu Buffu presided over the meat slicing machine close to the cash register and the revolver he kept there. The narrow space for customers was the only exposed part of the floor. The store might have been a replica of his store in Racalmuto. The sawdust on the floor was the only concession to American ways.

In a short time Lu Buffu learned he could make a considerable amount of money selling wine by the glass or the gallon from the back room of his store. The room was large (in the remodeling an apartment house was built in what once was a garden and right up against Lu Buffu's back room, leaving it windowless), lit by hissing gas jets illuminating the large round table surrounded by a dozen chairs. The back room became a club of sorts where men from Grotte and Racalmuto met to play *briscola*, drink wine and exchange news and information. Lu Buffu soon was making his own wine from grapes he bought in the New York markets. He learned quickly to offer a cop on the beat a glass of wine, sandwich, and later, as the back room business grew, to pay him money.

On the eve of The Great War, the Don Baldassare family was settled in New York, their network of relationships with relatives and other Sicilians was growing, their children were beginning to speak English and were on their way to becoming American. None of the immediate family was left in Sicily. They had all come over. Then too, the Great War closed the sluices to the Sicilian immigration. From a high of 146,000 in 1913, it dropped to 16,000 in 1915, and to 2,000 by 1918. The war separated many families for good.

***

When the sons of *Lu zi* Giuliano left Racalmuto they went to Naples where they took a German ship for New York. They took the German liner because the schedules of the Italian ships were erratic and most of their runs were made to South America. Only the "Vagabond ships" which went from port to port picking up cargoes, sailed to New York. Domenico learned this from Sicurella, the shipping lines' agent in Racalmuto.

Then too the German liners were quicker, had better accommodations and were more stable. The ship he left on was remembered as the "Onigerbergh".

Domenico was the tallest in the family, about 5'10". He was remembered as having a fair complexion and hair that was "almost blond".(Most immigrants in America in their old age, expressed and admiration for fair complexions and hair, something they did not express in Sicily.)

At 19 he was a serious young man with thinning hair and a sternness, if not sullenness, he had inherited from the mother Crucifissa. He liked to be well dressed and the pictures found in old albums show him dressed in a finely tailored suit, narrow trouser and a high bowler hat, its sides flared up in the stylish manner of the times.

He was clean-shaven in a time when most men wore thick drooping moustaches. He was not one to *fari brutta figura*—like those *cafoni* in Racalmuto who shaved only once a week—a sign of the uncivil man.

His younger brother, Sebastiano, was shorter and tried to copy his older brother's ways and manners. They both moved in with a family from Grotte by the name of "Five Hands" who had come over the year before. They were in the produce business and had two push carts near City Hall where they sold quality pears, apples and oranges.

It was no doubt through the "five hands" family that Domenico and Sebastiano found work. Domenico met a certain Mr. Bruzzesi who had his own small wholesale produce shed in the markets. He specialized in tomatoes and was already thinking of ways of producing tomatoes all year round. Domenico's knowledge of fruit and his serious talk about grafting made him work well with Mr. Bruzzesi, who later became the tomato king of the Mid-West where he reestablished himself after he was forced out of New York by excessive police demands for money. Sebastiano remembered this. For the moment, Domenico sorted various qualities of fruit and went with Mr. Bruzzesi. on buying trips to New Jersey and the surrounding farms on Long Island. Sebastiano, who took to horses worked as a truck loader and driver. Domenico's business dealings Americanized him: he began to dress elegantly, he spoke English more frequently than Sebastiano, until by the eve of the Great War, he spoke fluently, although with a marked Sicilian accent. He retained his stern manner which at times took on a threatening tone. "He looked tough and smart, Sebastiano remembered, "But then in those days it was a good idea to carry a gun around the markets. We all did."

Domenico's tragic death, according to those who remembered him, came about because of a woman. In 1915 he met a certain Sally, a red-headed woman (this in itself should have been a warning). But even stern, elegantly dressed Sicilians who carry guns fall in love. This he did with all the passion of a man alone in a strange and not too hospitable land.

For a moment, it seems she returned his interest. They frequented each other, as the expression went, for about a year. They became engaged but soon after the woman broke off the alliance and took up with another man. Relatives never spoke of the woman again; whether she was Sicilian, Italian or American was forgotten. The humiliation for Domenico made him "lose his senses" and in 1917 he volunteered in United States Army and for the war in France. The family believed he joined the army for personal reasons. From this distance though, the enlistment was not entirely from personal chagrin.

History or events pushed him also. Since 1915, when Italy had entered the war, the Italian government was demanding the return of all Italians to come join the fight for the Fatherland. The expatriates were treated like, or at least made to feel like, traitors; their relatives were refused permission to emigrate. Domenico decided to do his military service in America. There was a complete lack not only of nationalism of any kind among most Sicilian immigrants, but also a lack of feeling Italian. Where was this war in Europe? in France? It was as alien to them as the 19th Century war was alien to the characters in Verga's *I Malavoglia*. Domenico's sister, many years later, said mournfully, "Instead of doing his military service over there, he decided to do it over here," in a tone of voice implying that one army to her was the same as another.

Domenico joined the Seventh Infantry Division, took training at Fort Dix from where he sent a souvenir silk handkerchief, took part in one of the last battles of the War, was severely wounded in Chateau Thierry, "Between June 15 and June 22, 1918" and died soon after. The remaining family in Racalmuto, already making plans to leave for America, cancelled their plans upon receiving the news. *Lu zi* Giuliano was inconsolable when news of his son's death arrived. He stopped singing around the house he drank wine more often, so much so, his daughters would secretly cut it with water.

He wore black ties on Sundays thereafter and when he wore his shawl in winter it was black. The women went into mourning also. It was the first death in the family; the mother Crucifissa, the elder daughters Rosa and Pippina, were stunned by the news. The two younger children, Salvatore and Teresina were dutifully grieved by the death but were equally afflicted by the decision not to go to America. They were both young: Salvatore 18, and Teresina 16. In her old age Teresina remembered, "Eeh, life was good for me in Racalmuto. We were not poor nor rich. I had gone to school. I was a champion in lace making and embroidery. But youth is curious and I wanted to go to America were everybody was going."

The three middle sisters had already made marriage contracts with men who had gone to Buffalo, New York and were on the point of leaving. Giovanna had gone to marry into the Five Hands family.

All of this activity and preparations made Teresina, like all those left behind, sad and restless. She was a broad-shouldered girl with large luminous eyes. She had the self assurance which came from her mother and, no doubt, from having been brought up the youngest of a large family. In her speech she always retained the phrases and expressions of Racalmuto which gave her a reflective almost philosophical air. Of a bitter woman who left her drunken husband, she said, "it was in the time when she threw her one stone at the world." Later she would tell her children in America, "There is nothing in this world." But this only after 40 years of working in the dress shops of Brooklyn.

Salvatore was stocky and barrel-chested with a nose almost flattened which gave him a snarling look when he smiled. The two youngest were eager to go a year after Domenico's death, the three older girls left to fulfill their contracts and marry in America, men they had only heard of, but had never met. They knew their families—Terranova, Licata, Matina and that seemed to be enough. The two youngest pleaded to go soon after. They argued that they had part of the family there already in Sebastiano, Giovanna. It would not be as if they were going alone.

In 1920 the body of Domenico was brought to Racalmuto by a Captain of the United States Army. The captain stayed for three days, saw Domenico's remains buried in the cemetery Santa Maria and left a huge wreath of flowers with gold lettering—which read, "Domenico.... died in battle for his country in Aisne, France, 1918."

The Victory Medal for the Aisne defensive sector with its inscription, "The Great War for Civilization" was put away on the shelf of the armoire. The wreath was kept in the room lined with chairs for weeks, then moved upstairs where the children slept and finally moved into the shed behind the upstairs terrace where things of the dead were kept. The wreath was destroyed in 1942 for fear the Germans would take offense if it were fond.

Two other men from Racalmuto died in the United States Army and each home still has those medals, preserved in their boxes marked, "One Victory medal unassembled, with pin. The Art Metal Works Newark, contract no 9080-12. Mar 27, 1920." Surprising—There were anywhere from 250,000 to 300,000 Italians in the American Army, and 20,000 were killed in battle. The effect this had on towns such as Racalmuto and Grotte was devastating.

The war itself had a disastrous affect on these Agrigentian towns. It contributed greatly to the desire to go to America. In the fall of 1915, many remembered, began the long line of men trudging up to the station in Racalmuto on their way to the front. Every day women followed behind their husbands, brothers, and sons, crying in pain and anger, *Figghiuzzu di mamma, ti portanu a muriri.* Oh son's of mothers—they're taking you to your death. Some women brought children still in swaddling clothes and held them up as the train moved out loaded with men for the Northern trenches. The women pulled their shawls around their eyes and walked home alone.

The men left with medallions of the Virgin of the Mount and of San Calogiro around their necks which the women had sewn into little sacks. "Many men were found dead on the battle fields of the North, the sack of medallions clinched in their teeth."

The war was not popular in Racalmuto. The songs were bitter *Mi hannu fattu abili di prima catiguria, e m'hannu destinatu a la macelleria.* They've found me fit and able, I'm headed for the *abattoir*. The women sang:

> Na criatura chiangiva sta matina
> c'avia spiersu lu spusu—a li fruntieri—
> e di lu chiantu faciva na lavina
> e mancu cchiù c'è cu la spusa arreri.
> Picciutteddi nun chianciti accussì forti
> vi pigghiati a un vicchiazzu s'un c'è picciotti.

> A woman was crying this morning
> She lost her young husband at the frontiers
> Her tears were a torrent
> And there's no one to marry her again.
> Young women don't cry so hard
> Take an old man if the young are all gone.

The lack of men limited the harvests to the point of causing famine. The arrogance and incompetence of those in power infuriated the women and provoked demonstration against the war. Raffaeli remembered how the women of Racalmuto stormed police headquarters.

An A.W.O.L. soldier awaiting trial had been tied to the grill work of the front door of a building temporarily being used as headquarters for the Military Police. A certain Carmela Fichera, saw the young soldier tied and bound to the grill, began to shout in rage, "Look at our sons, they've tied them up like dogs. Oh son of your mother, what have they done to you." She continued shouting. Women came from all over town hurling insults at the officers inside; *figghi di cani*. The crowd grew, the soldier was cut lose, and the military court had to leave Racalmuto. The town was then designated as anti-militarist.

The women's anger was understandable. Wives of soldiers were given 14 *soldi* a day in a time when all the necessities of life were lacking. There was no flour, wheat, bread; no clothes or tobacco, let alone sugar. Fourteen cents a day couldn't buy a slice of bread. In such times the millers decided to close all the mills except one and raise their prices. The women were in the streets again, broke into the closed mills and forced them to stay open. But the war went on, food became more and more scarce, until famine set in. Hungry women with their children gathered around the City Hall, a delegation went in demanding flour "to bake our bread and kneed our dough."

A man by the name of Alaimo, who was acting Mayor, either out of stupidity or arrogance came before the women and said, "Do your kneading from the dust in the streets."

"And your women, do they knead with dust?" A woman shouted.

And then others, "Let's go see what his women do."

Led by La Pupina the mob of women went to the acting Mayor's house and tore it to pieces.

Famine caused such debilitation among the townspeople that they easily succumbed to disease and infections. When the world wide epidemic of influenza hit the area hundreds died in a matter of days. Whole families died, many fled to the Country side, only to die there. Many of the deaths could have been attributed to starvation.

Teresina remembered her mother not permitting her to leave the house during *lu morbu*— the plague as they called it. From her window she recalled seeing the *carretti* coming through the streets loaded with dead, "And people brought out their dead and put them on the carts, without any ceremony. Many, many died. "In our house we were lucky. No one died," Teresaina said.

When the soldiers returned at the end of the War to find their towns devastated by famine and plague, banditry became a political statement, a cry against the war through out Sicily. Racalmuto was no exception. Cattle, horses, sheep, goats were not safe even in day light; rustling became as common as hunger. Stolen animals were taken to fairs in Favara and Agrigento where they were sold—no questions asked.

Other returned soldiers plunged into the politics of the town. Unions were organized, strikes called. One such returned soldiers, Eduardo Romano, had come back from the war a convinced Socialist. He had known Togliatti and Gramsci. He became a Marxist leader in the area. Romano was a *muraturi*—a mason—builder who, through his contacts with the Marxists educated himself and dedicated himself, "to his fellow humble brothers of work" He spoke in the *chiazza* and wine houses, "with his open smile, lively eyes and his hands and fingernails tipped with white plaster." He spoke of equality, justice, and the inevitability of revolution. He founded the Proletariat League and a co-operative of workers. Socialism and Marxism, all but forgotten since the suppression of the *Fasci*, once again took hold in Racalmuto. There was talk of taking over the land.

The church, in response, led by the socially minded Father Cipuddra who was to be such a disaster for *lu zi* Giuliano, organized the Popular Party. Its members were nick-named the Luigini Little Louis—after Luigi Gonzaga who had founded the national chapter which later became part of the Christian Democratic Party. But for the moment it considered itself revolutionary and anti-Capitalist. The war, famine, disease had polarized everyone, the Church included. All agreed; the war had benefited no one but the capitalists, the bourgeois, the rich. The people had been duped.

In Racalmuto strikes broke out regularly, followed by demonstrations, and finally the seizing of the baronial lands.

In September 1919, led by Romano, a crowd, some on horse back, most on foot, a band a their head playing the revolutionary *Bandiera Rossa* seized the lands in Cometi. There was no resistance.

A few days later the crowd marched out to the feudal holdings in Villanova. But when Romano and his group arrived, they found Father Cipuddra with a banner of the Popular Party in his hand, had already seized the land in the name of the Church and the poor. A fight broke out. The Socialists assaulted the banner of the priests, tore their placards and replaced them with the red flag bearing the hammer and sickle. In the lead of the assault were two women, La Pupina and Alaimo (no relations to the acting mayor) who lead the attack holding up red banners on whose spear-like tips was a crust of bread.

These were the *malanni* so often spoken of, the evil years. They were particularly hard for women whose lives revolved essentially around marriage and children. But the towns had been emptied of young men first by the pre-war emigration and now by the war which decimated the rest. There were 196 men killed in the Great war from Racalmuto alone, with its population of 14,000. 33 were lost in action and never found a total of 229. It was tragic for the women whose lives without men became meaningless.

One understands why the eldest women of the Giuliano family, Rosa and Pippina, stayed behind, and why the younger women went to America. Since Rosa and Pippina were older their chances of marriage were slim. The choice had been made for them, and in a land and time where life revolved around marriage and raising a family, they simply said they chose not to marry. The younger may have said they were curious about life and America, but this meant they were going where the men were. It is no accident that the female migration rose dramatically after World War I. For the women of the Great War generation, to have remained in the towns and villages of Agrigento would have meant a shrivelling of life itself. The lives of Rosa and Pippina, who spent their days caring for the parents and then turned their thoughts and energies to a religious life, bear witness to this.

Rumors that the United States government was about to stop immigration brought a rush of immigrants. Salvatore, leading his sister Teresina, boarded a scowl which took them to the ship waiting outside the harbor in Palermo.

It was February 1920, the year which saw 108,718 Sicilians leave for America. The following year Congress passed the Quota Act limiting the number of any nationality entering the United States to three percent of that nationality living in the U.S. In 1910. In 1921 Sicilians entering the United States was cut to 23,082. Teresina and Salvatore had just squeezed through.

Soon after the youngest children left, *lu zi* Giuliano received a simple white envelope addressed to him in primitive hand. Inside was a thin paper written in a different hand, demanding a hundred thousand lire if not, his life would be in danger. For a while *lu zi* Giuliano said nothing to anyone. When a second letter arrived he went to the police who posted guards around his house and family. Giuliano himself traveled with his shot gun slung over his shoulder.

Nothing came of the incident, except that Pippina said, "A few believed we were showered with money by the America government because Domenico died in the American army."

Raffaeli said the two who sent the letters were not very bright *picciotti* who had brought back these ideas of Black Hand when they returned from New York in 1919. "They were living on wind and smoke and they thought they could put it to *lu zi* Giuliano."

The trip across the Atlantic took Salvatore and Teresina three weeks. The parting had provoked the first pangs of melancholia. The first view of the new world added to it.

The "dark and ancient buildings," the hissing jets of gas lighting the dark halls, the cold, the snow. "I dunnow" Teresina remembered, "I thought it woulda' been better." She wanted to go back. The ship she had come over on now seemed very comfortable in comparison.

Sal as he was soon called—and Teresina found a small apartment of two rooms on the ground floor on Christie Street.

Giovanna, who had married into the Five Hands family lived on the second floor just above them.

To over come the waves of *malincunia*, a Sicilian way of saying depression, Teresina was advised to go to work.

Her sister would not hear of her returning to Racalmuto, "There's nothing for you there." A week after her arrival, the youngest of the *lu zi* Giuliano family went to work, embroidering the then popular sequins on the dresses. Each morning she was accompanied to the shop by her brother Sal.

He also picked her up in the evening and returned her to the flat where she cooked dinner for him. If Sal went out in evening, she was left alone to look out from her darkened flat to the strange streets almost at eye level.

Sal was the youngest *lu zi* Giuliano's sons and the most taken by the streets around him, crowded with more goods and people he had ever seen. Nino, of the five hands family, had taken him, a few days after his arrival, down to the markets where he helped unload and sort fruit for the two push carts. He was paid, "a couple a dollars" and given lunch.

Within a week though, Nino took him to a produce store run by a relative from Favara who also pedalled his fruit and vegetables from a horse drawn wagon in the streets of Brooklyn. Each morning Sal would ride the horse and wagon across the Williamsburgh Bridge a shout out in Sicilian "Oh look at my lovely broccoli, my lovely grapes, my spinach straight from New Jerse." In no time Sal was bringing home 30 dollars a week and from the broken boxes of grapes, he was making his own wine. He kept the large barrel of wine in his bedroom, in the rear of the apartment. He learned to sell whatever surplus he did not drink to Lu Buffu on Cherry Street, whom he had met through his boss and where he enjoyed spending his Sunday mornings, dressed in his best suit. He often walked through Orchard Street, listening to the throaty Yiddish and the angry Gypsy speech coming from the store fronts where the Gypsy women in yellow silk blouses, their breasts wobbling lose beneath, motioned to come have his palm read. Sal's mind then was crowded with visions of making money.He could make enough wine and Lu Buffu would take all he made. But whiskey was easier to make and with the coloring Lu Buffu sold, he could make, amaretto, anisette, orange cordial, and what could pass for Scotch whiskey in his own bathtub and his cellar. It was a surprise, they all said later, to see Sal turn out the way he did. He wanted to make money, that's all he was wanted, He wanted to move "O Jerse" as Teresina said. He wanted an automobile. He became *nu malandrinu*, which was a Racalmutisi way of say, "a tough guy." Toughness had become a necessity.

Both Lu Buffu and Nino of the Five Hands family began to have trouble with the *Ganghi Airici* (the Irish gangs). In the markets Five Hands found no one to sell him bananas, or, if they did they would sell him only the left overs: "Take or leave" was one of the phrases he learned quickly. Five Hands started going to the market with two of his cousins fresh from Caltanissetta, and with Sal. One early morning Sal and Five hands were set upon, beaten, money stolen and their produce strewn on the streets. The next time they went armed. Sal began to carry a 45 automatic.

Five hands remembered, as an old man of 82, after he had had both legs amputated as a consequence of diabetes, in his soft voice, "They were *ganghi* then, that's all, *ganghi* we got our own *picciotti* and we were bothered no more." Five hands went on to become a successful wholesaler of bananas, supplying most of the Italian grocers in Manhattan.

Anyone who spoke English was Irish to most of the immigrants. Sal, though, took to drinking whiskey. Why. no one really knew, or didn't want to talk about. Teresina remembered, "think that's why he took to that filthy whiskey."

"Why?"

"Eeh, because. They asked him to do things he couldn't do."

"What things? Who?"

"Things those tough guys who stayed around Lu Buffu's store. He wouldn't do. He wouldn't do."

"He worked for Lu Buffu?"

"Sure. He used to come home *spavantatu* —white like a ghost. Drunk. And he began to drink... *Mancu si fidava* he didn't have the ability. He didn't like to do these things."

"But what things?"

"I really don't know. I never talked about things like that. He never talked to me about things like that. There were many killings in the streets then. I once saw a man shot. I was looking out the window and I heard three shots and saw this man fall just in front of me. He was very scared.

"Then the police came and knocked on my door. I couldn't speak two words in English then. I was forced to open and they came in and searched the rooms. They put a long stick in Sal's wine barrel to see if anyone was there, even. I was so scared. That was some *bellu postu* in those days."

"But you never heard of Sal fighting or beating up people?"

"I don't know. All I know... he was asked to do things he was not capable of and this made him feel humiliated and he drank. He just wanted to see me *sistimata*."

The word *sistimato* permeated the speech of immigrants. The word meant to be at ease, in harmony in this world, settled. Sal had fallen into a way of life that made him *malu sistimatu*. He was out of harmony. He was well aware of his own difficulty and for this reason, no doubt wanted to see Teresina, married with children of her own, with a husband with steady work—He wanted to see her *sistimata*.

Five Hands prodded Teresina's sister, who went to Lu Buffu and asked if there was anyone eligible for marriage among the *paisani*.

Mike who was now 23, the eldest son of Don Baldassare, was, *scattru*, smart, Lu Buffu said, and asked who the woman was. Sal said it was his sister Teresina, the daughter of *lu zi* Giuliano of Racalmuto. She was strong, healthy, never sick. She could have been a teacher of sewing and she was from that part of Racalmuto known as *La Baruna*.

"They gave me him," Teresina said with some regret. "He saw me and it seems he liked me when he saw me and they gave me him. That's the way things were done then."

"Who was they?"

"Eeh, My sister and her husband, Five Hands and my brother. They talked to me. They wanted me to take him. They gave me him. He saw me and liked me."

The oldest son of Don Baldassare married the youngest daughter of *lu zi* Giuliano in the Church of the Nativity on Second Avenue, after obtaining a marriage license at City Hall. Their wedding pictures were taken at the Rappaport Studio on Second Ave. and Fifth Street, on a crisp October day in 1922.

LU RABBI SCHWARTZ

Raffaeli liked to tell the story of lu Rabbi Schwartz. Where he had heard the story or read it, he never said, for all I know he may have made it up. But then there was a resentment about Raffaeli, as in many of those who remained in Racalmuto, towards America and towards those who went there. Raffaeli resented those who came back elegantly dressed talking of *la beefa stecca* and *lu whiskey*. They were reminders of his own indecision and his hardships in Racalmuto. He, like most *Racalmutisi*, never knew the hardships of those who went to America.

If ever I grew too proud of America, Raffaeli would ask, "Did I ever tell you the story of lu Rabbi Schwartz?"

No matter what I answered he would go on to tell me what happened to the Rabbi. Although some time it was enough for him to ask, "Did I tell you the story...."

Lu Rabbi Schwarts arrived in New York, with a long beard of a religious scholar and settled around Delancy Street among Sicilian immigrants. He was a young man, hardly 30, who had married at 18 and now had four children. He taught Hebrew in a school where the Jewish immigrants sent their children. It was on Division Street not far from where Don Baldassare lived.

On day he began to trim his full beard and little by little it became a little *pizzu* like the Fascists liked to wear, not all together a rabbi's beard. Pretty soon he opened a kosher delicatessen in a nicer part of the city. But he closed on Friday evening and he did not re-open until Saturday, after prayers. Schwartz was "mister" and president of his congregation. Then, in two or three years, "mister" Schwartz was a partner in a shirt factory where everybody worked on Saturday. He shaved his beard and he moved his family to the Bronx. He began to smoke, even on Saturday, and eat ham and bacon. His workers, who were mostly Sicilian now, went on strike one day— they called him a blood sucker, assassin.

He hired nothing but Italian workers and he changed his name From Solomon Schwartz to Sam Black. He moved again. This time to an even more fancy part of New York where there, "weren't so many Jews". When his daughter was grown she married someone who was not Jewish. The metamorphosis of Rabbi Schwartz was complete. He rode the train every morning from his elegant home to his factory. Until one day the railroad workers went on strike and the good people of his elegant town decide to run the railroad themselves. These wealthy men manned the trains. Mr. Black came every morning, working men's cloths under his arm, prepared to scab. But the three men in the locomotive would not permit a Jew in the cab.

Nor would they permit him to scab as a conductor. They would permit him only to ride as a passenger. Soon after that Mr. Black grew his beard full length again and allowed his daughter in the house again only when she had divorced her gentile husband and she married a Jew.

***

Every immigrant from the Puritan Fathers to those families from Racalmuto sought to make themselves secure "externally internally and eternally" in that order. In the 60 years which the Don Baldassare and *Lu zi* Giuliano families had to become, in their version of the Puritan objectives—*sistimati* they had little time or inclination to be preoccupied with eternity. What distinguished the two families from the Puritan Fathers was that the *Racalmutisi* had to change their identities—the Puritans created their own. And at times the *Racalmutisi*, like the rabbi Schwartz, as willing as they were to give up their old identity for the new, were not permitted to do so. The external environment seemed as hostile to the two families as any primeval forest.

Teresina had heard of the cold, the snow and of the fires. But the reality of the cold appalled her, "Oh the cold, the cold!" And the seven storied tenement house that smelled of urine, subdivided, gerrymandered really, into flats without water, heated only by wood stoves or gas heaters, frightened her. The hissing gas lights on each landing, the back houses (called *baccausu* by Sicilians remained in the mind of men and women until they reached old age: the trips down dark flights to the alley where a metal cabin served as a toilet. Some had great nightmares about earthquakes in these many storied buildings. Those who lived in wooden houses feared fires. Many women spoke of sleepless nights watching their children sleeping in wooden houses.

Wood was made for burning. In looking for apartments later the first thing Teresina looked for was stone steps and then for sunlight. Her great desire was to own a brick house. Everyone remembered discrimination or as Teresina said, "Sicilians were not appreciated." Al, the youngest of the Don Baldassare family, often saw his application for jobs torn up before his eyes because of his Italian name. At times the men were beaten up by roving gangs they learned to call *Airici*, Irish. The first reaction many had was to stay in the tenements, doors locked. To any one who knocked they answered, "No home." Many of the women admitted: "I cried and wanted to go home, to Racalmuto."

In face of this hostility the *Racalmutisi* or *Grottisi* had no one to fall back on but themselves and their families.

This strong sense of family did not come from some innate meanness or anti-social instinct. There was no other alternative. The Consuls of the Italian government spoke a dialect Sicilians from towns such as Racalmuto did not understand and who in many instances looked down upon the Southern emigrant as dirty, ignorant, animal-like, a disgrace to Italy.

They told the "watermelon stories" about Sicilians—Garibaldi brought soap down on his Sicilian campaign and the Sicilians ate it, thinking it was jam— genteel smile. Italian was the language of the rich and of the powerful and the language which put up signs in Italy stating, "Workers needed except Southerners"

The consuls were set up by upper middle class aristocratic minds which had little understanding of the needs of the immigrant and in many cases had little interest in finding out what those needs were. The immigrant was an embarrassment to his sense of Italian glory. Marco, always spoke of Italian bureaucrats as men "who lived in a cocoon surrounded by guns and look out at the people in fear. They are vicious wolves."

A kinder voice wrote of them, "Products themselves of a narcissistic culture which molded the Italian ruling class, it seems that, save a few exceptions....(they) were unaware of the distortions of the socio-cultural structure of the emigrant community. Many among this ruling class told themselves.... that many wept when they were forced to take out papers."

The American view of Sicilians varied. In the abstract Italy was admired as the mother of the arts. Their sons and daughters were sent to colleges where Italian scholars were brought to teach Dante and Petrarch. Nonetheless in 1924 an Italian immigrant could write, "It is a rare American who does not feel superior to a foreigner." Even the most sympathetic writers who wrote of the brutalizing affects of the work Sicilians engaged in concluded Sicilians had little mental ability in the first place. Their endurance in work, he explained, was due to their sense of timelessness.

"They spoke of events which had taken place weeks ago as if they had happened the day before or hours before." This writer, Foerster, also spoke of Sicilians as being: "fond of vegetables instinctively, miserly, sober, tricky, lazy, docile, passionate, an enduring worker, enthusiastic (but it fades quickly) suspicious, secretive, a time server."

There is as great a gap between the sub-human view of the Italian held by these cultured men of America and the reality of immigrants, as there is between the history written by some and the experience of Sicilians themselves. The gap of course in both instances is created by prejudiced opinion.

With the waves of new immigrants the pejorative image of Sicilians grew. It was understandable. Around 1900 it seemed as if America was not a nation split into North and South but an area where all the tribes and clans of Europe were camping in the cities, towns and villages of America.

There was great fear that these new groups, with their own newspapers, clubs, churches and with their great numbers, could challenge America's own identity.

The fear affected all manner of men. Woodrow Wilson wrote of Southern Italians as being the "lowest class, having no skills, no energy, no initiative or quick intelligence; the Chinese were more to be desired."

For Jacob Riis, the Sicilian was clannish, knife wielding, no squealer, and worked for nothing and inherently happy. In the South, Italians were not "white niggers" but just plain, "niggers". One employer could say, "It makes no difference who I employ; negro, Italian or white man." On the piers of New York, there was often heard—One white man is as good as two or three Italians.

Don Baldassare, his wife, the older children had little contact with this bigoted part of America. Don Baldassare lived more and more in Sicilian circles. The spaghetti factory he started was for the Sicilians in the area. A religious man, he stopped going to the church on Second Ave because he could not abide the Irish priests there. His leisure was spent with Sicilian friends and relatives. Entertainment for most families was each others company. Don Baldassare's entertainment was to gather at Lu Buffu's home or in his apartment and listen to the stories of Racalmuto. Sunday evenings the families gathered in the kitchen and lu Buffu would begin to tell a story while the children played cowboys, hiding under the table, roasting raw spaghetti over a candle—imagining themselves around a campfire somewhere in the Far West. Lu Buffu began his story with, "Do you remember the story of 'Rabieli?"

There once was a street peddler in Racalmuto whose name was Gabriel, but everyone called him 'Rabieli. He sold anything he could sell or convince people to buy. On day he decided to sell bedbug powder which he made by pounding the soft gypsum that abounded in the countryside around Grotte, into a fine powder. He went through the town shouting, "I have the best powder for your bugs, powder for your bugs, ladies."

To those who bought it, he explained where to put it and promised that shortly they would be rid of the pests. Of course nothing happened. And when the women surrounded him and angrily demanded their money back, 'Rabieli with a great air of innocence and concern asked, "Did you follow my instructions?"

"We put the powder around the bed as you said."

"Eeh and that's all?"

"What do you mean?"

"Didn't I tell you? You have to drop just the slightest pinch in their mouths. After all, my ladies, you can't expect miracles."

For a long time thereafter the people in and around Racalmuto used the 'Rabieli whenever some expressed the obvious.

On those evenings they told story after story of the legendary character, Giufà, who is often sly and cunning, often a simpleton whose only defense against the powerful is to play the fool. With his mother he played the simpleton.

One day his mother told him to meet her at Church around the time of the Angelus and "and don't forget to pull the door after you." Giufà of course, took the door off its hinges and arrived at the church with the door on his back.

On another occasion Giufà— he was known for his ability to avoid work— when he was loafing about the house, he was told to go out to the young fruit trees and raise mounds around each one. This process was known as *fari la mamma* to the trees. A lunch was packed for him and he headed out early the next day. He was gone all day and when they went out to see how he was doing, they found him in the shade softly saying to all the trees in the area, "Mama, Mama."

I remember hearing the story of Giufà and the ram while I huddled under the table with my cousins, all of us roasting spaghetti over a burning candle and Lu Buffu's voice vibrating as if it were coming from a great distance.

Giufà one day decided to go hunting, just like the gentlemen of the town. He took the old arquebus that had hung on the wall for generations, and asked the men of the town how to load the gun and how one went about going hunting. Which animals would make the best game. Everything of course was explained to him, *alla Giufà*, that is clumsily and in manner that was sure to court disaster. The best game he was told, was a large red-headed bird, the hunter's called a cardinal. (In truth, of course, these were the worst of scrawny birds, not worth the shot to kill them, all bones and feathers.) He was shown how to load the gun, and the next day, when his mother went to hear mass, Giufà took his ancient gun and went hunting.

Just outside the village, he sat behind a stone wall and waited for the red-headed bird. It was a lovely day, the countryside green and fresh, was filled with birds of all colors. None of the red headed variety. Giufà really didn't know whether it was bird or animal whether it had two legs or four. He waited, the old gun cradled in his arms.

Suddenly, just above a green hedge, he saw a brilliant red crown, more like the from of a mosque, move in his sights. It must be the red headed game, he thought, the most tasteful of game as he had been told, and huge at that; enough to feed a regiment. He saw the lovely platters of tripe his mother would make as only she could, with pepper and salt; and the soup made of the head; the sausages.... He pulled the trigger.

There was a shot like a cannon, loud enough to be heard as far as Grotte, and Giufà was sent back on his seat by the recoil. In a moment he was up and ran to the game he had dropped with one shot. The carcass was big, all right, almost as big as a man; two soft plump white paws that might have been hands, and two feet with fine shoe-like coverings. But after that cannonade of a shot, the carcass was beyond recognition.

And there was enough to eat there for months to come. Giufà carried the carcass home on his shoulders and in the kitchen laid it on the table.

He would surprise his mother when she came back from church. She would no longer be able to call him lazy and useless, not after this grace bestowed upon him by God.

His mother, of course, almost lost her senses when she saw what he had shot and brought home. She tore her hair, beat her head against each of the four walls, waiting in high strident whispers for fear the neighbors would hear,— would hear, "You've killed a Cardinal! You've killed a Cardinal!"

Giufà, seeing his mother carry on that way, didn't know what to do. Then suddenly he became furious by his mother's unexpected reaction to the game he had had the good fortune, by the grace of God, to bring home.

He angrily seized the Cardinal's carcass, put it on his shoulders and took it out to the courtyard and there he dumped it into the well.

His mother's waiting and crying became louder and louder and Giufà became so furious that he seized a young ram that had the misfortune of being in the courtyard and dashed into the well also. Then, not to hear his mother's wailing, he fled the house.

The Cardinal's absence was soon noticed. Rumors began to fly through the province. Police *sbirri*—spies were looking everywhere for him: in haystacks, in mounds of stones. They dipped long sticks in the huge casks of wine. Nothing. A reward was offered for any information leading to his recovery ten ounces of gold. And if some one denounced the guilty one, the amount would be ten times as much. The *sbirri* were every where: in the streets, listening behind the doors of every home for the smallest fart. If nothing else, in this way they learned that the courtyard near the house of Giufà, there was an awful smell coming from the well. *Sbirri* have a nose for such things.

Each *sbirru* attempted to look down the well, but the smell was so bad that their eyes teared, their noses burned and they became so nauseous that had to retreat. But the Captain of the police noticed that Giufà walked about the well without the slightest discomfort.

"We'll give you an ounce of gold if you will let us lower you down the well to look around for us."

Giufà for an ounce of gold would have jumped in head first. In a moment they tied a rope around his waist and lowered him down into well where he was soon up to his chest in water. He felt around with his hand under the water and then shouted up, "I found it."

"His Eminence?" The Captain shouted down, holding his nose as he looked down.

"What's this eminence" Giufà shouted up.

"The Cardinal, his Eminence, the Cardinal."

"I've never seen a cardinal. And who's ever touched one? I might be touching a cardinal. Then again, I might be touching a dog."

"Blasphemer!" shouted down the Captain. "I'll show you the difference between a Cardinal and a dog with a good whipping."

"Well, if you're going to talk about whipping. You can come down here to see for yourself."

"Alright, alright, I was joking."

"That's better." Giufà continued to feel beneath the water with his hands.

"Hurry."

"Hey I'm touching something hairy and wooly. Did the cardinal have wool on his back?"

"I don't know."

"You don't know! But how many feet did the cardinal have?"

The Captain was furious, "Christ! You have the courage to ask how many feet our Cardinal had." He turned to his men and shouted, "Bring him up. I'll give him a whipping that will make him walk on all fours for the rest of his life."

But the *sbirri* steadfastly refused, for the knew they would have to go down if Giufà were brought up. The Captain realized there was no other way. "For the last time, stop joking."

"Who's joking." Giufà called up. "I don't know how a cardinal is made. And all I want to know is if the one we're looking for has two or four legs."

The Captain holding in his anger but not his confusion shouted down "Four".

"Two" All the other *sbirri* shouted down, almost immediately. And the police began to quarrel among themselves.

Giufà shouted up, "Well, is it two or four?"

Finally the Captain shouted down, "Two. Imbecile!"

"This one has four. Therefore, it's not the cardinal."

"Two, four, tie a rope onto it and we'll pull it up." the Captain said.

"What for, if it's not the cardinal why go to the bother of hauling it up?"

"Do as I say."

"Hey, just a minute," Giufà cried up as he continued to feel beneath the water. "This cardinal, did he have horns?"

"Horns! His Eminence?"

"Is that not possible?" Giufà asked.

"I'll have you roasted like a suckling pig."

"Can't I ask a simple question? All I want to know how a cardinal is made and I won't have to ask you any more questions."

" Imbecile, a Cardinal is just like you and me."

"Nothing special, then?" Giufà called up.

"Nothing special."

"Then why are we looking for him?"

"Because he is an important man, because he is a prince of the church."

"Rich, is he?"

"Very rich."

"What does a cardinal wear on its head?"

"A fur hat, a red hat."

"But it has no horns. You are sure it has no horns?"

"Certain," the Captain said, shivering with anger.

"Just a minute," said Giufà who was fresh as a daisy in the water. "You say he didn't have horns. Did you know him when he was alive?"

"Yes."

"And he didn't have horns then?"

"No."

"How do you know he didn't grow horns when he died? I know that if one is sinful while alive, he will grow horns when he dies. Isn't that true? The cardinal, did he have many sins?"

"None. He was a saintly man."

"What did he do for a living?"

"Idiot. He was a Cardinal. He commanded priests. All the priests of the province."

"Even Don Pasquali, our parrish priest?"

"Even Don Pasquali."

"Then this cardinal must have horns. I'll send him up and you can see for yourself."

The men pulled up the cord Giufà had tied below and soon they had raised the rotten carcass of the young ram and Giufà after it.

The *sbirri* were speechless.

"Eh, is it or isn't it the cardinal?" Giufà asked.

The Captain kicked him in the backside and he and his *sbirri* left. The case of the missing Cardinal was never solved, for who would have thought to look in the same well where the young ram had been found.

Both Don Baldassare and Lu Buffu felt at home on those Sunday afternoons and evenings when they gathered around the kitchen table to listen to each other's stories. They felt secure and comfortable; they might have been back in Racalmuto in prosperous times. The Sunday meal of chicken roasted in lemon and oregano sauce, the home made pasta, mushrooms picked freshly in New Jersey, beef steaks, and wine, fruits and nuts—made the time of the green mice seem like a bad dream.

The old retained their sense of being Sicilian. The young had to find a new sense of who or what they were.

If you asked Lu Buffu or Don Baldassare what they were, they would answer, "I'm Sicilian." The older children led by Marco who had more contact with the outside world might answer, "I'm Italian."

The young children would say "I'm American" to their parents, but "I'm Italian" outside the home. Al, the youngest and only one born in America, would answer when asked what he was, "I'm a bricklayer."

Each one accommodated, emotionally, to America as he or she saw fit.

Soon after the birth of Alphonso, the last of the Don Baldassare children, the mother Caroline, after an attack of flu, lost her shape, she thickened and then shriveled into a frail old woman. Her hair dulled and grey wisps stood out about her head. At the same time she developed a great thirst which she blamed on the evil eye cast by some distant relative of Don Baldassare's and on this *maliditta* country. She began having fainting spells which weren't diagnosed as diabetes until much later. Then the strict diet she had to follow further shriveled not only her body but her mind which, more and more, centered around her disappointment in her marriage.

Many of the grandchildren remembered her as a complaining woman who punctuated her whining observations with "*Eeh chi*"— filled with disdain and tired superiority which can only be translated as, "Well, now look at that," as might be said by a woman who had once had been ambitious for her husband and felt he had become a failure.

If she learned that a relative had married a younger women, she would be quick to remark, "*Eeh chi*, he acts as if hot oil and cold water can mix." She had a good word for no one, and belittled any *paisano*'s success. But then America, for her, had quickly become a step down in status and aspirations. She had little too look forward to.

She knew too that her own daughter mimicked her with "*Eeh chi*—you'd think the world was round the way people act in America."

Caroline didn't understand that it was her daughter's way of showing affection. Nor did her daughter see that bearing ten children and two miscarriages, one perhaps an abortion had taken a toll on her body and her mind.

The confusion in the streets, the strange languages, bewildering manners, those first months, completely disoriented Don Baldassare. He yearned for the open quiet valleys outside of Racalmuto. The impossibility of returning made him think of ways of making a living in New York. With the help of Lu Buffu he bought some machinery to manufacture spaghetti which he set up in a empty loft. With help of the older boys he began to make all kinds of macaroni—from cavatelli to linguini, packaged in tough blue paper under the brand name of San Calogiru. No one spoke of why it didn't work out, but within a year the machinery was sold to pay off debts. "Your father is not like other men," the mother Caroline said to her daughter, "He can't do anything right. All he would do is go hunting. He'll have us all starving."

Don Baldassare withdrew to the flat after the failure of the business. He remained a kind man who, more and more, quoted the proverbs of his childhood— "Woe to him who changes the old ways for the new." or "From fire, heavy seas, and women, may God preserve us."

If the boys came home late they would often find him in the kitchen with his night cap tightly around his head, his shawl over his shoulders, seated at the large round table and looking out towards the window.

To the boys, "What are you doing up so late?" He answered, "I'm saying a couple of prayers to the infant Christ."

If Carolina found him this way as she went to the sink for water, she would quietly say to him, "But what are you doing, sitting here like a soul in Purgatory"—he would answer, "*Pensu a la morti*—I'm thinking about death", with that mocking tone *Racalmutisi* used when they spoke of emotions that troubled them.

During the day he cared for the children, did the shopping, set the table for the children before they came home from work. He never had a harsh word for anyone. Before any of the children married, when the house was still crowded, Don Baldassare would leave the house at night, saying he was going for a walk. He would not come back until early morning his pockets filled with candies which he produced out of his side pocket, his back pocket, and vest pocket until, to the children, he seemed stuffed with candies. He would open his fist and, as if by magic, there was a candy for any child who came to visit. Soon after Marco's marriage, he stopped going for his nightly walks, although the candies continued to appear. Much later it was learned that he had taken a job as a night watchman in a candy factory of a man from Palermo. It was the mother Calogira who let it out with, "*Eeh, chi*, we came here to work for *du caramelli*— a couple of lollypops."

Although it was rare, at times he grew angry as if his own disappointments were too much to be born in silence or kindness.

Late one evening he sat in his oak chair near the coal burning stove in the kitchen, whispering his rosary, while every one else had gone to bed. The boys Sal, Joe, and Al were playfully fighting in bed they shared. From time to time, between a Hail Mary and an Our Father, through clinched teeth he would shout, *"finiscila"*—stop it. The boys continued their brawling.

"Hail Mary full of grace....*finiscila*." A second warning went unheeded. And he shouted, "*Assassini*, are you going to let me finish my rosary or not. I'm storing it up for you." He returned to his prayers. The boys shouted, grunted and tumbled on the floor. With one last shouted, "as we forgive those who trespass against us." he rushed at the boys with the rosary in one hand and his leather belt in the other— whacking at them as they scurried under the bed. Al could see his white moustaches around his mouth and as he shouted *assassini*, his missing eye tooth. His shouting brought the mother Caroline, shouting from the front room— "Leave my dear children alone," while Don Baldassare brushed her aside with, "I'll teach them to have respect for their father and their elders. How could the Lord hear my prayers with all those interruptions."

Once order and serenity was restored, the boys came to say good night with, *Ssa benidica*—bless us father. And Don Baldassare, answered, *Santu*—"blessed be".

The boys returned to their bed and from there began repeating *Ssa benidica*—bless us father and Don Baldassare continued answering *santu*. The boys kept this up for a while waiting for their father to answer *santu* each time they said Benidica . Don Baldassare got out of his high double mattress bed, in his long johns and wearing his home made night cap, quietly came over to their bed and with an open palm slapped each one across the face, and with each slap he shouted, *santu, santu, santu*.

As the children grew and the older children married and left home, Don Baldassare slipped into the gentleness of a man who had willingly relinquished all power. The children could carry on. No one spoke of him as Don, there was no one and no reason to. Then, too, "Don" was being encrusted with new meaning in America—it no longer evoked a man of some accomplishment, of a certain bearing in living, a status, a well-being, a man whose very presence called for respect. He was called *lu papa* Baldassare or simply, Papa. He lived to be an old man, hardly talking except to say, from time to time, "People think the world is flat, with no oceans or mountains to cross." Or, if a son or daughter showed some laziness, he would say, "When I was your age I jumped the four jumps of the dead." No one really knew what he meant by the phrase. When asked, he would smile or laugh knowingly.

Josephine then, in her own mocking tone, using one of his own proverbs, would say, "*Eeh ch*i, you haven't lost the egg shell on your ass and you want to understand such things."

She married a former police man from Palermo who worked the rest of his life as a presser for Rogers Peet. She filled his life with six boys and the many proverbs she inherited from papa Baldassare.

Louis, a six footer, remembered as being in "perfect physical condition," introduced acrobatics to the family by doing stunts on the ledges of the roof. He went to Pittsburgh to work in the coal mines. The house was emptying, to the relief of the younger children who had more space and organized their lives in a more "American Way". The middle children lost the influence of their brothers and sisters who had been brought up in Sicily. They were more and more attracted to the world outside the tenement house.

Thomas, Angelo, Anthony and Grace all went to school P.S. 10. Thomas a short 5'5", well built, of fragile health,constantly played hide and seek with the truant officers who often found him driving a horse and wagon, for a coat and pants factory on Allen Street. A number of times he had to leave the wagon, as he was chased by truant officers over the roofs and through the alleys and stairwells of the tenements. To avoid these chases, he resorted to a trick many immigrant children used, to quit school before the legal age.

An underage boy would tell his school principal that his family had moved to Brooklyn or the Bronx. The forms were filled for his transfer; the principal told him to be sure to bring the papers with him when he arrived at the new school. Of course, the boy never did and he was never bothered again. Thomas was free in this way to earn his twelve dollars a week, all of which was turned into the family coffers. The small amount he was given in return he used to buy all the accessories needed to perfect the art of ballroom dancing. Thomas became the first local champion dancer. Even as he worked loading and unloading his wagon, he practiced moving like a bull fighter which, he told his brothers, was the way the tango should be dance. "You have to think you're in a bull ring, your shoulders back, you head not looking at the bull, but your eye is on him and you're proud. Your legs move like this, your shoulders don't... ."

He taught his brothers, and made Angelo into a champion dancer who remembered him as "a George Raft type". The movies Americanized Don Baldassare's children. Grace went to the movies religiously. She read novels based on films; her favorite was *Our Dancing Daughters*, starring young Joan Crawford, whom, she was told she resembled. These younger, middle children were Americanized too by the attractions of Saturday night along Second Avenue—the great white way, the Times Square of the lower East Side.

The boys came home from work on Saturday afternoon and the rest of the day was spent preparing for the evening. Angelo, worked in a laundry, but his heart was in dancing. Tony was the tallest, 6'1, well built, a little flat footed. He had the ambition to be a movie actor. His stage name would be Tony Wallace. In the meantime he worked as a plasterer with *compare* Totò and helped build the Empire State building. But Saturday afternoon was a preparation: the suits were carefully inspected, the shirts with detachable collars and cuffs were laid out, shoes well-heeled and shined. They dressed in the dark, windowless bedroom where they all slept: first their garters to hold up their black silk socks; suspenders more comfortable for dancing; over their shoes, *..Uspats; a white shirts, a silk tie, tie pins, and handkerchief in the breast pocket.

Once dressed, Al, the youngest would fetch them a whiskey flask and a hand warmer, a small tin container covered with red felt which held chunks of burning charcoal. The flask and warmer in their back pockets, the three brothers were ready to enjoy Saturday night on Second Avenue.

Second Avenue was a state of mind which began with the brother shaving, their shoes shined on the throne-like boot blacks stand made of marble with upholstered leather chairs from which they could survey the crowds. There were no cars then and few left the area; Second Avenue was their community. Strolling up Fourteenth Street or down to Houston and Delancey, they did meet many friends. There were bars and saloons, restaurants and dance halls, theaters, some with 13 acts of vaudeville, ice cream pallors and cabarets, movie houses. They passed Polish cabarets, Hungarian and Ukranian restaurants. The Russian Bear was one of the most crowded restaurant-cabaret in New York. It catered to those wealthy Russians who had fled the Revolution. Al, the youngest of the boys, remembered looking down into the restaurant, four steps below the street level, and seeing an opulent crowd gayly dancing opposite the Russian Bear was the Royal Cafe with its cut-glass windows beautifully designed and the heavy, carved mahogany doors. Inside the huge crystal chandeliers picked up the reds and greens from the thickly upholstered furniture.

The Royal attracted the rich and elegant who if they were inclined could go to one of the whorehouses on East Fifth Street, run by an old women in a brownstone sandwiched in between a synagogue and a settlement house. The famous came to Second Avenue: Al Shane, the singer, Arthur Tracey, Al Jolson, Sylvia Sidney and young Johnny Weismuller who was training at the Boys' Club on Tenth Street and Avenue A. His trainer was a man named Kojac, Al remembered. For the immigrants and their children Second Avenue was the *chiazza* of the New World.

It was not unusual for the boys, playing craps in the alley of the Public Theater on Second Avenue and Fourth Street to see the back stage door open and out came Molly Picon, who rolled—the dice once with them and went back in.

If Saturday night proved to be a debauchery, there were always the bath houses catering to those who lived in bathless tenements. The really bad drunks who could afford it would always go to the Second Avenue Baths on First Street, just opposite the tenement in which the Baldassare family lived, for a "lavage". The "lavage" had become fashionable.

This consisted of having "a tube stuck up your ass and another in your throat and you were flushed out with warm water." Men swore by its quick sobering effects. On hot summer days, the boys could watch the procedure through the open windows.

From their dancing the brothers, now in their late teens and early twenties moved on to acting. They wanted to make films. They wanted to make money.

With books from the Tomkins Square Library, they studied acting at home. In the evening they retreated to their bedroom and learned how to apply make-up. They practiced, "emotions: fear, joy, happiness, sorrow and grief." which resounded through the long flat, provoking the mother Calogira to shout, "*Eeh chi*, they have lost their senses."

Angelo enrolled in acting classes run by a Neapolitan in a loft on fourteen street. In classes with him was Joe Bonanno, Al remembered. Angelo, Thomas, and Tony Wallace now had their portraits taken with soft back lighting which they circulated to agents. Thomas also studied photography, taught himself really, at the Ficalora Photo Studio on the Bowery. For about a year they raised money to make a film. They borrowed from friends, put in their own savings, and finally incorporated as the Silver Eagle Productions and sold stock. Among their papers I found dozens of one hundred dollar stock certificates, fresh as the day they were printed in 1926. with the money they raised, they rented equipment and started filming "The Sheriff of Eagle Canyon." It turned out to be a comedy filled with a Sicilian sense of humor. The sheriff, representing authority, was ridiculed. He was played by the small, almost frail, constantly coughing Thomas whose incompetence as a law man reflected his disinterest in law and order.

"He was acrobatic, the Montgomery Cliff type," Al recalled. The villain was played by Wallace, "a Joseph Cotten type", who was over six feet tall. The villain, too, was incompetent but did manage to steal from the rich—huge amounts of money—which he later shared with the poor. However, the film made the point of showing the villain giving very small amounts of the loot to the poor, and on the way out of their homes, he stole a dish or a spoon which he later sold to an antique dealer.

The film was shot in Central Park and in the backyards of the Lower East Side. Thomas did the lighting, directed the film and the editing. *The Sheriff of Eagle Canyon* was distributed in New York and was still being shown as a silent film in Third Ave. movie houses in the early 1930's.

The brothers though, lost the rights to it. "Being naive," as Al said, "Although with the coming of sound, it did not matter much."

A print of the film was kept in the closet for many years along with "the things of the dead." When the mother Calogira, with her fear of fires, learned that film then was highly flammable, she insisted it be thrown away. Al, one day in 1936, took all six reels and one by one, dropped them into the East River.

To see the pictures of them all, taken by Thomas, is to be reminded of their energy and their eagerness and desire to be Americans. I am still struck by this whenever I set their photographs beside the picture of Don Baldassare, dressed his black suit, high leather boots, his long Semitic face, peering out at me like a young, wild, but sad pony. In the ten years they had all spent in America, a gap had opened up between father and sons, that might as well in time have been a century.

The sons' faces looking out at me reflected the vitality of Second Avenue, of a young people let loose in a highly competitive society who believed in the possibility of instant success. The enthusiasm of the twenties was reflected by all the children. The enthusiasm, one is tempted to say exhilaration, coincided with their youth as the Depression coincided with their maturity.

The leader of this middle group was Thomas, filled with energy and ideas. In spite of his frailness he served as a model to all his brothers, especially to the younger group, Sal, Joe, and Al. The brothers admired him, even when he grew sickly, perhaps because of this, for he seemed to acquire more energy and ideas as his health deteriorated.

Mike, the oldest son, from a picture taken at the Ficalora Photo Studio at 230 Bowery and the corner of Prince Street, was a tall, well proportioned man, with the pony face of his father, a strong cleft chin and full sensuous mouth. His right eye, if one looked closely, turned inward slightly. He had the air of a confident man, of one who bore no ill will, and if anyone bore him any, if he noticed it at all, he ignored it. His straw hat, Irish tweed suit, woven tie and pin did not seem alien to him. In the picture, Marco or Mike as he was now called, had become American. Yet he was much closer to Sicilian culture. He still spoke Sicilian at home, whereas the younger children, answered their parents' Sicilian in English. He frequented Sicilian and Italian friends. He worked with Sicilians, Calabrians, and Neapolitan. When his aspirations grew they grew within the Italian community. The younger boys looked to the vast America for their projects.

Mike had his own ambitions. Working in the suit factories, having lunch on the roofs with other operators, was not enough for him. He explored the streets picking over the used books stores and with a new made friend in the *paesano* Pitruzzella, a cement mixer on construction jobs, the streets of New York became a vast *chiazza* of the New World.

Mike and Pitruzzella often walked on Saturdays from Fourteen Street up to Central Park, talking about Capitalism, America, Henry George and Anarchism. It was Pitruzzella who told him, "If you can't help organize workers, you do better to get out and work for yourself—sell fish in the streets if you have to. Working here will kill you, mind and body." Pitruzzella was much like Raffaeli, he mocked authority but with a rage lacking any sense of humor. He raged against Jimmy Walker, J. P. Morgan, the priests who put turnstiles on our fears, baseball the true opium of the people. He always carried a gun, "because no one is going to put it to me". In 1938 there was a hold up in a Brooklyn Ice Company—a half million dollar robbery. Soon after Pitruzzella moved to New Jersey. Many years later he had a whole sale fish distribution company, a fourteen-room home, automobiles, servants and his daughter was in Medical School. No one spoke of the robbery, yet it was understood Pitruzzella had taken part in it.

Vendors often came through the shop where Mike worked, selling candies shoe laces, razor blades and condoms. One man came regularly soliciting accounts for a local bank. Mike asked the man how he had gotten the job.

The next day he became an account salesman for a bank on Eighth Street and Broadway. He sold on his lunch hour, on the roofs of the shops,to the piece work men who ate at their machines. The first time out he sold sixteen; a dollar was his commission on each one. In a half hour he had made sixteen dollars. It astounded and encouraged him. He sold on his way home along Broome Street and up to Stanton, from store to store, house to house, until he had sold sixteen more. When the shop was slow he continued selling. He laughed incredulously when he stood with a check for 150 dollars from the bank in one hand and the pay envelope of 20 dollars in the other. One hundred fifty for "a couple hours work and twenty for a hundred hours". Pitruzzella was right. The world was dishonest!

Sun was important to the *Racalmutisi* when ever they looked for an apartment.

After their marriage, Mike and Teresina took a three room apartment on the seventh floor of a tenement on Christie Street. They were close to the roof, the three rooms were sunny and they had good neighbors. Here more than anywhere they became aware of being Sicilian. Outside they were Italian.

The tenement was filled with people from Abruzzi, Naples, Puglie, Bari, and Calabria. For some reason they all referred to the tenement as *Lu Vaticanu*— The Vatican.

On the narrow seventh floor landing there were two flats; on the left Mike and Teresina set up house; the right a larger apartment lived the family of Don Cicciu and whose wife was comare Rosalia. They were from Bari. They had five children who were in their late teens and early twenties.Don Cicciu was a curly headed man, constantly smoking a pipe and carrying an ash tray that the could snap on to a cupboard or a chair.

He worked as a presser and had that moist pallor pressers often have. In the evening when he came home, his black pepper—like beard stood out against his wet white face. The Children—Joe, Sam, Jack, Jennie and Mary—were all musicians. The had been trained by their father who had once played the mandolin but had given it up because, "you need two to play anything worth listening to" and no one played the mandolin anymore. The boys played the trombone, banjo, drums. They played for weddings and dances held at the local Democratic Party hall.

Mike and Teresina were taken under the protection and guidance of the older family. They joked about each other's dialects, learned each other's recipes and Teresina taught the girls embroidery. In April of 1924 the first son was born to the young couple. The birth certificate recorded Mike's nationality as Italian, his occupation—Laborer. The first born, as was the custom, was named after the paternal grandfather, Baldassare.

The birth tied the two families on the seventh floor closer. The girls of Don Cicciu's family cared for the boy lovingly, he was the only child on the landing which, in a way was the via of an Italian village. For the young couple, Rosalia became *comare* as she showed Teresina how to care for the child, helped her with the cooking and, in general, was good company for the young woman. She became, in the Sicilian word, *comare* like a mother. For the girls, the boy, a sturdy happy child born almost nine pounds and quickly growing, became a loving plaything to be cuddled, caressed and cared for with all the tenderness of young girls brought up in a community whose principal of life was to procreate and survive. The women, of course, never thought of life but as bearing children, caring for them and seeing them *sistimati*—well settled in life.

The boy's name—"Baldassà" echoed in the halls and stairwell. The girls fought so much to hold him, that once or twice he was dropped, but he seemed to just bounce and not even cry. Nor did he fear being held on the window sill at the open window in summers to look down to the streets seven stories below. The boy child was showered with love from the women and the girls who took him to bed with them and taught him his first words of English, read from comic books by the beam of a long silver flash light.

From *comare* Rosalia, sitting by the large black coal stove, he learned his Italian, while Teresina went to work. The boy listened wide-eyed while the older people told him stories of Sicily and Italy, taught him to tell time, read a calendar in Italian so that the days, weeks, and months—time itself— became Sicilian. From the young he learned English. The boy grew up in two families; *comare* Rosalia soon became *mamma* Rosalia.

He would run to her offering hugs and caresses as he did with members of his own family. In the evening Mike would sit by the window and croon to him "Baby shoes..." or Ramona, the mission bells are ringing..." tunes popular then. Time then developed a texture of affection in which tenderness and love were not rationed. The women were open with him, something his own family wasn't. If little Baldassare surprised the mother Rosalia in the bath, she simply let him watch, and if he touched her, she laughed, "Your little ass is much more beautiful," and she would pitch his bottom *chi beddu culu*.

Yet the women whispered among themselves, knowingly, of the day the child was born as "my sin". In anger they might say to a naughty child, "You are my sin. You were always my sin." But where could all that affection and tenderness ever be found again in the outside world?

Everyone remembered "The Vatican" with great affection "where the doors were always open." For the child it was a comforting, secure place, filled with festivities, with Joe and his band playing in the halls, with young faces flushed from dancing and with smells of food that seemed filled with sunshine. For Mike and Teresina though, outside of the comfort of the comare Rosalia, the cold flat, the seven flights to climb with the heavy Baldassare in her arms provoked arguments. The winter of 1928 was grey and cold. Teresina remembered her life in Racalmuto which seemed more and more attractive now and fell into a deep depression which she recalled *Io ero quasi sempre ammalata di malinconia*—I was nearly always sick with melancholy. As a cure she, along with the child Baldassare who was then 4—returned to Racalmuto. It was the first of many prolonged visits as the family hesitated whether to stay in America or return to Sicily. For the boy it was the beginning of a tug-of-war between the two cultures. The mother and Sicily on one end— the father and America on the other.

Mother Sicily. Father America.

In the year and a half that Teresina and Baldassare were away, Mike became aware of America.

While selling his accounts for the bank, he met a salesman in the store of lu Buffu who told him of the marvels of real estate. "If you sell two lots in Jersey for 500 each you get 10 per cent. You make three hundred. Why bother with the small things?" He gave Mike the address of a Realtor on Park Row who was looking for Italians capable of selling. With his experience selling accounts he became an asset to the Kirkland Realt m(.U.

Mike sold lots to the land hungry immigrants almost sight unseen; lots of 25 by 100 feet in places they knew only as "Hacksack," "Woodridge," "Hasbrook," and "Wineland." On one occasion, in 1928, he sold a property of 10,000 dollars. The commission of 1,400 astounded him and made him admit to Pitruzzella, "A man could lose his head."

Alone now, his friendship with Pitruzzella tightened, as they say in Racalmuto. Pitruzzella who was Baldassare's baptismal Godfather was one of those gentle and at the same time intense anarchists with a determined sadness about him, as if he understood the great odds of ever achieving the fraternal order of liberty, love and justice the anarchists desired. He had come to America from Grotte where he had worked in the mines as *carusu* and where he had learned to read and write through one of the evening schools organized by the workers. He had discovered anarchy on his own. He was one of those souls, too, who although he did not read many books, the few he read were important to him. He understood them thoroughly and they became part of his life. Then too, books were a form of power and he suspected them too.

In their long walks around Manhattan, Pitruzzella's words were avalanches of ideas for Mike as they walked through the canyons of the newly built skyscrapers. "*Potenza e potere*. Authority and power can't put up with a rival; it's like God. Power is consuming us all.

115

Look what *a schifio*—what a filth of an atrocity they did in the War. Power! They threw tinsel in our eyes. The Fatherland! As if it is one big family. A family is natural, we have ties to it like the fingers of the hand, and the powerful use it to cut our throats and the throats of our brothers.

"They put that manure in our heads: The American Nation, The French Fatherland, the German Fatherland. So they can grow rich on our deaths. Power is a tuberculosis and Authority lives on it. And anyone who takes power, the lungs of his mind, become spotted and the rot and sooner or later he will die of it as a human being."

Marcu remembered those empty valleys around Racalmuto where he never had a sense of belonging to anything but the family. What Pitruzzella said made sense.

Anyone who wants power wants to use others for his own advantage. Look at the Communists, Pitruzzella said and became angry, "You know, when the Socialists around Grotte came down from the North and talked about taking power through the strikes, they were using us to get power that they could not get without us, they were using us. This Marx, this Lenin, they are murderers, power-hungry murderers. With this dictatorship of this and dictatorship of that. This Trotsky who organizes huge armies, will never, never help bring about liberty and justice. The tuberculosis of the mind has touched them all. As soon as you take power you are doomed. Those *camurrista* will be the death of workers. I can only withdraw from authority, work for my brothers, withdraw from a system that makes uncaring wolves of us all. Look what they have done to our brothers Vanzetti...(*Camurrista* was used by Sicilians then who had never heard the word Mafia. Pitruzzella no doubt would have seen the power of the state and mafia as one.) "and Sacco, two anarchists who wanted to be left alone, to live in freedom. And you know Mimi, without that freedom, there can not be love. Where there is power, there cannot be love. *Nun ci pò essiri amuri.* It seems to me."

"If Jesus Christ had a battalion of soldiers, he wouldn't have had a drop of love."

With Teresina and Baldassare in Sicily Mike was free to attend meetings in Webster Hall, to meet new people. He attended evening classes at Washington Irving High School twice a week, to perfect his English. He copied poems out of anthologies on love. He used old grammars to understand the structure of English. But the principal impulse for learning came from his friendship with Pitruzzella. He read the anarchist, Malatesta, and Carlo Tresca. His ability to read Italian or English always remained faulty and he often read more into a text than was actually there. This made his reading as powerful as his imagination. The Anarchist movement helped perfect his English, politicized him. He became aware of American hatred of radical European thought. What was done to Sacco and Vanzzetti frightened him. The Anarchist movement too, introduced him to the intellectual life and gave him a love of poetry and painting which would stay with him the rest of his life. In his last years when doctors were caring for him, he wrote, mocking even this last authority in his life:

My finger knows more about my nose

than any doctor can diagnose.

But for the moment he was politicized by his friendship with Pitruzzella. With his friend he attended the *meetincu*—a Sicilian way of saying meeting— Cooper Union and those halls around Irving Place where all manner of philosophies were discussed in the innumerable accents of Europe. He discovered the radical world of ethnic New York and it was assimilating him. Anarchist ideas began to pepper his speech—"Priests have put turnstiles on our fears and we must put in coins for them to comfort us." "Capitalists make wolves of us all. We eat each other and there is no affection." The phrase he repeated most often as he grew older however, was "They're all a bunch 'a racketeers.'"

But as a young man, alone in New York, he was energized by America and Anarchism. He took courses in science and in drafting. He attended lectures on Personal Magnetism and Yoga. In a political club (in later years he no longer remembered its affiliation), he took part in plays in which he had the role of an anarchist about to be executed. Later, it was apparent that he had felt a great fear in those days when Sacco and Vanzetti waited to be executed. He never spoke of this activity when he was older. It would be hard to describe or become aware of the affects of such governmental anti-radical measures such as the Palmer Raids, deportations, the execution of Sacco and Vanzetti, had on individuals, on Mike. The intent seemed to be the silencing of European radicalism and these actions were effective in America of the 1920's as the English silencing of European radicalism in 1790's. Like William Blake who wrote in that period, "Tiger, Tiger burning bright in the forest of the night..." Mike (who had copied much of Blake's poetry in his note books) wrote himself:

Oh little bird high up in the tree

Why I have so much fear?

Just because I read for thee.

In a year and a half Mike crammed haphazardly, pushed by an intense curiosity of the new world around him, readings, lectures, discussions and experiences to equal a liberal arts education. But the language barrier filtered it in such a way that, passing through a mixture of Sicilian, Italian and English and some Yiddish, it emerges so contorted he had to embellish it with his own vision and this caused malapropisms of the mind and language.

This angered him until he learned to make use of it in humor. Poetry became "poultry"; kid became "kit"; Washington "Washing a ton"; Herbert Hoover became "Erbeti 'Ova".

At age 28 Mike was undergoing an identity change which most people undergo in their teens. If only it had happened sooner. The sentiment of having missed out on something stayed with him for the rest of his, life touching it with a mysticism and a melancholy which he exorcised through a creative world he built for himself; his inventions, his poetry and finally, his painting.

Teresina's conflicts, as a woman, were more disturbing. The values which gave meaning to her life were as simple and ancient as Sicily itself—to have children and to bring them up in a civilized way which would show the community that she had fulfilled herself as a woman. What people thought of her was important to her and material things were for her a mirror in which she could see her value in the community. Being the last of a large family, she had always had this reflection from her brothers and sisters who cared for her as the lovely last child of the family.

She brought with her to America all the emotional structure of Racalmuto; it was wrong for women to walk alone in the streets, you showed deference to older people; and yet she saw women walking alone, working alone and old people, lonely and ignored in empty apartments. She too believed that her son Baldassare had been conceived in sin, and often dutifully said to him in moments of anger, "You are my sin, my sin."

She missed her family's attention which made the absence of signs of affection between Mike and herself all the more confusing. She had had no illusion about marriage. The word love was never mentioned. If Mike used such words, was the word "huhney" in English, and then only to mock and to tease her and the English language. Love and affection seemed to be reserved for Baldassare. The husband-wife arrangements may have worked in Racalmuto. In America where Mike was exposed to so many distractions and Teresina was forced more and more into the isolation of home and work, it caused a festering unhappiness. Both yearned for something better. They never talked about; it simply was understood.

Terasina withdrew to resentment and melancholy which, once she returned to Racalmuto vanished.

Lu zi Giuliano's family to which Teresina and Baldassare returned in the late 1920's had little opportunity or desire to change. In Racalmuto they suffered neither exhilarating nor mental disorders. The family seemed to be enough for them; but if one separated them, they grieved.

Upon her return, Teresina lost her depression and became a happy, radiant mother, proud to exhibit her American-born son. She was not aware of the great changes taking place in Racalmuto.

Mussolini and his Fascists had come to power in Rome five years before but had made little headway in Racalmuto. On two occasions the Black Shirts raided the Socialist headquarters just off the *chiazza*, destroyed pictures and literature, but they had to go to Ravanusa, 30 miles to the East for recruits. As Fascism took hold though, jobs and privileges became tied to loyalty to Fascism. Many "who had not found a place in the established parties and who were the greatest opportunists" joined the Fascists. They brought with them all the pompousness and spitefulness of those hungry outsiders.

The Socialist tradition was too old in the region to be stifled, quickly. Then, too, the Socialists and Communists thought Fascism was a passing reactionary trend. They would wait it out, go underground. Alphonso Tirone, secretary to the Workers Party, continued to collect dues and keep records of his group all the years of the Fascist dictatorship.

On his death bed, he gave the records and 300 lire of dues money to his children who, in 1945, turned it over to the Communist Party of Racalmuto.

Calogiro Picone Chiodo had a more adventurous time of it. He was the son of poor peasants who had somehow managed to educate him. He received a diploma to teach elementary school which he quickly gave up to become a journalist. In the early days of Fascism he protested against Mussolini, insulting him for having betrayed the working class. He was a happy orator who attracted crowds of young people whenever he spoke.

He was often seen wearing the broad brimmed hat of the Socialist of his day. Of course, he was one of the first the Fascists went after, once their power was consolidated in Racalmuto.

Special tribunals were set up to try such dissenters as Chiodo and he was forced to flee. He wandered throughout Italy, working as pedlar, living with friends. In Bolzano, he took refuge in the home of a childhood friend who now was a questore—Fascist title for police commissioner—for that Northern Italian town.

Chiodo stayed with his friend until the evening his friend the questore returned with a telegram he had received from his Fascist superior. It read: "Wanted—Antifascist Calogero Picone Chiodo, said to be in the environments of Bolzano. Notify all posts to assure justice before he crosses frontier." The telegram was from the Minister of the Interior.

The two men finished the evening meal when the qestore showed him the telegram. The next day his friend gave Chiodo a false passport and two agents who escorted him to Innsbruck. He became one of the earliest anti Fascists — a *fuoriuscito*. He went to Austria where he married and lived until the German occupation; then he moved back into Switzerland. He died in Milan in 1943, not far from the square where Mussolini and his mistress were strung up a few years later— not far from an apartment where years later one of Raffaeli's boys, Pino lived. Pino who took me to see where the Duce had been strung up.

Raffaeli remembered Chiodo as a man of many interests a Marxist and a spiritualist, a medium himself who once had communicated with Saint Just, the French Revolutionary. He wrote many tracts, now lost, but remembered as, "The Truth About Spiritualism," "The Immortality of the Soul," and "Bolshevism," in which he criticized Lenin and Leninism.

Soon after the Fascist murder of Giacomo Matteotti, the anti-fascist parliamentarian, the Black Shirts in Racalmuto began to ape their friends in Rome.

On January 2, 1925, while Eduardo Romano, one of the organizers of the Communist Party in Racalmuto, was walking home, a man stepped out of the shadows and fired three shots at him. None hit home. Romano recognized the would be killer, a petty Black Shirt, but refused to denounce him, saying, "Under the present regime it would do me no good."

Soon after elections were held. There was but one list of candidates: the Fascists. Only the Fascists were permitted to campaign.

The Black Shirts saw to it that the vote was gotten out. In spite of this, Romano, the Communist, received 400 votes which impressed the local Fascists so much that they avoided any further "ferocious persecution".

The 400 Communist votes encouraged resistance. One evening Romano went to the theater. He chose to sit in the center seats. Before the performance began, the Fascist hymn "Giovinezza" was played and everyone stood, took off their hats and looked respectable.

Romano remained seated, his hat still on his head and a cigar hanging from his lips. The local teacher, Don Niniddu, as he was known, rushed up to him and shouted, "Get up, take your hat off, and stop smoking!"

Romano, in a voice to be heard in the whole theater, answered, "I will not stand, I will not take my hat off and I will not stop smoking."

The Fascist Mayor from his box shouted down, "Arrest him!" The carabinieri moved towards him when the whole theater burst out in a chant of "No! No! No!"

It was the local Fascist leader who intervened, stopped the carabinieri, saying, "Don't bother. If not, we won't be able to go on with the show." There was a Pirandellian quality to the scene; the Fascists in a sense avoided reality when it was contrary to their illusions.

I heard these stories years later, from Raffaeli. If they had a anti-Fascist bias and exaggerated anti-Fascist activity it no doubt came from Raffaeli instinct to mock all authority.

Although Mussolini was now in power, bringing with him an air of operatic bombast, Teresina noticed little change in the house on the Via Cavour which she had left six years before. She did remark that she had gone to America on a German ship and returned on an Italian ship, the Conte di Savoia on which she felt much more at home.

The trip was a delight,the food astounded her with its variety and abundance. She was introduced to Italian civility on board ship and little Baldassare was treated like a little *signorino* by every one on board. The ship anchored outside Palermo where they were ferried into the harbor on a small boat. The reunion with *lu papa* Giuliano who had come with one of his workmen to meet them, was joyful and tearful. Young Baldassare was more curious about the train which smelled of coal tar much like the roofs of New York in the sun.

The reunion in Racalmuto was tearful and joyful. Pippina shrieked her welcome frightening Baldassare. But once the first emotions had subsided, the boy was the object of much affection and attention, as the "little *Americanu.* "

Teresina found Papà Giuliano as he was called in the family now, grieving more than anyone for his children who had left for America, especially for Domenico killed in the war. He consoled himself with work which accumulated some wealth. A pension given by the United States Government, in dollars, contributed to the family's well being. But his son's death confused Giuliano. He often fingered the medal left him by the American Captain. Pointing to it he asked Teresina, "What's written here?" And Teresina translated: "The Great War for Civilization?"

"For what?....Civilicia, civilici... Eeh, I can't manage to pronounce it." He turned the medal over, "And what's written on this side?"

Teresina, not knowing where or what Aisne was, pronounced it in Italian *asine*. It sounded as if she were saying donkey. "We really are jackasses, my daughter," Papa Giuliano said, "That's true."

It was remembered as a bitter joke to the end of all their lives. For Teresina it was a coming home. Baldassare could hear her laughter and her singing as she helped with the house chores, something he had rarely heard in "the Vatican". For the boy it was a visit to relatives who lived in a sunny land where he rode horses, was taken through fields of wheat so high he seemed to be in a golden forest: where he could collect sweet fruits from trees and vines which his grandfather led him to with much care and love both: for the boy, the trees and the vines. These days filled with sunshine and family love implanted in the boy a sentiment of secure happiness which once back in America he associated with Sicily.

Teresina brought them news of the family in America: the sisters in Buffalo and Hamilton all had children; the men steady jobs in steel mills. Sebastiano had opened a grocery store in *Brookulinu*. His produce was the best and he found a clientele among those working class Brooklynites in Gravesend Bay. She described the tree-lined streets, the homes with gardens just behind the wooden houses. And there were farms, not far from the beach on Bay 13th street and Bay 9th street. Bastiano's store was on Bay 25 street, *due blocchi* from the beach where in the in summer everyone went to sit by the sea to refresh themsem*.Ues.

"But don't they burn themselves?" Rosa asked.

"No, the sun is not that strong as here and every once in while they go in the water."

"How, with all their cloth? They'd catch a death of cold!"

"No, there are bathing suits."

"With their thighs showing?" Pippina cried out. "Oh Beautiful Mother Mary!"

"Eeh, that's the way things are in America:"

Teresina told them of *lu trollecar* and *lu trenu* which took an hour to get from Stantoni Street to Bensonhurst and to Coonisle where there was a confusion of people, a mountain of people on the beaches.

The sisters listened and Rosa would say from time to time, "Eeh, for me, I wouldn't like this America."

"Me neither," Pippina chimed in.

The year was spent as if Teresina was staying for good. Baldassare was the center of social life in the family and for all those who came to visit. He learned to speak a Sicilian *ncarcato*, a heavily accented Sicilian. Teresina had to repeat her stories about America to all who came and tell that Sebastiano had a store and three sons all born in America.

They asked about work. "Work there is, but I tell you, you work and life is not good. There is a cold that bursts the heart. People are crazy. There is a confusion and a *schifiu*—a filth. The houses never see the sun. The men drink *lu Whiskey* and become *bumi*."

"What is a *bumi*?"

"The Americans say *bumi* for those who drink so much 'wiske' they are drunkards, crazy."

"But you say there is work?"

"Eeh, work there always is. But you must give them your blood." The conversation was repeated over and over again in the homes she visited.

That Spring and Summer they lived in the *aria*, papa Giuliano's lands where they would sit with neighbors in the evening freshness and watch the lights of the fishing boats rocking in sea, way off in the distance.

Papa Giuliano pointed to the lights, "See, Baldassare, there are the fishermen. They're catching fish. Tomorrow we will go get some marlin. And we will eat them. And look over there, there's Favara, and there is Montedoro."

Sitting close by the grandfather Giuliano who smelled of snuff, peaches and the sunshine he had been working in all day, the words settled in Baldassare's mind along with a sense of loving wonderment for the people around him.

The time for leaving was bound to come. Everyone came to the station up on the hill.

The sidings were lined with blocks of yellow sulphur. The papa Giuliano, mama Crucifissa, Rosa, Pippina and the servant girl

Giovanna—they were all there. The sisters were crying and mother Crucifissa, dry-eyed and stern, kissed Baldassare. He was hugged, almost violently, by everyone, although he seemed more fascinated by the sulphur blocks along the siding.

Papa Giuliano gave his last reminder for greetings to all his sons in America and with "you must make yourself some courage, daughter," no doubt addressed to himself as well as to Teresina, he put Baldassare on the train. They all believed it was the last time they would see each other.

The Racalmuto Teresina and Baldassaro saw slipping away through the train window was firmly in the hands of the Fascists. The City Council was all Fascist and it elected Enrico Macaluso as Mayor. Mussolini had spawned hundreds of mayors, replicas of his own strutting.

Enrico Macaluso, pharmacist turned Fascist, was no exception. His pharmacy at one end of the *chiazza* facing the Mother Church became a center for the public officials—all Fascists now, who looked out scornfully to the "cuckold populace" and to Macaluso with respect and admiration.

Don Enrico demanded it. If a barber did not greet him with, "Kiss your hand, Don Rico, "he soon found himself without customers. If men insisted on frequenting his barber shop, the barber found his sons expelled from school.

One had to buy one's medicaments at his pharmacy, if not, a son or relative might not enter college, or, as happened to one boy, be prev06Uvented from ing a job. Don Enrico's motto wa*schi sbaglia, paga*—who makes a mistake, pays. He enjoyed strutting in the *chiazza* followed by an entourage of Fascists, functionaries and job seekers. Behind him was the power of General Mori who had been sent to Sicily to "eradicate" the mafia but who, in reality, used his power to wipe out the opposition of antiFascists. Men were murdered, whole families persecuted, exiled to desolate islands, without accusation of any offense. With such terror any opposition was stifled. These Fascists, as one aging school teacher later said, had no political experience, no constituency, they had raw power, they were responsible to no one and it went to their head. The Fascists found freedom while everyone else found humiliation. Any slight to the

Fascist Mayor or his followers was to be paid. A Socialist merchant who had offended the mayor found himself out business. His son, hounded out of Sicily, went to America where he settled in Virginia, it was heard years later, where he became a union organizer! This was Salvatore Greco known as *Cinniredda*—Little ashes. Appropriately the family scattered; there was no place for them in Racalmuto. A Student who contributed a lira to the flowers for the murdered Socialist leader Matteotti was thrown out of his final exams at Medical School in Palermo. When he asked why, he was told to go to his home town and ask. An old Socialist, Michele Di Niro, despairing, committed suicide by stepping in front of a train. Another Socialist who had led the demonstrations of 1893-94 went from person to person in the *chiazza* collecting enough money to buy the suicide's widow a sewing machine.

For the most part, opposition went underground to rise up in fits of personal anger, more a refusal of the individual to be humiliated and dominated by the arrogant and primitive minds in power. Arrests and imprisonments continued to be made on whims or the pleasure of Don Rico. But his honor the mayor slept badly and noises disturbed his sleep.

The peasants coming in from the fields at night always loaded, their plows on their mules; their handles dragging along the ground could be heard long distances late at night. Because this disturbed his sleep, the mayor decreed "That all plows handles will not be dragged along the ground." Some men were so intimidated that they carried the plow themselves when they neared town. Others, however, were not so easily intimidated.

One morning the mayor found on his door step a pile of shit with a note which read:

qua la faccio
qua la lascio
merda al Duce
merda al Fascio
Here I do it
Here I leave it.
Shit to the Duce
Shit to the Fascio

All the forces of Fascism were unleashed to discover the culprit.

Giuseppi Collura was arrested, given a trial before the special tribunal and sentenced to the prison of San Vito in Agrigento. The Mayor-Duce in a gesture of petty arrogance handed the prisoner 10 lire and said, "Buy yourself some tobacco in San Vito" Collura took the money in his manacled hands and threw it in Macaluso's face. This was not the end of it. When he returned to Racalmuto after having served his time, he was accused of having committed a murder, of which, of course, he was innocent.

But then this was a common practice of the Fascists. Whenever a crime was committed, the local Fascists would pick up a anti-fascist or anyone against whom they held a grudge, accuse him of the crime, and before the special tribunal quickly sentenced him. The method gave the world the impression that Fascism effectively fought crime.

The truth was that crime went unpunished and injustice flourished. Collura was tried and of course Mayor -Duce Macaluso came to testify against him. All that Collura could do from his cage in court was to spit squarely at the Mayor as he passed him to take the witness stand. Collura was condemned to prison again.

Sometime later, the murderer, on his death bed, apparently, confessed. Again Collura returned to Racalmuto where he demanded money from the Mayor-Duce, who gave him weekly sums until he could find a job.

But the Fascist Mayor never refused the poor or the sick money. His generosity extended to everyone who was willing to take it. Many could never pay for the appliances he began to carry in his pharmacy.

If one came to pay an overdue bill, he was quick to say, "Let it be. We will talk about it later." The unkind said it was his way of tying people to him or like most bullies he had an inordinate need to be liked. Nonetheless, Macaluso was one of the few Fascists who did not profit from his position. He would have died impoverished had it not been for his daughter who looked after him after the war.

***

Teresina and Baldassare returned on the Conte di Savoia in September 1927, just a few weeks after the execution of Sacco and Vanzetti which had disturbed Mike visibly. The execution was no less disturbing to him than the sight of the grandiose funeral accorded a murdered gangster, which was attended by judges and politicians and by the rich and powerful of the city. He began to use the phrase, "They're all a bunch of racketeers" more often.

Baldassare often lulled himself to sleep in his crib-like bed with the chant he had heard in the fields around Racalmuto.

Sugnu na addrina spersa
ma nuddru mi chiama.
I'm a lost chicken
but no one calls me.

MALANNI OR HARD TIMES

One night soon after Teresina's return from Sicily, Mike, returning from a meeting at Webster Hall, heard a voice coming from a doorway, "Mike, take longer steps." He had just turned into Christie Street when he heard the shoots. He rushed up to the apartment.Teresina and the boy were already asleep. The next day they decided to move to Brooklyn.

Mike sold real estate full time now. There was enough money to permit the move. Pitruzzella had moved there a few months before and told him of an apartment on Bay 13th Street in the Bath Beach section. It was on the fourth floor rear and constantly flooded with sunshine. The move took them away from the Vatican, a totally Italian immigrant neighborhood and brought them to area where there were many Irish, Germans and Jews.

On Benson Avenue there were gas lamps still, lit by lamp-lighters, a board-walk (which made Baldassare think they had moved to the far west) fronted the A and P. it was small store run by a pudgy man who always smelled of coffee and vanilla. Nest door was a butcher shop which smelled of cool sausageand pungent sawdust on the floors run by a German accented man.

The beach was only a few blocks away, along Cropsy Avenue, lined with large family homes with vast porches encircling them and large lawns.

They were being abandoned then and one had become the play ground where Baldassare played his first games of baseball.

In the summer it was just a short walk to the beach on Bay 9th Street and the whole family would meet with the *paisani* on week-ends there. Huge rocks had been set out all along the bay to form squares of break waters about 300 yards out in preparations of the building of the Belt Parkway. On "The Rocks" as it was called, there Mike and Pitruzzella netted crabs and the odd lobster and in the evening when the families got together there would be a feast of spaghetti in crab and lobster sauce. And each string of pasta would taste as tender and sea-sweat as any lobster.

There was Pitruzzella with his new bride from Grotte and Totò, a little hunch back, a *caruso* from the mines around Racalmuto who now worked making artificial flowers.

In 1928 soon after the brothers in the Don Baldassare family had lost the rights to their film THE SHERIFF OF EAGLE CANYON Thomas organized a stock company for a new film he had in mind—Spanish Tango. He would come home after a day's work as a sewing machine operator, change and go on a hunt for money. Relatives and friends still have certificates stating that they own a 100 shares in the Silver Eagle Productions Company. At night Tom wrote outlines and scripts for more films. He showed them to prospective share holders and a film maker in Long Island. His short wiry frame vibrated with energy when he danced his tango on a Saturday night in the dance halls around Second Avenue. One night while dancing he had a fit of coughing and spit up quantities of blood. Within a year he was dead of tuberculosis. He was 26 years old and it was the summer of 1929.

Without telephones the news of his death had to be passed along by messengers, letters and symbols. Al, the youngest, was sent to Brooklyn to tell Mike. "Thomas died and my mother says if you can come over." He gave the same message to relatives in the Bronx.

In many of these aging tenements around First street, if you look closely, there is a nail set in the door frame of most entrances. It was here that a floral wreath, decorated with purple and black ribbons was hung. Those who passed by crossed themselves. Those who were related recognized a death in the family and came to pay their respects during the three day wake.

The Mother Caroline demanded an honorable funeral for her son. Tomas was given one of the last ritual *Racalmutisi* funerals held in New York. The undertakers chosen for Tomas were *paisani* from Racalmuto. They took the body to their establishment for embalming. The family gathered, the shades of all the windows pulled down and waited for the body which was brought in a casket and set in the front room. The methods of embalming were crude and poor. It was a hot day and for the three days of the wake it grew even hotter. Al remembered: the corpse was placed in a casket and left on display for three days in the small living room. The dead body laid out, all the window shades were down tightly in all the rooms of the railroad flat, the temperature soared to 95-100 degrees. The 30 or 40 people present perspired, the living filled with flowers for Tomas, the rooms illuminated with dim 25 watt bulbs threw a jaundiced yellow glow on everyone's face giving everyone a dead pale look.

On the second day the corpse began to sweat and his beard showed signs of growth, a putrid odor of death blended with the scent of sweet carnations. To this day I still can smell it whenever I pass a funeral parlor. I had to run up to the roof tops for some fresh air.

The women sat by the corpse and rocking back and forth cried openly and wailed, led by the Mother Caroline, "*Commu pozzu suppurtari* .... How can I bear this thing the little Jesus has brought me."

The men sat stoically, unshaven. They would not shave until Tomas was buried. The more distant women relatives took care of feeding and housing the families who had come long distances for the wake. Mattresses were laid out in the homes of near by relatives and the children all slept together. Bennie was delighted to sleep at Mama Rosalia who still lived near by on Stanton Street.

The night before the burial the men stayed up through the night and watched the corpse. In the dim light their unshaven faces took on the same look as the corpse who's beard had also grown in the three days it had lain at rest.

At 9 the next day the funeral director arrived and when the coffin's lid was shut the Mother Caroline fainted. The coffin closed the pall bearers began the careful descent down the narrow staircase.

By the 3rd floor the men were shouting, "Lift his head end up a bit. Watch it. Turn it. Bring it my way." One pall bearer had a bad cough and in a coughing fit almost dropped his end.

Waiting in the street were all the relatives. Bennie waiting at the Curb was frightened. He had not been permitted upstairs for fear the tuberculosis might infected him. He imagined all kinds of ghosts and ceremonies taking place in the apartment he knew so well.

Three uniformed musicians, two drummers and a cornet waited also and the moment the coffin, carried on the shoulders of the men appeared in the door way, the drummers rolled a slow ra-ta-ta-ta. The casket was slid in the hearse with its stained glass windows, and large gas-lit lanterns on the side of the rear doors. As soon as the horses took the first step the cornet sounded a mournful note and the relatives fell behind the hearse as it moved away. The music intensified the grief. The women cried, the men wept openly.

Friends or paisani crossed themselves as the cortege passed them. Men took off their hats.

After the ceremony in the Second Avenue church where Mike and Teresina had been married, those going to the cemetery rode in the automobiles rented for the occasion. The body was transferred to a motorized hearse. The procession slowly rode past the tenement where Tom had lived, as if to show him his earthly place for the last time. It then headed for Brooklyn where he is buried. All of Tom's cloths, dancing shoes, tuxedo, the sheets he slept on were thrown away. There was a silence in everyone's mind that was never filled, Al remembered.

***

Bastiano, of the papa Giuliano family, in his new acquired grocery store on Bay 25th Street had quality produce which he bought twice a week in markets where he still had contacts. In the back room he made wine which he sold by the gallon and the glass. With the help of wife, Angelina, a woman from Racalmuto and the first of three sons, Giuliano, the store prospered. He lived in a six-room apartment above a pharmacy, but soon bought a spacious home in which he was the first to install an automatic oil burner and a player piano.

Bastiano became an admirer of Mussolini, if not Fascism. He was a-political before the rise of *Il Duce*. But then to those who had felt the humiliation of prejudice of that time Mussolini gave them a sense of pride and identity— a pride and identity they probably never felt in Italy.

The sympathy for Fascism s encouraged by *Il Duce* himself who saw the Italian-American Community as a political force for his own foreign policy. It was encouraged also by many Americans in high places who saw Mussolini as a political genius and brilliant leader of his people, a man who had brought stability and well being to the Italian people. Jimmy Walker, the mayor of New York, Congressman Fish admired the new regime. Walker was welcomed in home and given a one half hour audience with the Duce. The Fascists addressed themselves to the feelings of hurt among the immigrants. They played lip service to their problems. The Secretary of Foreign Affairs, Dino Grandi, declared in 1927, "Emigration tends to diminish the strength of our race. We must have the boldness to assert that the emigration of our citizens to those countries which are not under direct Italian sovereignty, is a danger. Those of our citizens, especially those of the lower classes, who are forced to live among other races, are inevitably and violently assimilated with them. Why must our race continue to be a sort of human reservoir at the disposal of the other countries of the world? Why must our mothers continue to furnish soldiers for other nations?"

By such words many Italians in America, Luigi Barzini, editor of the Fascist *Corriere d'America*, among them, were attracted to Fascism. Fascist speeches in America were filled with such phrases as, "The Fatherland should not be defrauded of so many precious energies.... The sons of Italians abroad should be brought up to feel, to think, to love, to act and to hope as the sons of Italians at home."

"Young people are the prey sought by preference by nations eager to assimilate foreigners." These were the words of Mussolini's brother Arnaldo. And Dino Grandi could declare, "The sons of Italians abroad must be trained to feel that their material absence from their country of origin has no importance; they must feel to be not only spiritually but almost physically united to and included in the great national family."

Even from this distance one must wonder; were the Fascists deluding themselves? What loyalty could the humped backed Totò living in Brooklyn and now making artificial flowers have for a land that had put him in the sulphur mines as a *carusu* at the age of ten. What pride could men have who remembered Crispi (one of the Fascist clubs in Brooklyn was named after him) putting down the Fasci movement, who remembered famine, plague and starvation which brought on visions of green mice?

Certainly a few Sicilians had more love for Mussolini in America than they would have had if they had remained in such towns as Racalmuto and Grotte.

For most the Don Baldassare's family and Papa Giuliano's Fascism meant little to them. But in Bastiano there was a visible change.

133

On Sundays he would open his store for a few hours in the morning. Clean shaven, dressed in a dark suit, a tie folded over once loosely set in a white shirt, a fedora hat with the rim turn up all around, he stood in front of his store smoking a de Noboli cigar. In his pockets he had a role of bills as thick as a birch log which on the slightest occasion, perhaps to pay a delivery boy, he would take out and peal off a bill slowly, watching the effect his gesture had on those around him. A wiry bricklayer from Tuscanny who lived alone above the store, often told him. "Sir, I wouldn't flash money around like that."

"Who should I be afraid of? Of what?"

"One never knows...in America."

Bastiano faithfully read Il Progresso, a Fascist oriented paper, published by Generoso Pope a man dedicated to *Il Duce*. Bastiano could be made cheerful for weeks reading of an Italian triumph such as Balbo, the Italian aviator who flew to New York in 1927. The then governor, Franklin D. Roosevelt's welcoming speech honoring the aviator honored Bastiano also. His admiration for Mussolini grew. The Italian station WHOM carried the commentator, V. Comito who was deeply involved in Fascist activity. He was one the directors of the Benito Mussolini Fascio, an inspector of the Fascist League of North America, and editor-in-chief of the Fascist review, *Il Combattente*.

Bastiano was often glued to the small radio he kept high up on the stacks of sacks of beans in the corner of the store. His language soon became peppered with words such as *razza, potenza,* race and power—and *sciabola*, this last he translated as side arm. He too began to carry a gun.

When his brother Turiddru or Sal as he was called, disappeared, and rumors began that some one had seen him as a bum around the Bowery flop houses he blamed this on the filth of undisciplined America.

***

For the middle group in the Don Baldassare family (Tony, now Wallace, Sal, and Joe) Tomas's death was a harbinger of the great depression. Their energies, for the moment, though, rose much like some one afflicted with tuberculosis. Wallace, tall, barrel chested continued to act in amateur theater. Sal, six years his junior entered Seward Park High, made the football team, enrolled in drama classes and talked about becoming a radio announcer, a *metier* he saw as a way of getting before the public which he felt necessary for a political career. He had the stature for it and a deep baritone voice.

He saw his future clearly and this the others envied and admired. "The Italians will be voting soon and they'll vote for one of their own." he repeated often. He won a football scholarship in his senior year to Rutgers. The brothers seemed to be, waiting for something to break for them, in the meantime Wallace worked as a plasterer and Sal drove a truck, part time for a meat packing company on Horatio Street.

The financial crash of '29 came at a time in the lives of the brothers when they were reaching their maturity, when everything and anything seemed possible. The Crash deepened to Depression. Listening to their remembrances one can almost hear the doors of possibilities slowly closing in their faces.

Wallace worked more and more as a plasterer, did less and less in theater. He married a beautiful redheaded woman of whom every one predicted disaster. Sal graduated in 1931 with a scholarship to Rutgers. But it would have coast the family a considerable sum.

His absence alone would have been costly. The mother Caroline said, "*Eeh, ch*i, at almost 20 he still wants to go to school."

Sal took his mother in his arms, "In five years I'll buy you a brick house in Brooklyn," and he laughed.

"It was always good to see the big man laughing like that," Al remembered. Sal was to start college in the fall of 1932 when Wallace took sick. It was the plaster, they said, it had gotten to his lungs.

Mother Caroline sat by the dark round table, crying endlessly, while dipping a Unita Biscuit in a bowl of milk. "*semu consumati*—we are in trouble." The sight of Wallace, tall and heavy in the door way made her suppress her tears. How could such a strong big man (he could carry a board as big as a table loaded with plaster in one hand, balance a pile of bricks on the back of his extended hand and walk up a ladder whistling)—be ill and dying. Everyone in the family was stunned by his illness. The year of hoping, despairing, hoping, despairing, along with the ups and downs of his illness, dominated the families energies. Grace who loved him, could not bare to be in his presence. The brothers brought him money and cared for his child and wife when he entered the hospital. Sal decided to put off going to college; he gave part of his salary to his wife. Wallace died in 1932 of tuberculosis at the age of 31.

To all the family it seemed as if their youth was buried with Wallace. The mother Caroline cried for three days, "Who knows where the cemetery is here in this *malidittu paisi*. Papa Baldassare prayed for ever after it seemed, holding the rosary beads in his long boney fingers, ignoring the cat that jumped on his lap and fell asleep while he said his paternosters and avemarias. They both grieved with a special grief of the old who see their grown children die before they do.

It was Sal who consoled them both, holding the mother Caroline up on her feet. The funeral was the first to be held in a Funeral Parlor on Second Avenue, a store front sort of place where a curious crowd gathered; men with the plaster of their trade still in their finger tips, young people from the settlement house, and the now aging Sicilians and Italians dressed in black. The bouquet of flowers and purple ribbons hung for days on the door way of the tenement house.

With the death of Wallace the middle group of children lost their leader, their model. Angelo resigned himself to working in the laundry a job which seemed more and more appealing as others could find no work at all. Then too, he had married and a child was on the way. Al, the youngest was in Junior High School 64 and worked afternoons from 4 to 8 for a lithographer at 4 dollars a week.

Marriage and the Depression evaporated the aspirations of the brothers. The depression stunned them, literally. Like most immigrants who came of age between 1929 and 1935 their aspirations and their talents, shriveled into a cautious fearful attitude. They scurried for secure jobs in the Post Office, Sanitation Department or later, in the Police Department.

Sal did not seem disappointed for not going to college. Although he began, soon after Wallace's death, to dress in ways he imagined a college man would dress and act. He wore bow-ties and smoked a thin stemmed pipe with a small round bowl. Through the settlement house on East 5th Street he got a job with the radio station WABC as a general helper and driver. It wasn't much, but it was a beginning.

Just looking for work was not easy. When Al graduated Seward Park High he was made aware that certain jobs were not for him. He remembered, "Some days we would start on Fifth Avenue and put in applications in the big publishing houses from 14th to 42nd Street for stock clerks. We never got a break because of our Italian names."

It was the same with the Department Stores, Con Edison and large corporations. Our applications went right into the waste paper basket as soon as we walked out of the office. One man even tore up my application in front of my face.

"You applied with at least 35 other kids for the same job.

"That went on day after day, month after month. Our parents would give us 25cents for looking for work, 10 cents care fare, 10 for eating, and 5 for newspapers—for the want ads. We walked and used the car fare for a movie or a burlesque. One had to be very flexible in his hopes, play each day by ear, resign oneself to reoccurring disappointments.

"I worked at blind alley jobs... Grocery clerk, night laundry work, toy assembler, construction, welder, carpenter and lithographer's helper. I got into art by accident—but I was good at it."

All of the Don Baldassare family were high strung. In their youth it was energy and ambition, creativity. As they grew older it turned to *nerbusu*, a Sicilian way of saying nervous. It was most apparent in Mike. A frightened look came into his eyes, after Wallace's death. The birth of a second son, Giuliano, on a sunlit day in April, up on the fourth floor of the apartment on Bay 13th Street added to his nerbusu. It became more and more difficult to make a living in Real Estate. Italians or anyone else for that matter were more interested in putting food on the table than buying lots in New Jersey. But real-estate had been good to Mike. He was able to invested, how much he never told anyone, in the Huppemobile Motor Co. and when the company went bankrupt in 1930, he said to Pitruzzella, "I should have know that something was going to happen when they let the little suckers into their rackets. "The next year the company of Dorsey Realtors closed its doors.

"Get yourself a gun, Mimi." Pitruzzella said. Mike was not ready to give up on free enterprise. On those nights he sat at the kitchen table divining numbers to play in the Italian lottery, "I tell myself, you don't make anything working for some body else in this country. You gotta make it on the suffering of other people. That's the way it is." He decided to start his own Cosmetic Company called MARCO ENDS.

From a bankrupt distributor around Canal Street he bought gallons of lotions, shampoo, perfumes, soaps, bottles, and razor blades. A printer Pitruzzella knew printed on gold paper labels which read: MARCO ENDS

Dandruff

Flaky Hair

Leaves Hair

Lustrous & Fine

Smell Good

He mixed shampoo and perfumes in the bath tub and filled his bottles on the bathroom floor. In the kitchen he dried the bottles and pasted on his labels. Every day he went out to the shops in the garment district where a few men still worked and in the streets where men waited for work and peddled his wares. In the evening he went from door to door in his own neighborhood. It kept the family in food "and tooka my mind off things." Mike said. But as the crisis lengthened, prospects became bleak. Teresina had had difficulty giving birth to Giuliano. She grew more and more depressed and often greeted Mike when he came home with "Who's going to buy your nick nacks, nobody but our relatives." But then Teresina had found condoms in Mike's sachel that he was selling these vulgar things embarrassed her.

When the Mother Crucifissa wrote offering to pay their return to Sicily, Mike who thought he would "Just looka around," they decided to return to Racalmuto.

There had always been a coming and going among Sicilian immigrants in general. At times those returning out numbered those coming. People returned for may reasons. Before World War I those who had contracted tuberculosis returned with the hope that the Sicilian sun would cure them. Others returned disillusioned to walk in the *chiazza* and curse that damn country. Mike, Teresina, Baldassare, now ten going on eleven and Giuliano four returned to Sicily on the newly launched liner, The Rex, pride of Fascist Italy. The ship's elegance impressed Teresina while Mike discovered the waiters and seamen all were Fascists. This disturbed him. He learned to keep his mouth shut.

The deck hands and waiters called Baldassare, Benito who suddenly felt very American.

"They call me Bennie," he told the deck steward who insisted on showing him the superiority of Italian Fascists by pounding his bare fists against the ship's railings. And if he answered their Italian "These are Italian fists..." at all, it was in English, "I'm Bennie Moreli. I'm an American. I was born in America."

"If you have Italian blood, you're always Italian."

"I'm Bennie Moreli. I was born in America."

"*Sempre Italiano.*" The deck steward laughed and pounded his fist against the railing.

RETURN TO SICILY

The Fascist Parenthesis

When Marco and his family returned to Sicily, small cities and towns such as Grotte and Racalmuto were gong through what some *Racalmutisi* called *La Parentesi Fascista*. The Fascist parenthesis.

The office of mayor had been abolished and in its place was put the *Podestà*. The new title made the pompous Don Enrico Macaluso, Don Rico as he was known, all the more arrogant. His manner and the nature of Fascism prevented the realization of many projects. In the time of Marco's return, he had proposed a union of Grotte and Racalmuto. The Communists, who had gone underground, worked against it. They did not want Don Rico to have more power especially in Grotte which had a radical tradition. As one man put it "There were ethnic differences" between the two towns.

Yet most people had to admit to his honest and concern for the public weal. He profited in no way from his office as did so many other Fascist officials. Nor did he take advantage of his contacts with men in power. He was scrupulously honest. He was in debt to no one, but he loved, insisted almost, that others be in his debt. If someone, no matter of which political persuasion, bought medicaments or appliances in his pharmacy on credit and later came to pay, he gruffly would say, *"I conti a casa mia li debbo fare io*. I take care of my house accounts."

He aspired to aristocratic ways and this was his way of binding people to him. Then too, he enjoyed saying of someone who maligned him—and he would announce this loudly in the pharmacy or in the *chiazza*—"Why doesn't he come and pay me first?"

Don Rico was a lover of trees. He planted rows of eucalypti running along the road to the cemetery of Santa Maria. When Arnaldo, Mussolini's brother died, he planted acacias trees along the public highway. They were later all cut down, whether in hatred of Don Rico, Fascism or the supposed traditional dislike of shade trees is hard to say. But even in a dictatorship the consent of people is necessary if not to do good, then at least to plant trees.

Don Rico proposed the building of a sewer system and although begun on paper in his time, it wasn't finished until 1956. Life just seemed to get in the way. When the Ethiopian War broke out Don Rico and his cohorts spent more time with map of Africa he kept in the window of his pharmacy, decorated with little Italian flags which he moved about as he heard reports of the campaign, than he did with public affairs.

Don Rico was overthrown by a 19 year old girl named Giovanna d'Arco.

Don Rico was a bachelor and had a reputation as a ladies' man, which had its perils in Sicily. At the height of the Ethiopian campaign Maria M. a 19 year old girl accused him of having seduced her and now she was pregnant. She brought her grievances to the court in Agrigento. She demanded marriage. All the support and influence of his friends in high places could not prevent a sentence of three years in prison being imposed on Don Rico. He was stripped of his office of Podestà and secretary of the Party. The Reign of Don Rico was over. Maria M. was dubbed Giovanna d'Arco. Couplets were sung in her honor:

> Il popolo di Racalmuto
> saluta Giovanna d'Arco
> che ha voluto immolare il suo
> onore per la salvezza della Patria.
> The people of Racalmuto salute
> Joan of Arc,
> Who in immolating her honor saved
> the honor of the Fatherland.

Maria's real name was politely forgotten and she is remembered to this day as "Joan of Arc of Racalmuto."

With the new Podestà Mattina, Fascism settled uneasily upon Racalmuto. The Fascist Commandments declared:

1. Punishments are always deserved.
2. The Fatherland is served even in guarding a can of gas." etc.

More and more men faced imprisonment, house arrest, beatings or penal service in military camps.

The lives of the young were regimented, advancement and careers depended on their enthusiasm for Fascism. In elementary school they were marched about as balilla, later as *Avantiguardisti*, then as young Fascists and finally, as mature men, as Black Shirts. Certificates of attendance in these groups were needed to enter schools or obtain the most menial government jobs. But some in Racalmuto, used to a brawling democracy, protested. Don Rico's nephew, an anti-Fascist, refused to join these groups and was hauled before the Fascist tribunal. There, the young man declared, in phrase still remembered: "Well, arrest me. The comrades in prison need the company of the younger generation."

Lu zi Giuliano was not a political man. He was hardly aware of the political turmoil. His work and the Church, occupied enough of his time. On winter nights, sitting a little apart from the women, he said his rosary and thought of his dead son Domenico. His lands prospered, the pension of the United States government made him financially comfortable. When news came of Teresina and her family's coming to Racalmuto, he had the house repaired; the upstairs was re-plastered and the stair wells were painted blue, a color, it was believed, which acted as a fly repellent. He contracted with a mason, Campanella to have a toilet installed. This meant digging up the length of the street at his expense and laying a sewer pipe down to the slopping road where the waste would be carried on the surface down to *La Baruna*. For help in carrying out the project, *lu zi* Giuliano confided in the *arcipreti*, a tall elegant man who had lost a brother in the Great War. This alone brought the two men together. *Lu zi* Giuliano took his advice as to which men to hire for the work. The *arcipreti* was a well-read man. He spoke French, knew his Latin and read widely in these languages. He had spent many years in Rome where he had made the acquaintance of a French priest who invited him to visit his home in Cluny, in Burgundy. Out of this friendship the *arcipreti* was able to spend a number of years in France. His travels and education did not make him unhappy to return to Racalmuto. He plunged into his work caring for the *Matrici*, the twin-towered Mother church that stands at one end of the *chiazza*. Along with Father C., in 1919 he had been involved in the seizing of lands in the name of the people. He sincerely believed in political activity and was much concerned, in his later years, with the image of Sicily and Sicilians being manufactured in many of the newspapers—an image of mafia and backwardness. He harbored a disdain for Sciascia whom he considered responsible for this image, although he never said a word against him in public. He lived simply in a rambling one story house on a small rise hidden in the narrow alleys of the town. It was kept immaculately clean by his mother and, after her death at age 98, by his sister, a serene, fine complexioned woman who seemed to enjoy serving God by serving her brother the *arcipreti*.

When Marco and Teresina arrived with the two boys, they were given the entire upstairs. Pippina and Rosa with the help of Donna Giovanna, who had been taken on as a servant on the recommendation of the *arcipreti*, (she was a war widow and had a son to care for) prepared the upstairs rooms. The front room was large and gave out to the narrow Via Cavour and to the cube-like houses with curved tile roofs rising gently up to the distant railroad station. The women had washed the walls, put new straw in the mattresses and set them on the boards resting on iron pedestals. On the wall they hung a large picture of Christ tearing his chest open to expose a bleeding heart crowned with a wreath of thorns. They dusted everywhere, chasing out the small lizards lying in the cool corners and the white washed doors.

The smaller room had been a storehouse for grain, medlars, apples and melons which often lasted well after Christmas. They had cleaned it all out, washed the walls and floor, scrubbed the corners where the *municeddri* (little nuns—small ladybug—like insects which fed off the grain and whose bites left large welts) loved to hide. Rosa and Pippina would sleep downstairs, on folding beds. The upstairs would be for Marco and his family.

The whole *vaneddra* knew of their coming; women sat on the balcony in the evening and when a neighbor passed he was sure to ask, "*Zi* Giuliano, is it true your daughter and her family are coming from America?"

"*Si*, it's true." And the neighbor disappeared up the street where the houses overhang the street so much they almost form an arch.

The family arrived in the Spring and settle in the upstairs rooms. Bennie rushed to the back window and could see the ochre tiled roofs slanting down to the Baruna, the Norman Castle looming up against the sky, the rolling hills, and way in the distance, the *Castiddruzzu*, the Saracen Castle of Al Minsar. He heard the bells of the Mother Church ringing. He never had seen anything like this in the streets of Brooklyn. The image remained with him and twenty years later he remembered it in this way:

The evening bells rang from the steeple of Father C's church of the Munti and then Vespers. The thin angry sounds spilled down over the cube-like houses clustered around the road and out to the valley where, in the plain, lay the sulphur mine of Farubi, quiet, still, the one tall chimney pouring a thick olive-oil-yellow ribbon of smoke. The smoke rose above the valley and the flattering winds of summer scattered it to the east where the high dark mountains protected the valley from the sea; and the smoke swept back to the west and there stood the *lu Castiddruzzu*.

For the moment the room smelled of whitewash and straw. He heard a rooster crow a jackass bray mournfully. He felt abandoned by Brooklyn. The image, the first look at that room remained with Bennie for years and he never understood why that room provoked such strong emotions for him.

Years later he felt once again the emotion.

"I sat dirty, weary upon the stiff bed and I wanted to cry. A bare bulb had been covered with fly-speckled crepe paper. Upon the freshly whitewashed walls were images of Christ—Christ tearing his chest open to expose a thorn-ringed heart dripping blood. I got up and walked to the bureau to put my clothes away. I looked into the mirror and saw Christ gazing at me from beneath a ring of blood. Papa Giuliano was dead. Mama Cruciddra was dead. I wanted to cry. I numbly put my clothes away, then lunged onto the bed. Downstairs I heard the voices of Rosa and Pippina praying, chanting, 'Our Father who art in Heaven... We thank thee for the arrival of our own blood...'"

I sobbed and an infinite shame and pride grew in me that had something to do with love and humility.

For the first few days strangers frightened Bennie and he would talk only to his mother and father. They spoke to him in Sicilian but he answered in English. He grew sullen. But as he grew accustomed to the house, he began to answer his mother's "Tell them something in American" with *"Chi vuo ca ci dicu*—What do you want me to tell them?" which made them all laugh. Rosa clapped her hands and said merrily, *"Buonu, buonu.* See how well he speaks." Slowly, inevitably, he slipped over into Sicilian. The affection shown him by his aunts and grandmother coaxed more and more Sicilian out of him until he soon was speaking fluently, amusing them all with expressions such as, "There is still eggshell on my ass..."

Papa Giuliano won him over once and for all with his happiness and gentleness. Within a few weeks he spoke Sicilian a tight Sicilian.

Although at first Bennie would never go near the horse—he had a mortal fear horses remembering Lu Buffu's story he did ride the jackass and the mule. With Mike and Papa Giuliano they often went riding to the aria. The mare was kept for longer trips. On the way home Bennie often sang along with Papa Giuliano, those Arabic chants he was to remember years later.

> Sugnu n'addrina spersa,
> vaiu fannu cro cro tutta la iurnata
> ma nuddru mi ciama.
> I'm a lost chicken
> I go crow, crowing all day long
> but no one calls me.

The summer was spent at *l'aria*, the family's lands in the section know as the *siruni*. The stone house was on rise shaded by walnut and almond trees, overlooking the road about a half mile below. There was no end to the variety of fruit. In morning Papa Giuliano and Bennie would go down to the garden and, feeling beneath the broad green leaves, they found round Persian melons. They picked figs so purple they were almost black. They arrived up at the house, their arms filled with fruit. For breakfast there would be figs, melons and goats milk, and bread spread with olive oil, pepper and salt. The noon meal was light: bread, cheese and fruit. In the evening there was some pasta, lentils, sauce, escarole or carduna. There wasn't any meat except on Sunday when, because of the Americans, the family would kill a rooster or a rabbit.

Mike had come to Sicily to see if there possibilities of returning to the mining business. One day early in the stay, Mike and Papa Giuliano went to Cianciania a sulphur mining town up in the western hills. Bennie went with them. It was a long trip and Papa Giuliano took the *giumenta*—an auburn—colored mare he kept for such journeys.

Bennie would not ride on the mare, no matter what Papa Giuliano said, until the boy asked, "is it a male or female?"

Papa Giuliano did not understand.

"The horse, is it a male? a stallion? or a *giumenta*?"

"A *giumenta*."

Only then would he leave his father's side on the mule and ride behind Papa Giuliano who was wearing his black leather boots and carrying a shotgun across his back.

In the early morning Bennie could smell the spices in the air: thyme, oregano, fennel, warm straw, and the pungent snuff—smell of his grandfather. He heard him say "*Teniti*—hold on" And the mare just then seemed two stories high and vibrating beneath him—sprang up as if to fly away. Suddenly they were galloping, and once he knew he could hold on, he felt an excitement and an affection for the country-side that moved swiftly on either side of him in a blur taking his breath away. At the cross road they stopped and turned to wait for Mike who, smiling, came towards them on the jogging mule. The rode all morning stopping to eat beneath a cluster of olive trees by the road where a shepherd talked with them. In the afternoon they moved slowly and paused by a water source with a trough where the horse drank deeply with its lips tight, straining the water to prevent drinking in the leeches that Bennie could see swimming in the clear water. In the evening they arrived at the stone hut of an old couple, friends of Papa Giuliano, where they spent the night. The old woman welcomed them heartily saying that they hadn't seen anyone for days.

She fed them great bowls of lentils and wild chicory, heavy damp bread and watered wine. Some straw was put in what looked like an old manger and Bennie was put to sleep, covered with a heavy peasant's cloak. Before falling asleep he heard the elders speak of wheat and sulphur and the town they were headed for.

"What are you going to that lost *paisi* for? There's nothing there but four *beccamorti* with two *tabbuti spasciati* (Four grave diggers with two broken coffins.)

Bennie went to sleep thinking of Santa Claus astride a great auburn *giumenta*, two horse pistols strapped around his red tunic. He was suddenly awakened by a series of furious bites. Bedbugs as big as the lentils he had eaten for supper swarmed up from the manger where he slept; his calves and ankles were burning, his buttock were covered with red rings. By morning he had welts all over and when they rode into the town it seemed even more brooding than it was because of the burning bites beneath his cloths.

The town loomed up above them on a slight long incline guarded by a square, box-like fortress, with narrow slits for windows. There were no trees, not one! All was stone. It had begun to drizzle.The cobblestones and the mortared houses clustered behind the fortress glistened grey in the morning light. The horse slipped but quickly regained its footing with a loud clap of its hooves echoing loudly in the morning stillness. They were in the town of Cianciana, Papa Giuliano said.

They spent the night with relatives where Bennie burned with fever. When they returned to Racalmuto the fever had not abated. It was the filth of those bed-bugs, Rosa said. Mother Crucifissa felt it was the milk he had been drinking. After two nights of numbing sleep in the darkness of the upstairs room, he was well again and he was introduced to wine as a tonic, which brought strength and opened the appetite.

Marco had returned to the mining areas to see if it were possible to buy into a mining operation. He talked to his uncle in Palermo who told him the industry had never really recovered from the set backs of the early decades of the century "You' d do better to look at something else, Mimi," his uncle told him. They would have liked to find some thing else themselves. Then too, they invested their money in their children's educations; one son was in medical school, the other was preparing law. Marco thought he would distribute Sicilian wines, and with this idea in mind, made trips to Rome, Genoa and finally into Southern France; he left the family in Sicily.

In the fall, after the harvest and vintage, Bennie discovered the boys of his street. He made particular friends with *Bacareddra*—which he understood to mean "Little Bucket" With him he became part of the boys that roamed the town and the countryside. They taught him games, how to make toy pistols, spin tops and to trap those yellow canaries that sang along—*la Baruna* which they later cooked over a fire of rosemary brush.

He became part of the life of the boys growing up in the Sicily of the 1930's. It seemed natural to Teresina for him to go to school. It would do him no harm to learn Italian. He was enrolled in the elementary school, the long barn stone building not far from the Mother Church. From the first day he felt uncomfortable; was made to feel uncomfortable really. Certainly, although the boy was not aware of it then, the teachers were all chosen for their Fascist enthusiasm. He was aware of their hostility.

He was an American in their eyes, or at least one of the children of Italian immigrants who was losing his Italianness to the foreign assimilators, as *Il Duce* said. The teachers prodded him with the superiority of Italian things; the children took their lead. Bennie believed in Sicily, that he was an American. The blabbing of *A, E, I, 0, U, e sceccu ca si tu*— and the donkey that are you" as a way of learning vowels, annoyed him. He remembered the individual questions of the teachers in the Bath Beach school and the damp, shaky benches he was sitting on now— how airy and neat the class rooms of Brooklyn. He forgot that in those schools he was made to feel Sicilian.

When he was taken to the *Balilla* demonstrations and made to march with swinging arms, and he caught a glimpse of the smiling men watching, he said nothing. But the next day he refused to go back to school Nothing the women could say would make him go back. He decided there and then that he was an American and he would act superior, mature, and he would never say *merda, cacare* or *piritare*, and when he grew up he would live like a good American and never fart.

But the family was loving to him and there was Christmas seeping into his head with the sound of troubadours singing at the wayside shrine, along with the sound of *ciarameddri*—the bagpipes of Sicily—all to comfort Mary, he was told.

"There were three wise men who brought gifts to the infant Jesus and one of them was called Baldassare."

"They brought them oranges and hazel nuts for the infant Jesus to play with."

In the streets the children played marbles with hazel nuts; the myth mixed freely with reality.

Towards midnight of Christmas eve as they walked to the Mother Church with the sound of the shepherds' flutes coming in from the fields, and the light of the church seen through the darkness of the *chiazza*, it was hard for Bennie not to believe that the shepherds were not coming directly from Jerusalem and that he was not part of a ceremony that his namesake had taken part in a long time ago.

The Church glowing in the darkness of that Christmas eve, became imbedded in his mind. Then too, there was Donna Giovanna's son Don Arrigo, who was at the seminary in Agrigento where he was studying to be a priest. He would come home more often now that the Americans were there.

Carrying a pistol in his black tunic, he would take Bennie to the edge of the cemetery of Santa Maria and whip out his pistol and pick off the canaries in the bushes. It pleased the boy that the priest to-be never hit one.

Don Arrigo's father had been killed in the Great War and this had given the son the privilege of becoming a priest, or at least entering the seminary. This he did with the help of the Arche-prete who had tutored him in languages. Not that Arrigo had much of a calling for the priesthood; he was in the tradition of those rascal priests abounding in Agrigentian history. He himself often said, "If I didn't have this tunic on, I'd turn this town on its head." He was almost to do that in later years. Now he was a slight, short young man in his late teens who had entered the seminary at age 10.

In the spring, the Archbishop of Agrigento made his round of the towns and villages of the province and when he came to Racalmuto Bennie was confirmed with Arigo as Godfather. As his Godfather, Don Arrigo taught him much about Sicily and little about God, with that comic pompousness that could take the Fascism he professed to admire seriously. The same year he confirmed Bennie, he said he also confirmed Leonardo Sciascia. Years later, when he was close to death after several strokes, he called for his two Godsons' return to the Church. He reminded them that John Kennedy had God in his heart and therefore was loved by all and touched all men's minds, whereas his Godsons', Danilo Dolci and Quasimodo were, "paralyzed by the fashion of the times."

The little father suffered from the restrictive nature of the Church in Sicily. No radical element was ever permitted to enter.

If some priests such as Casuccio and Cipolla attempted to seize lands or set up co-operatives, the Archbishop in Agrigento quickly squelched them. Then, too, such men were rare and eventually, in their maturity became conservative men. The leaders of the Church were never drawn from poor families; they were men of means whose philosophy centered around the parables, "The cake is too small to be divided equitably" and "The poor will always be with us." The seminary instilled this in the young boys who were taken from their families and returned, as men, not to their towns but to a far off city where they had no personal ties with the people. The Church always remained a class institution. No men or group of men could look to it for social change then. It was natural for one such as Father Arrigo, who had little calling for his priesthood, to frequent, proudly, those elements known as malandrini. In his first parish in the town of Favara, just south of Racalmuto, which had been founded as a penal colony, he was always found in the *chiazza* in the evening admonishing the bachelors to "Marry, marry! Don't remain a capon all your life!" and to the young women who might be sitting in front of their doors stroking a cat, "Marry, my daughter, marry. You need to have children, not cats on your lap!" All his speech seemed to end in exclamation points.

As he walked with the men who controlled the town, he told himself that he was priest of all the people; that if these men had no spiritual guidance they would be lost to the Church and he would be left with a few old ladies and sickly men to come hear the Holy Mass. So he packed a Berretta pistol and was proud that these men around Christmas and Easter always left him a quarter of a kid wrapped in muslin at his door step. Once or twice he was in affairs, "that ended badly, badly!" as he said. A man came pounding at his door late one night only to be machine-gunned down. In the morning when he opened the door, the body fell into his arms. He loved to tell such stories as he liked telling over and over again the pleasure he found in returning to Racalmuto in the uniform of Chaplain to a Division stationed in Bari where he had spent the war. He shed his Fascism easily soon after the war however, for at heart he had not believed in it, as he did not believe in any authority. not even his own, an attitude which permitted him to open a movie house and show Lana Turner, "with her tits hanging," as some of the more pious said, in spite of the fact that priests were not permitted to see films. His housekeepers were always young. And in his maturity he became a supporter of the right of priests to marry. His attitude was to permit him later to travel to Paris to see his godson and to make trips to America from where he returned wearing a black double-breasted suit, a black fedora and smoking Camel cigarettes. He returned also as an ardent anti-Communist predicting that Cardinal Spellman would be the next Pope and joined the sixteen other priests of the town who had never spoken out against Fascism, but who now were preaching against Communism.

Don Arrigo became an amusement to the whole town later, when he walked the *chiazza* saluting everyone with a blessing and invoking Tulumello's old slogan *Popolo cornuto* —The people are cuckolds.

***

Dressed in a light gabardine suit, in the morning, Mike would take a walk around the town, up the steep incline to Via Garibaldi leading to the *chiazza*. Sometimes he would stop at the cafe of Taibi to buy Bennie lemon flavored ices, then on through the square where he met men who were sure to ask him about relatives in Argentina, Peru or Brooklyn. Such walks would always end up in the tailor shop of Raffaeli, his cousin.

The shop was on a street just parallel to the *chiazza*. Men of a certain literary and political inclination always ended their walk here. Mike often found a number of men watching Raffaeli cutting a piece of cloth, a cigarette hanging from his mouth. When he saw Mike he stopped whatever he was doing, and with a calm voice so in contrast with his warm gestures of hugging Mike and Bennie would say, "So you finally made yourself seen. Sit here, Bennie, that I can give you a *caramella*. Okay boy, come on. Time to eat." These last expressions he had learned from returning emigrants. Mike shared his green package of Lucky Strikes with the men in the shop who took them cautiously.

Some sniffed them and put them away to be smoked later; others lit up and smoked deeply while they spoke of Africa, America and the Roman poets Raffaeli loved.

Raffaeli had just opened his shop with the financial aid of his brother Mimì in America, who had a cleaning store on Delancy Street. In the shop there were books of elegant models sent from Rome and New York, with cloth samples attached.

One afternoon when an unusually large group had gathered at Raffaeli Mike, without much thought said, "Why should the sons of mothers go have their throats cut in Ethiopia for the benefits of the capitalists?"

"It doesn't seem to *Vossia*, " a small man said, using the polite *Vossia* without sarcasm, as Raffaeli caught Mike's eye, "that Italy was made *cornuta*—700,000 killed in the Great War, a million crippled, and we were given crumbs by the men who were supposed to be our friends... and they took everything."

Mike, ignoring Raffaeli's look said, "To me it seems nothing has changed here; the poor will live on wind and smoke, and the rich will still break their asses watching their almond trees bloom."

Later, as they walked in the *chiazza*, Raffaeli said in a calm whisper, "That one can make trouble for you, Mike."

"What trouble?"

"Eeh, Raffaeli said and shrugged his shoulders and put his hands together as if to say, "Do I have to spell it out for you?"

"I'm an American citizen."

"In America you are an American citizen. Here you are an Italian. Your sons are Italian. That's the way He wants it."

Mike was irritated by what Raffaeli had said, then he grew fearful as he realized how America had changed him. He dressed differently, he shaved every day whereas most men in town shaved once a week. He loved to take showers; people laughed at him here because he would go down to the *raffo*, the fountain where the women washed their clothes and he would wash his hair. Now when he talked to

Raffaeli about his meetings in New York, his yoga and politics, he felt apart, even from Raffaeli who told him, "Go back then, Mimi. There is nothing for you here. *Li malanni* awaits us all." Then, too, Mike became aware of his manner of dress being more elegant, and he responded to people who pointed to him and said, "*chistu di l'America veni.*—That one is from America." And he compared himself with what he saw, with other men in the *chiazza*. Then too, the view of Don Macaluso who had so little reason to be strutting in the *chiazza* the way he did, did not appeal to him. When rumor had it that men of his age, even though married and with children, would be called up for the war in Africa, Mike began to feel uneasy in Racalmuto. He began thinking about returning to America, no matter how hard times were there. The mother Crucifissa wanted the family to stay and was offering to buy them a house there. But there would be little here for the boys they were already outsiders. They would stand a better chance in America.

It was Teresina who wanted to stay and when Papa Giuliano asked Baldassare which he liked best, Racalmuto or America, the boy answered quickly, "*L'America.*"

In the summer of 1935 they all took a trip to Rome where they stayed in a hotel near the Vatican: attended a papal audience, kissed the foot of St. Peter's statue, bought souvenirs, and, almost by accident, stumbled on to a Fascist rally in Piazza Venezia. The square was filled with people who were shouting "*Duce! Duce!*" raising their arms in salute. A tremendous roar went up that made Bennie disoriented and frightened. He looked at the crowed around him and he wanted to run. He felt alien. His father held him and he caught a view of a pudgy man in a black uniform, a tassel dangling from his cap, gesturing jerkily on a stone balcony. The view was imprinted in his mind by the dozens of newsreels he would see of the scene later in life, until he never knew whether he had ever really been there to see the man they all shouted for, "*Duce! Duce!*" But the crowd had been real. He felt a great relief to get back to the hotel and watched the white frail curtains blowing out gently in the Roman evening light.

***

The Atlantic crossing in September was stormy. And Mike, already anxious for fear of being taken into the Italian Army, held the rocks of Santa Rosalia, patron saint of Palermo, in his hands as the Rex bucked and rolled in the heavy seas. Teresina, who did not mind the heavy seas, said, "And now you pray to the Saints!"

"And when should one pray to the saints?" Mike smiled sheepishly.

> Quannu vidi ca la fortuna
> nenti ti dici
> iettati 'n terra e cogghi babbaluci.
> When you' re down and out
> throw yourself upon the ground
> and start collecting snails.

HARD TIMES

The Depression hastened the assimilation of Sicilians. The families from Racalmuto were no exception. Hard times made them give up the idea of ever returning to Sicily. They were in America to stay. The *malanni* had to be accommodated to in an American way.

In the afternoons, the young Baldassare now came home and fell asleep letting the book he was reading fall away. He drifted into a warm feeling that permeated all his body; he could relax and fall asleep. He felt comfortable in Brooklyn; the school, P.S. 200, was new he had been welcomed back and within six months he was in the "Rabid Advance" as it was known in the accents of Brooklyn.The school had a comforting presence of its own.

Once he asked for the wooden pass to go to the boy's room. He walked through the quiet corridors filled with the humming of voices vibrating through each door he passed. He wandered through the halls and up and down the stair cases which smelled of fresh paint and iron. On the third floor he stopped to look out the window; the street was empty, the sky bright, the wind was howling through the leafless trees. At that moment he felt a great affection for those of P.S. 200, for Dr. Pullman the principal who played the violin for them at the assemblies, for Miss Borger and for Mr. Heller who picked his nose carelessly and left bits of snot on his face. The moment stayed with him all his life and rose in his spirit producing a sense of trust—and he could fall asleep.

Around four or five o'clock he was stirred out of his sleep by Mrs. Bloom calling her boys in for the evening meal: "Mutten—youuuu, Calvin—youuuu, Shimin—youuuu, Hymn— youuu...."

The family had moved into a three room apartment of a tenement house whose name, "The Providence" was chiseled above the entrance, on a tree lined street close to Cropsey Avenue and the beach. The apartment faced the street and Bennie could easily climb out the window, grab a branch of the tree and swing down to the sidewalk, where his friends were waiting.

The America to which Mike and Teresina had returned was bleak. Only Angelo and Sal were working in the Don Baldassare family: Angie in a laundry and Sal part-time for a radio Station. The family had returned to eating escarole and lentils. Louis, married, living in the Bronx, was on W.P.A.; Susie's husband had come down with tuberculosis and then died of a heart attack. Petruzzella, Mike's anarchist friend, had not worked in a year and had moved into a dark flat above a butcher store on Bath Avenue, not far from Mike's place. Mike found him sullen and brooding.

Bastiano was prospering in his store, although most of his trade now was kept in a large accounting book—on credit. Mike and Teresina were in great debt to him. Mike could find no work and his selling of cosmetics brought little if any money. Like everyone else in the neighborhood, he went on W.P.A. and he began a series of jobs, measuring the tides below the Brooklyn Bridge, cleaning up dumps along with mobs of men, waiting on long lines outside the warehouses of Bush Terminal where clothes were distributed, early morning line-ups for cheap milk, dried meat, canned milk, beans that Teresina did not know how to use. The family went on a steady diet of lentils and escarole, spinach and spaghetti, bought on credit from Bastiano who also gave them the tissue paper fruit came wrapped in to be used as toilet paper. At times, as a joke, one of his sons would include prickly pear wrappings.

There was the constant presence of the home relief investigator who came and looked through the cupboards and smelled, disdainfully, the simmering dinner pots. There was never hunger in the house but a great deal of anxiety.

One afternoon Mike did not come home from the city and Teresina came into the store where Bennie now helped out, looking mournful. Uncle Sal had been in an accident. Teresina and Bennie went to a hospital close to the Brooklyn Bridge and found the mother Caroline, small, weeping, frail as a bird sitting before the bed on which her giant son Sal struggled to free himself from the ropes that held him tied, feet and hands to the bed. His head had been shaved, there was blood caked on his nostrils and cheek bones. He was breathing heavily and arching his back off the bed, his powerful muscles knotting and swelling as he tried to break free. The sheets fell off him and his naked body pushed upward as his breath hissed out of his blood clogged nostrils. He fell back. His breathing remained constant and furious, inhaling and exhaling angrily. His eyes were closed and he made no sound but his angry breathing. The Mother Caroline, weeping stood up and covered his body; the sheets fell off of him again; his body was beautifully shaped, long strong legs and deep chest heaving, powerful arms. Again Mother Caroline covered his body and let her hands rest on his shoulders. Sal struggled this way until two in the morning when he died.

Mike told Teresina how it had happened. Bennie listened from his bed. Sal, Joe, and two other friends had been driving off the Brooklyn Bridge when they were hit by another car. Sal's car was totally wrecked, yet no one seemed hurt. Sal had gotten out to help some of the people in the other car when the police arrived. He was polite. Then all at once he began to hit every one in sight.

It took three officers in another squad car to subdue him. He was taken to the hospital, head shaved for x-rays. He had suffered brain damage. They could not tell how much. Early the next morning it did not matter. He was dead and still tied to the bed when the undertaker on Second Avenue came for the body. Most of his personal effects—wallet and watch—had been stolen.

Everyone in the family felt as if their best had died. For Bennie a hero had died and for a long time after Sal's death he had a strange feeling. He could look at the most simple objects—a knife, an apple, a piece of bread—and in the pattern which the simple objects formed on the kitchen table, he understood, he knew he had seen them and used them somewhere else where he had spoken another language, breathed a different air.

For Mother Caroline it was America's final blow against her. The next year she died. Don Baldassare was left with Al, Joe and Grace in the apartment where just a few years ago the family had been young, numerous and filled with hope.

Mike was stunned by his younger brother's death. He could not accept it and often went to a medium who tried to communicate with the dead Sal, to no avail.

***

Italians we are told had the lowest incident of insanity among all immigrant groups. But then Sicilians detested hospitals and mental institutions; they took care of their own; Only the sever cases made the statistics. The Great Depression of course did not do much for the mental well being of the Don Baldassare family and their friends.

Petruzzella now began to speak on street corners up on 86th Street—against Capitalism, calling for brotherhood so raucously that one night he began to cry, pleading with the passers—by to come together. His speech became more and more strange, a mixture of Sicilian, Italian and English. To those who knew of the Socialists in Racalmuto and Grotte he would have seemed like a caricature, a resurrected Socialist of the Sicilian *Fasci*—gone mad.

One evening, Bennie heard him shouting in the street where he had stopped and, as if addressing a large crowd, shouted, *formaggio, tumazzu*, and after a great stuttering effort, blurted out, "Cheese." The effort made him shake all over, as if the three languages were fighting as to which way of saying cheese— the Italian *formaggio*, the Sicilian *tumazzu* or the English cheese. He was often seen in the neighborhood thereafter, walking alone, talking to himself, shaking violently, until he could blurt out a word— just one word.

One day he came out in the streets with a cane and broke two store front windows on Bath Avenue. He would have broken more but a lone cop saw him and Petruzzella's fury was directed against him. He had the cop pinned on the ground and was driving the splintered cane into his chest when the squad car arrived and cops scrambled out and beat him senseless. He was taken Kings County, where he remains to this day. His wife who could not speak a word of English, a timid fair-skinned woman with shinning black hair and blue eyes, lived alone with her two children for a year. She too then went mad and was taken to Kings County, where she lived close to her husband although never seeing him for thirty years. She died of pneumonia in 1963. The children went to orphanages where, no doubt, they were assimilated quickly into American life. No one heard of them again.

For Bennie, however, it was a time of discovery. The area of Brooklyn they had moved to was a mixture of Italian and Jewish families. There was the Harpo family (no one called them—or knew —their real name) whose father was a carpenter. He left every morning with his saw wrapped in a brown paper bag and returned in the evening looking like a tired Harpo Marx as did his five boys. Father and sons were all one more quiet than the other. Bennie liked them and took on their gentleness. With the Bloom family he discovered new meaning in books. Mutty was his age and the youngest son in that family whose father was a playwright for the Yiddish theater. Bennie taught Mutty to play ball. Mutty shared his books with him. He read Tolstoy and Dostoyevsky at an age when he could read them as adventures of the mind. From Iggy Lapidus, a neighbor whose father was a baker from the Ukraine., who often came home in his rolling gait of a bow legged man, his arms filled with bread still warm and he himself covered with flour and sesame seeds, Bennie learned still more about books. There was Gorky, Chekhov, Sholum Alecum, and Sholokhov. No one seemed to know father Lapidus's first name. To everyone, his dark curly headed wife who always smoked holding her cigarette like a pointer, to his daughter Shalamus, with natural buffant russet hair and to his son Iggy—he was simply called Lapidus.

Summer nights on that street in Brooklyn, the street lamps shown down on mock boxing matches, real fights and talk about books that went on into the night. Iggy spoke of justice and Jewish hurt that made Bennie aware of his own sense of inferiority of being Sicilian.

The reading of Lenin, Marx and Engels came as shock to Bennie; not only did these words give him a feeling of uniqueness as one of the down-trodden who would inherit the world, but at the same time made him aware of the power of books. He read Lenin with a dictionary beside him. He learned such words as "nascent," "bourgeoisie," "conflict" and such metaphors as "seeds of its own destruction" and the realization that the word "thus" was always followed by a conclusion which was an absolute truth. Marx's *Anti-During* and *The Poverty of Pure Reason* gave him an awe about the human mind; how could anyone write words so profound that after three readings with a dictionary beside him, he still could not understand what was written? But one day he would, he was sure. This was the important thing. One day he would. He felt the same mental exhilaration as when he played ball well and he knew that his playing and his thinking could only get better. For this reason he knew he was the fastest runner in the neighborhood, because he never ran as fast as he really could. He could always run just a little bit faster. These were happy days for Bennie.

For Mike they were the *malanni*. The relief programs gave barely enough to live on. His efforts to make money went to extravagant ends as the depression deepened. He played the lottery every week. He began to work on his inventions. The first, and no doubt his favorite, had infinite possibilities. The basic design was a circle of outer "energy points," dots, connected to inner circles by lines or "rays." These energy producing or collecting points turned inner circles connected to diamond—shaped propellers, and this whole circular source of energy was connected to distant circles, smaller, larger—four in all. The pattern was repeated on hundreds of sheets of paper. Later they were photostated. Each sheet had its own possibility. One was labeled, "Winter generator with copper plates", and other "Florescent tube lite (sic), another, "ray gun" or "vehicul (sic) for earth and space," with the added explanation "Space ship to collect the sun's rays stored in floating batteries in space, to b used when needed."

Still another invention could be used to "Picking up vibrations in the air like when you drop a pebble in a small pond and the vibrations come back, you can tell where the vibrations have been." When radar became known during the war, Mike felt his invention had been stolen.

There were designs for lunch pails in the form of books for unemployed college professors on W.P.A., he said, who where ashamed to carry regular lunch pails.

He worked on these inventions late into the night on the metal kitchen table covered with his papers, a compass, a triangle, pencils and a ruler. He ended the night with yoga exercises his "vibrations exercises" often waking Teresina who would whisper, "But what are you doing? You'll wake the boys. Go to sleep."

If Mike's aspirations were grandiose, reality was narrow. Home relief just did not bring enough to buy clothes, or to make a trip to New York, or to buy enough food, let alone such luxuries as a radio. At times food for the next week could not be bought. Bastiano would grumble over the accumulated bill. It was a god send then when the family took in work distributed by a family living a few blocks away.

It was the vestiges of the home work people were accustomed to on the Lower East Side. Each morning Bennie would go pick up a bundle of cheap stamped-out broaches, a package of rhinestones and a bottle of glue which had been shipped from a plant in the City and take them home. Bennie, Mike and Teresina would start work on them right after supper, never during the day for fear the home relief investigator would find them making the extra money. It would be sufficient cause to take them of the rolls. Bennie, years later remembered those nights this way.

"I used to go get the work and when I brought it back I'd put it in the closet. After supper my mother would clear the table, take, three of the glass protectors off the wheels of the furniture, and put them on the table. She'd take the bottle of glue from deep in the closet and pour some of it in each glass coaster. It smelled like nail polish remover and gasoline. My kid brother put to bed, we all sat around the table quietly. My father brought the pins and spilled them on the table. They made a huge pile. I could see my mother on the side, putting on her glasses."

"Well, let's begin," my mother sighed.

We'd work until after midnight, but never after one. At least I wouldn't, for I had to go to school in the morning. Yet sometimes I'd hear my mother get up, because she couldn't sleep with that thought in her head. And then my father would holler at her, "*rimbambita*—old senile idiot... you'll kill yourself!"

And my mother would answer, "Shhhhhhhh. The children are sleeping."

"Go to sleep, *scimunita*! Dummy, you'll ruin your health."

I could hear the sound of the diamonds falling into place, click, click, click.

"*Stupida*! take yourself away from that filth and get to bed right away."

"Quiet. There are not many left," my mother would answer. "I tell you to go to bed, *rimbambita*," and he'd get up and go to the kitchen. They would argue for a while and then my father would sit down and work, hollering and arguing all the time. From time to time my mother would whisper, "We can't leave them for tomorrow. What if *l'investigata* came?"

And my pop would holler, "It is not important to me when the filth comes!"

"Sh-h-h-, the children will wake. But that was all right, because I wasn't sleeping anyhow. They went on like that until it was finished, my father hollering and my mother trying to calm him.

On one night like that we made about two dollars and fifty cents. This too was part of assimilation. The fear of being caught by the investigator created an anxiety within the family that made school seem all the more comforting to Bennie, a refuge from the Irish-accented investigator who was not much different from Father Donagon.

But then all the priests in the Church of Saint Finbar's were Irish and the parishioners spoke of Jews and Blacks in such disparaging terms that Bennie could not reconcile their views with the Harpo family, or the Blooms, or Iggy who Bennie remembered years later in the way.

"As the men moved our furniture I stood close to the wall, out of the rain, and I looked at Iggy. He was wearing sneakers —Keds, they were the best—corduroy long pants and a lumba jacket. He was just a little bigger then me and he had blond, tight curly hair—the kind you don't have to comb because it's always in place. He was older than me, I could tell my his lumba jacket; on the back was written 'Lincoln's Blackjacks' and then in little letters below, 'Seniors'. Iggy had been responsible for the Lincoln part. The other fellas had just wanted the club called 'The Blackjacks'. But Iggy had said, 'We gotta have a name based on America's democratic heritage.'"

He had wanted to call the club "The Youth for Lincoln A.C." Well, finally, they compromised for they needed Iggy on the team, so they named it "Lincoln's Blackjacks."

In this time, Bennie stopped going to church and frequented the street corners with the Jewish boys who didn't go to church either. These were the impressionable years, between 13 and 17, when Bennie was observing people, concepts, relationships and feeling emotions within his body for the first time. The first look at any thing is startling and these people and feelings would never be seen or felt that way again. No wonder those images remained with him to his old age.

Sicily was fading, was not part of these impressionable years. Sicily remained behind in an age of innocence, a land without the disturbances of puberty and because of its innocence, it took on an aura of wholeness, the purity of a lost world. America became reality, reason, materialism. Sicily took on an importance which, as Sciascia was to remark later, "his parents never invested in it."

Puberty for boys who discover the explanation of the inexplicable feelings which provoke swellings between their legs, is, literally, a shocking experience. Can it be possible that his mother and father whom he loved and trusted engaged in such foul actions? Is that what those angry words his mother blurted out in the darkness were all about?

That afternoon he walked back across the sunny street to the apartment, "The Providence". With the street he discovered knowledge that he was the result of his father's fucking his mother and it angered him. The happiness he had felt evaporated; he would have to deal with girls in a different way now. He could no longer go to bed with many of them and they would not fondle him as a child and read books to him by the light of a flashlight under the covers with their warmth rising all around him. Comare Rosalia could not let him see her ass anymore; he could not look at her and say, "What a beautiful ass". All the affection women had shown him as a boy, unselfishly, would never be found again. He began to grow pubic hairs as if that swelling was ashamed of itself and would hide. He knew one thing—he'd never be able to do it with an Italian girl, not even married. He had known them all when he lived in *lu Vaticanu* and where they all could go to bed without provoking the swelling. He would marry an American.

That night he put himself to sleep with the song:

Sugnu na addrina spersa

ma nuddru mi ciama.

I'm a lost chicken

but nobody calls me.

And the memory of Cianciana as they approached it on horseback, he holding on to his grandfather and the fortress looming up in the rain and everything shining and clean....

The place where these thoughts were lived and experienced became reality and they were thought in the English language. He could wince to say fuck. The Sicilian word ficare, because he had learned it when it meant nothing to his body, simply evoked a fig. Assimilation was taking place creating an American inner moral climate.

Bennie left the house then, mentally and physically. He spent his time in the streets and became an American. His father and mother remained behind—Sicilians.

Teachers at P.S.200 gave him an image of America by flash cards with answers in the back which told him America was the land of the free, of equality, of the brave, of Washington the honest and the brave, of Lincoln the wise. The teachers left him their personalities too; Miss Borger a large loving woman who always wore a red pin with a hammer and sickle engraved in it. Miss Meane taught him punctuality.

If ever any of the boys came late she would put them under her desk and nonchalantly throw pencil shaving and scraps of paper in their faces as she went on with the lessons. One such day while huddled beneath her desk for having come late, squeezed in beside the wicker waste basket, Bennie could see Miss Meane's knees. She spread them apart and beyond and he discovered, with a gasp, the difference between grown men and women. Thereafter he climbed the high fence in order never to be caught coming late again.

Teresina became pregnant again and a depression set in, which became more severe after the birth of the girl who was named after the mother Calogera. Teresina's depression was called a "nerves break down". She was taken with fainting spells and fits of weeping which nothing seemed to alleviate. Angelina, Bastiano's wife, who had brought her mid—wifery skills from Racalmuto, diagnosed it as *na iettatura* attributed to the *mal'occhio*—the evil eye. In order to break these spells, Bastiano's wife performed her ceremonies. She came first with her cupping instruments: a copper penny wrapped in muslin which she dipped in a solution of olive oil and kerosine. She lit it and set it in a dish. Then held a glass cup over the small flame until a vacuum was created and the cup was quickly set on Teresina's pale flesh. There was a soft sucking sound and the cup stuck to the body and the flesh rose inside the cup. Angelina placed cup after cup on Teresina's shoulders and her sides; the red welted flesh rising in them made her look like a grotesque stained glass window.

After an appropriate time, as Angelina sat by her side and told her, "You mustn't discourage yourself in this way. These are trials the Lords sends." she began to remove the cups. They made a popping sound much like the sound children make, in puckering their lips.

The 'nerves break down' persisted and Angelina returned with leeches she had brought from Racalmuto and set them on Teresina's thighs and let them suck out the poisoned blood. Then she blessed water and oil and chanted a prayer to San Calogero. Only the severity of Teresina's anguish prevented Mike from shouting against such stupidities as he called them, while he muttered in the kitchen.

Teresina had difficulty getting out of bed in the morning.

In this time Bennie and Mike did the cooking and shopping. Bennie cleaned the floors and scrubbed the woodwork. When Mike was away on the W.P.A. job he did the cooking and even brought Mike his lunch as he sat with the W.P.A. crews on an empty lot used as a dump around Bay 50th which then was a desolate part of Brooklyn.

Teresina did not get better. On the suggestion of Angelina, they went to a reputed saintly woman in New Jersey who was in touch with Santa Teresa. Each night of the Saint's day, the shadow of the Saint, it was said, fell across the woman's body. She had great healing powers in *iettatura* and evil eye. With the help of Bastiano, Teresina with the baby Calogera went to stay at the retreat of the holy woman. Mike and the boys were left alone.

Left to themselves, the boy and his father came to know each other: besides the small conflicts of over the cleaning and dishes, the father and son were soon arguing politics.

Bennie began to frequent the Communists, although his father's Anarchist feelings provoked arguments. Yet Communism was America, it was in the streets, Anarchism was Sicilian. The Communist Club's headquarters were on 86th Street near Bay Parkway, above a shoe store. Its large window gave out to the West End elevated line. The stairs leading up to it were narrow and wooden at the landing there were two doors, one leading to the Communist Club, the other, on the right, to the Sons of Sicily where through its glass door, Bennie often could see a few old men sitting calmly playing cards. The symbolism was too perfect to be imagined or even for the boy to be aware of: the empty Sicilian club on the right, the Communist Club on the left, filled with young men and women.

The Communist Party, assimilated the boy into American life. It introduced him to a society of men and women who were equal and moved with each other easily, in English. They were America. The men and women spoke of their origins with an easy assurance and for the first time he heard Italians spoken of with genuine affection and admiration.

If he learned to read *Anti-During* and *Lenin on the Women Question* he also read Schalum Alechum and Giovanni Verga and Thomas Wolfe, of whom, Iggy Lapidus used to say, "If he had lived long enough he would have become one us."

On the corners of Brooklyn he became aware of world politics. The Spanish Civil War, since it coincided with his discovery of injustice came to personify Evil—in the person of General Franco. The war in Spain and the reaction of the young Baldassare was a preparation for the idealism of the young Communists who fought in World War II, and a source of love which the ethnic children were to feel for America. For the boy, the Spanish Civil War was a struggle between Evil (Franco) and Good (the Republic). The songs of the International Brigade, reverberated in his mind for a long time. That America was not on the side of Evil, and later certainly was on the side of Good, played a large role in the assimilation of the second generation of ethnic children. For the radical young in the Communist Party loved America as the possibility of justice it represented which from Baldassare's point of view, never existed in Sicily. Those with no political affiliation became "patriots" in the 1950's and 60's. For them, assimilation, their identity, was associated with America in its war against the Evil Hitler. The lines were so clearly drawn here. The evil men in America were Hamilton Fish, Martin Dies, Father Coughlin, Westbrook Pegler and their newspapers, *The Journal American* and *The Daily News*. The good men Tom Paine, Crispus Atkens, Jefferson, Lincoln, Clarence Darrow, Sacco and Vanzetti, Eugene V. Debs, all resonating in the mind with the voice of Paul Robeson.

America then, had the possibility of being good and this coincided with puberty's need for stability afforded by goodness. The children of immigrants found their American identity during their puberty; they discovered it with the same ardor as the first love in high school.

Those who found their American identity through radical politics in a way took the road of Sacco and Vanzetti and the traditional Sicilian radical road of those Socialists of Racalmuto such as Vella, Baeri and Ingrao. Those who did not, had more difficulty and many went into petty crime. Not one of those who became known as criminals in America had any experience with radical politics in their youth.

Lucky Luciano was a "patriot". Al Capone often said, "America has been good to me."

The Communist Party brought Mike and his son into conflict at a time when they were alone in the house and when father and son antagonism seems natural. The conflict took the form of the Anarchist father arguing with the Communist son. It was no use the father pointing out that the Communists were worse than the Capitalists who would create a tyranny—greater than any of the Capitalists could imagine.

The son said, "Yeah, greater than Hitler."

"The Communists murder people who are not willing to be regimented into their prison."

"The Red Army became so corrupt with power they became murderers."

"That was Trotsky."

"He was the greatest organizer of mass murder, your Trotsky."

"It's only temporary. The Dictatorship of the Working Class is necessary. We have come from a Dictatorship of the Bourgeoisie, when a class controlled everything: the newspapers, the radio, the means of production. Thus, if we don't use the same means, there will be a counter-revolution.... The Workers will lose power."

"Power will make racketeers of all of them. Why do you think poets kill themselves in Russia?"

"They are Bourgeois Romantics; and poets kill themselves in every country. And Iggy says every country kills their poets."

"That's no reason to kill a man."

"No wonder Sicily was a mess. Between those Bourgeois biscuits, and those lumpen proletariats. .. "

Mike could not help but smile with some satisfaction when he provoked the boy's anger this way. The boy interpreted the smile as ridicule, which hurt him all the more, for he sensed his father to be right.

For the boy, the Anarchist father was Sicily and these arguments made it all the more easy to reject Sicily and the father and to embrace America, Communist Idealism and his own independence.

Many years later Leonardo Sciascia was to write of Bennie: "He identified Sicily with the father: and therefore he detests and loves it. And he feels like...a bearer of betrayal and at the same time knowing the necessity of this betrayal; which after all is the *etat d'ame* of he who has crossed the line of integration."

Sciascia's remark is close to Braudel's observation about identity and culture that, "Civilizations are stubborn and cannot simply transplant themselves bag and baggage plant themselves bag and baggage. By crossing a frontier, the individual becomes a foreigner. He betrays his own civilization by leaving it behind." Since two men bear witness to the fact, it might be true.

It certainly was true for young Baldassare who no longer wanted to be called Baldassare, let alone Bennie. Only Ben would do. Yet the conflict remained. Many years later when he returned to Racalmuto as an adult he was hoping to find, if not some Anglo-Saxon ancestors in Sicily, then at least a Norman or two. He remembered a conversation with his aunts Rosa and Pippina.

"How was grandfather Giuliano?"

Rosa was sitting by the table shelling fava beans and Pippina opposite her was smashing them with a shoe-maker's hammer.

"What do you mean, Bennie?"

"I mean, was he big... or...?"

"No, he was short, like you, but *forte*, strong."

"I always imagined him to myself tall."

"No. He was short like you, but solid, not fat. Solid."

"He had fair skin, no?"

"Yes, like yours. So fair a skin that you could see his blood in his face."

"He had blue eyes, then?"

"No, he had brown eyes, like you." Rosa said.

"In all cases, he was of Norman origin, no?"

"No. He came from Campobello."

"No, I mean—his grandfather came from Normandy— his ancestors ..."

"They were all from Campobello; that is all they ever talked of."

"I always imagined them from Normandy."

"But where is Normandy?" Rosa finally asked.

"In France."

"Is that farther than Caltanissetta?"

"Yes, farther north than Italy."

"Farther than Rome?" Rosa asked.

"Yes."

And Rosa threw up her hands, "Never, Papa Giuliano never went farther than Caltanissetta."

Residues of the conflict between Sicily and America for Bennie's loyalty remained and it wasn't until he returned as a grown man, that the conflict was in some measure resolved. He remembered his feelings then as he left Racalmuto.

"Every one had come to the railroad station on the hill to say goodbye. Father Arrigo was there, Rosa who hadn't been up to the station in years, Pippina. On the train as it was turning I leaned out. The station was gone and I could see part of the village scattered down in the valley, and beyond it the wheat fields thick, the wind running vein-like across the valley where the Saracen's castle stood brooding, eying the train as it once again turned, slipped into a mountain, and was gone, while a shepherd boy in the midst of his goats waved his cap furiously as if he knew I was on the train and wished me a merry journey and many good things.I was saying goodbye to the image of Sicily I had carried with me since I was a boy. I discovered that day more than ever that I was an American. I preferred it that way in spite of the affection, trust and comfort I felt for Sicily. It would always remain with me and I knew I would return to Racalmuto. There could be no other way."

THE WARS

The outbreak of World War II was not greeted with enthusiasm in Racalmuto in 1940. Even the Fascists felt a foreboding. The official radio announced that the glorious troops of Italy had invaded France and defeated the French armies. The war would be even shorter than the Ethiopian War. A few cheered the news.

In the home of the former Fascist militiaman, Carmelo Buruano who, because of taxes imposed by the Fascists had turned anti-Fascist, the young often listened to Radio London. Sciascia went there along with Massena to hear that in reality Italy had entered the war when France was already defeated and that it was no victory of arms for Fascism. Some wept to hear Radio Paris: a woman's voice describing the misery of defeat, pleading with "Italy, sister Italy, help, help!" and "Mussolini's answer was to join Hitler and invade." The young men left the radio listening post, humiliated and ashamed.

There had always been an affection between France and Sicily; Pirandello had been discovered by the French, the painters Caruso and Guttuso spent their youth there, Sciascia was to be honored there, the Mediterranean Club began in Cefalù, many French conscientious objectors in the Great War had fled to Sicily. There were bonds between aristocrats, radicals, and workers. Articles often appeared in *L'Humanitè* about the barbarity of the work in the sulphur mines around Agrigento.

The break with France was the first of a long series of humiliations for Sicilians, brought on by Mussolini's War. Those who believed in Fascism, wrote a former mayor, only served, "to humiliate a generation of Italians, brought death long before their time to millions and ruined a nation."

The pattern of disaster for Racalmuto was the same as in World War I, only this time, intensified and brought home. The young men were once again called up and soon the fields were left without hands, the mines without workers. The natural flow of money, (that from relatives in America also) dried up, commerce came to a stand-still.

Food staples disappeared from the shops. Rationing broke down and a black market developed. Soon everyone, to survive, was dealing in it: old men, women, children, priests, all took part.

At each railroad station there were check points and one had to have a pass for everything one carried. No morsel of food could move without a pass. But police were bribed many resisted and the black market flourished. As the war worsened, the trains became fewer. To travel people hung from windows, the doors, and some even rode the roofs, "in the Indian manner," Raffaeli said. When the train slowed down, hundreds got on an off; boys with boxes; women, their black dresses stuffed with flour and food stuffs. It was impossible to check passes. The black market became the only market. Some became rich.

Towards the end of the war clothes also became scarce; Army uniforms bought on the black market were restyled; from old saddles, cobblers made shoes. When every bit of old cloth was resurrected from trunks and armories, some turned to the wool inside old mattresses which was spun into yarn and then knitted into sweaters. The poor walked on wooden slabs with nailed on canvas to hold the foot. Hunger became unbearable and women demonstrated in front of the Municipal Hall shouting, "Bread and Peace." The mayor promised them more flour coupons, but the women left, spitting at the bust of Mussolini set in the entrance by Don Rico.

In 1942 the Army took over the administration of Racalmuto. And as the war intensified, the soldiers began to go hungry also, and the townspeople saw them simply as their own boys. Many deserters began to trickle into town. A certain Totò Morreale who had left as a young doctor, returned from the Russian front. He had deserted from an Italian Division around Stalingrad. When asked with some astonishment and admiration, "How did you do it, you coming all that way?" he answered, "on foot."

If he had done the feat in the name of some ideology, or a victorious country, he no doubt would have been a hero of Spartan quality. As he returned to a suffering town, he was greeted with, "Eeh, you came all that way on foot! Bravo!"

By late 1942 the official bread allotment was reduced to 150 grams a day. A school teacher made 706 lire a month; bread on the black market was 100 lire a kilo, 1 cigarette 50 lire. A month's wages then could buy 7 loaves of bread or 14 cigarettes. At his point, American bombers intensified their attacks and at times dropped soap on which was written, "Wash your underwear, pigs." And in schools, students were to sing:

"*Vincere, Vincere, Vincere!* and we'll win in the skies, on land and on sea, and the order of the day, let it be of one supreme will."

The official radio, filled with much military music, was now being cut into by a partisan transmitter built by the Communist Polano, which gave news of an imminent invasion. Messana remembered that, "We entered in the organization already operating in Italy by the doing of Leonardo Sciascia.... He was responsible for the organizing of a students Anti-Fascist group... He helped us all to become aware of the true brutality of the Fascist regime."

One night, as rumors of the American invasion increased, the *Arcipreti*'s church was covered with Fascist appeals, "*Siciliani difendetevi!* " In the morning men passed, looked at the inscription and muttered, "You threw yourselves in; now we must defend ourselves."

Those who would defend themselves asked, "With what and what for?"

In July P47s flew low over the town, straffed the Mother Church and peppered the *chiazza* with bullets. A train sitting in the railroad station was hit and a number of passengers were killed. Then on one hot night, soldiers and police came out into the streets, church bells began to toll, loudspeakers, preceded by the sound of trumpets, announced, "The enemy has landed in Licata." That night a German unit appeared and camped, sullenly, near *La Baruna.*

The sight of the Germans was not reassuring. The town would be a target for the Allied bombers. And it did. Rosa of the Papa Giuliano family remembered, "They bombed everything—churches, villages, palaces, hovels, women in the fields, and every hay stack." Many remembered, "In the night and in the day the fields smelled of burning wheat." A woodsman, Nicolo Ciuni, was strafed and killed because he was wearing a black shirt, Raffaeli said, and to be kind he added "How were they to know that he wore the shirt because he was in mourning for his mother'?"

When the Germans moved on, there was a sense of relief and more rumors. "The Americans are in Comiti!" And the *Arcipreti* Casuccio and the *Maresciallo*—the chief of police—where sent out to meet them, carrying a white flag. The Fascist began to cut off their insignias. Everyone waited. The priest and the *Maresciallo* returned after two hours, having met no one on the road going to Campobello di Licata. The next day they took up the white flag and went out again. They returned to the Racalmuto again, having met no one.

On July 17 the police chief was walking in the out-skirts of town when he saw three soldiers whom he thought were Germans. One of them had a basin-like helmet and shouted, "Put your hands up" As he raised his hands, he knew they were not Germans. One was English, the others American. Word spread quickly, shouted from window to window, door to door, "*Ca sunnu! Ca sunnu!* They're here! They're here!"

"There was a moment," wrote Messana, of that day when the American troops entered Racalmuto, "as if we were suspended in air, we moved about frantically without accomplishing anything, a moment I would not want to experience again. When the two Americans began to say, "*Ehi, paisà, finiu la guerra. Ora si mangia.*" and they began to throw candies, soaps, tins of meat. The feeling changed to one of euphoria.

The streets filled with people to welcome the invaders. Men ran to the City Hall to destroy the symbols of Fascism. The tricolor was replaced with the stars and stripes, amidst the cries of "*Viva L'America!*" and "Down with Fascism and the Germans!"

Agro and Cravero, Fascists of little consequence, were taken prisoners and sent to "American concentration camps." The American, a certain Tony, who administered the town, became good friends with Don Rico and on the whole the real Fascists survived. Many who were not Fascists, were denounced as such and sent to camps. It was the old Fascist method of doing away with opponents by denouncing them as criminals. The humiliation continued. Famine for many could only be avoided by women turning whores for the allied troops. A woman known as *zia* Pippina, organized the prostitute trade, sending the wives and daughters of men who would have killed for an indiscreet look at their women, to the American camps where they served the troops. As the war ground on, hunger and destitution grew. Only those who had American military or Sicilian friends of the Americans, survived.

The men began to return from the wars, trickling in, in twos and threes. They found little comfort in Racalmuto where only mothers and wives of men still absent came to visit and ask about their men whom they had not seen or heard from for years. When the men had nothing to tell them, they went to La Pipituna who had set herself up as a clairvoyant who could speak with the missing men. Women brought her bread and earrings to hear the voices of their men speaking through La Pipituna. When news arrived that Mussolini had been executed by Italian partisans no one grieved. Some said his collaborators should have been shot also. The war dragged on and the years it took to come to an end saw most people in Racalmuto hungry and anguished.

The roots of post-war politics were set by the American Administrator, this certain Tony—who appointed Don Baldassare Tinebre as mayor. It was not long before he was dealing in the black market, working closely with hustlers in the American Army. His house was stoned a number of times by the angry people of the town who often heard trucks in the dead of night leaving his house— trucks loaded with medicines, food stuffs and grain while their children went hungry.

It is understandable then, if such men as Tinebre became leaders of the Separatist Party which would have Sicily break away from Italy and become "the 49th star in the American heaven." The Separatists had a following among those people who for the moment hated the King, Italy along with Mussolini who had dragged them into this disaster.

On windowless walls of houses where once the image of Mussolini glared down at passerby, there now appeared new slogans: *Abbasso L'Italia!* and *Viva la Sicilia Independente*. America was *a la mode*. Many became *Americanisti*. The language became peppered with "very well," "all right," "yes" was replacing "*si*". Raffaeli began to use "Sure, sure" more often, whenever he agreed with anyone, in his mocking way. The Separatists sang:

Dolce terra baciata dal sole
O Sicilia, di canti e d'amore,
Sopraffatta dal giogo straniero,
Ti daranno i tuoi figli
la libertà.
Noi ti faremo
e rossa e gialla
la tua bandiera, nelle tre punte
sventolerà.

Sicily of love and songs,
duped by foreigners games,
Your sons will give liberty.
We will make the red and yellow
your flag, and to the three points
it will wave.

The Italianists answered:
E la bandiera Italiana
sempre è stata la più bella.
Noi vogliamo sempre quella,
noi vogliamo la libertà.
The Italian flag has always been
the most beautiful.
We want liberty

Politics had taken hold again. The Social Democrats settled in the Circolo Unioni which caused a splitting that club. Some of the younger members—Sciascia, Messana, La Mastra, Cavallora—protested the politicalization of the Unioni and broke away to form a *Unioni* of their own. They met in the back hall of Farrauto's cafe.

On the evening of November, 1944, while sitting chatting, half listening to the him of the huge crowd in the *chiazza*, these young men suddenly heard the crack of pistol—the sound of running people. Then another shot. This time they saw the flash also. The gun was point towards them. They all flattened themselves against the wall. It was deathly silent outside. Little by little they heard a voice and then more voices. Messana looked at Sciascia, then Romano who stuck his head out of the door heard someone shout, "Mayor Tinebra has been shot dead!"

He had been shot while walking between his friends —the chief of police, Iacono on one side, and the police officer, Amato, on the other. The mayor had fallen, a bullet in the back of his neck, one hand in his pocket, the other, closed fist, at the base of his back. It was his habitual pose as he walked in the evenings in the square. Who had done it, or who hadn't done it, as they say in Racalmuto, no one ever really knew. A certain Carmelo Mattina was condemned to 24 years of prison for the crime. He was convicted because, shortly before the shooting he had asked the mayor for a job and had been rebuffed angrily, and one of the mayor's aides had even slapped his face. Some, like Sciascia and Messana, were not convinced. They knew that one shot had killed the mayor; the second was fired by the police officer Amato in the direction of the splinter Unioni Club. The bullet was found imbedded in the door about the level of a man's head. Did the mayor's friend think the first shot came from the Unioni Club? Was it a warning to them? Or was it just a settling of accounts between American black marketeers, as others said. All in all, it was the stuff of novels—Sicilian novels.

The Communist Party grew rapidly as the war came to an end. Led by old leaders, Romano, Picone and Macaluso, it also found new leaders among the young, such as Tascarella, Leone, Grillo and others.

It became the most popular party in the region. The Social Party had little success. Many new parties appeared, no doubt reflecting the outpouring of emotions released by the fall of Mussolini. There were the Liberal Party, the Sardo Action Party, the Republican Party and the Democratic Labor Party, founded by the murdered mayor Tinebra.

The Christian Democratic Party was formed by the priest La Russa. All these parties had to contend with the post-war disasters:

soldiers returning from prison camps all over the world, after doing what Raffaeli called, "War Tourism." They found no work. They returned with little idealism, with a shattered sense of self, a deep felt humiliation. Fascism was to lay heavily on the conscience of all particularly of the intellectuals. That *mauvaise conscience* helped explain the sympathetic attitude towards the Soviet Union which had bled so much for the victory. It helped explain, too, much of the creative energies of Sicilian writers such as Vittorini and Sciascia or the paintings of Guttuso—a creative energy which seemed to come from a need to explain one's relationship to Fascism. The great mass of the young had been brought up under a dictatorship and lost any sense of dialogue with an opposition. The young in all parties wanted to seize power.

The Communists awaited the revolution which seemed just around the corner, but never arrived. In the meantime, they demonstrated out of a rage for past sufferings and menacingly, on all occasions sang:

>L'operaio italiano
>va gridando rivoluzione.
>Rivoluzione si farà.
>Rivoluzione si farà.
>The worker shouts
>Revolution
>And revolution he will have.
>And revolution he will have.

Sesa, the Communist leader from Agrigento, came to Racalmuto and spoke to the crowd in the 18th century theater. He succeeded in moving them, especially the young Sciascia and Massena among them. The coming of Sesa with his eloquent pleas for Communism alarmed the clergy. Every priest from his pulpit began to speak of politics. The Monsignor Peruzzo came from Agrigento. His message was simple. He said, "You want Communism? Then you will see your Virgin of the Church of the Mount with a cord around her neck and dragged down the steps of Her Sanctuary!" Women wailed some strong men blanched. The town was split. The Communist went their way, the Church its way. The Communists spoke of revolution, the injustices of the Bourgeoisie, the hunger of the workers, the example of the Soviet Union, and the leader of the great war effort against Fascism, Joseph Stalin. The Church spoke of God. In the midst of all this, the Fascist began to reappear in a party called, *L'uomo qualunque*—or the party of Everyman.

The "time of the war" was coming to and end and becoming part of memory. The sulphur mines re-opened under the directions of the Vinciguerra family, ardent members of the Everyman Party. Their mines were on a "first friend come, first friend served basis". Only those friendly to the Everyman Party were hired. But when the mine owners saw the political winds changing, they, along with other neo-Fascists, moved towards the Christian Democrats. It was rumored that it was Father Peruzzo, now ArchBishop of Agrigento, who counselled young Catholics to united with the old Fascists politicians and those "virtuous men" who through the U.S. army had returned to power. It was this coalition, many felt, along with Raffaeli, that became the basis of the Christian Democratic Party. Raffaeli added, "and the virtuous men took over the Party." If I asked him if he meant mafia by virtuous men, he answered "mafia does not exists here. It has never existed here. These are just simple business men who use ingenious methods to make money, create jobs, bring prosperity, and order and well being to deserving communities." He said this with only a hint of his mocking tone.

The old Fascists remained with the Everyman Party and campaigned on the issue of law and order, reminding everyone that Mussolini had done away with crime and mafia. It was no use pointing out as Raffaeli often did that Fascism had simply replaced the extra-legal methods which suppressed any revolutionary or reform movements with its own. Fascism had a mafia mentality. Respect and reputation was everything and had to be maintained at the expense of reality. Mussolini's manly strutting hid a trembling weakness. The supposed law and order brought to Racalmuto by the Fascists also hid a terrible reality. Under Fascism crime existed even flourished in spite of the fact that in the name of law and order houses were searched and pillaged, men tortured. salt water forced into their stomachs, electric shocks sent through their bodies, people brutalized with whippings and castor oil.

A certain Sciascia (no relation to the writer) was murdered in 1935. A Salvatore Giancani was barbarously murdered in his home a few years later. The Fascist had a special method in dealing with crime. They used in this case. By torturing a suspect the man confessed to the murder. The crime was solved. Unfortunately the real murderer escaped to Africa. During the same period, a prostitute was found, her throat cut, in her home on the Via Madonna Rocca; another was found in pieces near Acqua Amara. Many of these crimes were "solved" by accusing an Anti-Fascist or a personal enemy of the regime, then torturing him until he "confessed". It was a way of getting rid of any anti-Fascist and at the same time "solving the problem of crime."

Yet many believed and still do that Fascism had brought law and order to the region and to this day vote for the neo-Fascists in every election. The local church had supported the Fascist regime and many a prelate still believed in the good old days of Fascism. From the pulpit priests preached the dangers of a victory for the left: churches would be destroyed, children taken away from their parents, husbands would leave their wives, priests would be killed and property confiscated. A vote for the Democratic Christian Party was a vote for the Church, its preservation.

The isolated life of most women (politics was a man's affair) made them believe these predictions. It was in vain that a few women such as Clementina Vince, running on the Democratic Labor Party ticket, spoke in the *chiazza* against such arguments. She was considered a heretic. The school teacher, Emanuela Baeri, also spoke to thunderous applause as she spoke for labor. In church she was insulted.

The Communist and Worker's Party both worked hard in organizing demonstrations. Each of their candidates was met at his home with a band playing and he was escorted to the *chiazza* where he spoke to the crowd. Parades were held daily; mass meetings were organized in the theater where speeches exuded much spleen against Don Rico Macaluso—the mayor in Fascist times.

During one parade, the Democratic Labor Party, women candidates up front, met with the Communist Party candidates and joined their banner, with its three stalks of wheat, to the Communist banner with its hammer and sickle. The day before the elections, the old Socialist Romano, spoke to a roaring crowd about "this wonderful opportunity that is within our grasp."

The high visibility of the Communists and Socialists would have made a stranger believe that they would easily win. It was to be another way; women, their shawls held to their faces, praying, some shouting "Viva Maria," went to vote. Old women who had not left their houses in years, were carted to the polls. The convent was emptied and nuns who had sworn to silence and isolation came out "to vote for the Church." Rosa of the Papa Giuliano family, laughingly tried to pronounce Democrazia Christiana, after a few attempts said, "I can't manage it, but that's who I'm voting for anyway."

When the votes were counted the majority went to the Christian Democrats and its supporters with 3714 votes. The Democratic Labor Party received 940 votes, The Socialists and Communists a total of 842. Don Enrico Macaluso, the ex-Fascist podestà was elected Mayor! Only the laws prohibiting Fascists from taking office prevented Don Rico from ruling once again. The Christian Democrats took power and the Socialist Labor Party was in official opposition. The Communists had no voice. Democracy had returned to Racalmuto. Young Sciascia could, along with Messana, the future Socialist mayor, now run with their banner in campaigns for the republic, singing *The Marseillaise.* And Father Arrigo, young Baldassare's God-father could speak in favor of the Republic. He often pointed to the buxom woman representing the Republic and said she was the Virgin Mary really, "All you good women should vote for her."

About this time the list of war dead and missing was compiled. The names were echoes of the list of those dead in war of 1915-1918.

In both lists there were 4 Macaluso, 3 Morreale, 4 Sciascia, 2 Chiodo, 4 Picone, 2 Petruzzella, 5 Risso and one each Cimino, Campanella, Puma, Tinebra. The names ran the gamut of all parties from Fascists to Anarchists. The war ended and politics had been reborn.

***

There was no humiliation for Americans in the War. For Bennie perhaps there were small humiliations. For a moment during the Hitler-Stalin pact everyone in the upstairs club of the Communist Party was stunned by the news; some left the Party in anger, others, like Ezra were immobilized. An American Peace Party was organized within the Party. A few dispiritedly attended meetings muttering, "It's to protect the Worker's State." The invasion of Russia by the Nazis changed the view as if by magic. Suddenly evil was on one side and good on the other. Again Bennie could sign petitions calling for the draft of all 18 year olds. When the Japanese bombed Pearl Harbor and Hitler and Mussolini declared war on the United States, there was a sudden co-ordination of good will. Ezra was joyous, "There comes a time when you can only smash heads. Talking must come to and end." In order to be with the people, as he said, rather than volunteer, he waited to be drafted.

There was an a feeling of good will in the air. Old men buttoned up young boys' coats, knowing that it wouldn't be long before they would be soldiers.

Bastiano's two eldest sons of the papa Giuliano family, were drafted. Many of time young men enlisted to avoid the being drafted, some in the paratroopers, others in the Air Force, a few in the quarter-master corp. There was not a week that men, boys really, did not leave in clusters of two and three to meet at Pennsylvania Station where they were met by a sargent to be taken off to Fort Dix. No one thought of evading the draft. Bennie, 17 at the time, needed his parents permission to enlist. He demanded Mike's permission. And this caused great arguments between father and son.

Mike for a long time had detested Roosevelt, calling him *lu sciancatu*,—the gimpy one—because he was a man who humiliated workers with useless work, a man who was leading the masses into a disastrous war, all because he sought power.

"He'll take you over there and have your throat cut in the name of the capitalists."

"You are not going as long as I command in this house'" Mike shouted angrily.

But as the draft took more and more men, the only argument Bennie had left was, "If I go, I can choose my position. I don't want to end up in the infantry."

The year after Pearl Harbor Mike gave in and on December 7, 1942 Bennie left for Fort Dix where he entered the Air Force as an Air Cadet.

After basic training he was called into an office where an officer from the adjutant's general department interrogated him.

"How does your father feel about Mussolini?"

"What do you mean?"

"Does he like him?"

"What do you mean?"

"Is your father a Fascist?"

"My father loves the country where he makes his living."

"You lived in Italy did you not?"

"Not long."

"Our records show you were there for two extended stays both rather long."

"That was not Italy, that was Sicily."

Bennie remembered: "The officer looked at me sternly as if to let me know he was no fool. And the interview was over. In a week, Bennie and a number of German-Americans who had spent time in Germany as boys, were on a boat to New Guinea."

The war for Bennie then, was spent in the most desolate valleys; Tetsli-Tetsli, Ramu, and Biak where he caught glimpses of the most primitive people; flew in planes happily; was close to death once in bombing raid; and one time, caught on an open air-strip, watched a Zero strafed in a line with him, watching the puffs of smoke and earth bouncing up off the ground coming straight at him, the wings of the Zero winking like fire flies at him, and then the puffs stopped just at his feet as the plane pulled up over him.

He saw the Islands of Mindoro and Luzon and was in the Philippines where Ezra was killed, and saw MacArthur rehearse his landing on Luzon several times before the photographers were permitted to take their shots.

The great ideals of the war, of course, faded in the day-to-day reality of the war. What remained was a true assimilation into American life. He learned Texas politics from a small man from Crockett, Texas who told him of Pappy Daniels who campaigned with a country band, and when people asked how was he going to bring about all those wonders he promised, he turned to the band and said, "Play' em another tune, Hezzie!"

He learned Southern folk songs from Beasely of Union Springs, Alabama, and often sang with him: "The hair round her pussy was piss-burn brown and the last time I seen her and I ain't seen her since. She was trying to fuck a nigger through a barbwire fence."

With Bill Novadjec from Detroit, he argued politics and learned of hatred for blacks in the auto factories—the fear and anxiety over jobs. "You won't talk like that," he'd end each argument with, "when you get back and find some black buck has got your job and been banging your girlfriend." Yet with all these men, on board an LST going up to Okinawa, singing with them, "What a difference a day makes when you're going to NaHa, as the fleet turned at a right angle and he could see the line of ships extending in both directions as far as the eye could see—and in the sunlight the American flag—he felt a closeness with all those around him and an affection for America, his country—the just, the noble, the good, that the young in Racalmuto do doubt never felt and yet wanted to feel and this was at the source of their humiliation.

The army, the war, was the final assimilation for Bennie and for the second generation Sicilian. It was the good war to which they all willingly sacrificed themselves and it became the source of passionate patriotism for many of the second generation. America after all had asked them to serve "their" country.

The dead in that community of Brooklyn were two: Ezra (Iggy) Lapidus and a boy who had no friends in among the living. The wounded were Irwin Greenberg, a painter who lost an eye in Southern France; Bernard Lipman who for a while was paralyzed from the waist down from shrapnel caught in the spine while jumping across the Rhine with the 82th Paratroopers; Frank Albi and Julie (Giuliano) Melluzzo, whose parents were born in Racalmuto.

The losses and suffering of those in Brooklyn were nowhere near the losses and suffering of those in Racalmuto. Yet in both communities the young felt a political commitment to making a better world. If Sciascia, Messana and their friends turned to radical politics, so did Bennie and his friends.

In Brooklyn they campaigned for Vito Marcantonio and Peter Caccioni, the Communist city council man from Bensonhurst.

If the young in Racalmuto were defeated by the old and the clergy, in America they were defeated by the same elements joining together in McCarthyism. Then too Bennie began to see that his father had been right about Stalin and the Communists; slowly he drifted away and was left with the intellectualism the Communists had instilled in him and he gave himself to an American education.

ENDINGS

Papa Giuliano, born in 1859, tree surgeon, father of eleven children, nine of whom went to America, died in Racalmuto in the winter of 1943, at the age of 84. He was buried in the Holy Field of Santa Maria beside his wife, Crucifissa who had died a few years before and his son Domenico who had been killed in France. All three of the dead stare out at whomever passes by from pictures imbedded in their tombstones.

The news of Papa Giuliano's death was kept from the children until after the war, when the letter edged in black arrived. Oddly enough none of the men in America of the Papa Giuliano family lived to be really old men. Bastiano, who suffered from an undiagnosed disease for years, died in Brooklyn soon after the war and was buried there. Sal, who had disappeared in the early 30's and who would appear every once in while to ask for money, reappeared for the funeral. Soon after he took a cure for alcoholism and spent the rest of his days working as a railroad hand. He died in a small town upstate New York. Bennie went to visit him just before Sal died.

He remembered the visit.

"I was directed to Pullman Alley, just up the street, past the old company store. It's being torn down, you can't miss it. Then turn right. You'll see some old railroad coaches. He's living in there. The only one still lived in. You'll see it."

Pullman Alley was a triangular piece of land where cars had once been set on cement blocks and transformed into apartments for the miners and railroad workers. At one time there had been twenty such cars, some divided into two apartments. Now only the shells of two were visible, the roofs gone, the windows paneless and through the young poplars one could see the remnants of a long line of cars disappearing into the woods."

Sal lived in the only car still in good repair. For fifteen years he had worked on the railroad labor gangs recruited from the skid rows of New York and Albany. He had lived most of that time in Albany, then up here where he had spent ten years with the railroad servicing the mines in the area. When the mines closed down he became a caretaker, looking after the trains that came up once every six months to pull out the scrap the salvage company sold. He spent his time keeping his railroad car neat as a pin, as old men do who had been great drinkers; cleaning his linoleum every day, washing the walls, painting them each fall and winter, and taking care of his garden where he grew tomatoes, peas and asparagus. He really kept his garden more to protect himself from the woods that grew closer and closer to his car every year. Even so, the woods had over run the two wagons shells beside his.

As the cab drove into the dirt road dogs began to bark. I could see a bald headed man leaning over the sink, peering out into the darkness. I remembered Sal a being fairly tall, solidly built. The door opened and in the light stood a small fat man, wiping his hands on a dish cloth.

Salvatore, the son of Papa Giuliano, who had come to America with Teresina, died soon after Bennie's visit and was buried in Batavia New York.

Most of the women of the Papa Giuliano family lived on to their 80's leading vigorous lives, hardly aware of the great migration and transformation of a group of people that they had taken part in.

Don Baldassare died in 1947 in the apartment on First Street and First Avenue, where he had lived for over 30 years. He spent his last days pacing slowly in the flat, his shawl hanging on his shoulders, a cap on his large head, and saying his rosary which he interrupted every now and then with, *"mi gira la testa*—my head is spinning." At times he would sit in the front room in a patch of sun, turning his head only when one of his children came in. Joe had become a shoemaker, almost forty now, not married, his face and shoulders constantly twitching nervously. Al was attending Cooper Union at night.

None of the grandchildren came to Don Baldassare's funeral. Bennie who was a Brooklyn College now was hardly aware of his passing. The war and the army had created a gap between him and most of the grandchildren that seemed an ocean in time and feeling. The grandfather was buried somewhere in the Bronx.

With the post-war years those who had come as young men and women settled into jobs they would hold for the rest of their lives. No one spoke of making films, becoming movie stars, or starting a spaghetti factory.

Mike worked for the next 15 years as a sleeve-maker for Rogers Peet while Teresina worked as an operator in one of those store-front dress shops on Bath Avenue. Between the two of them they put aside enough money to buy a brick house on Bay 29th Street.

Mike grew more and more fearful of life and the daily trip to Manhattan was torture. The work, piece-work, was a frantic scramble. The evening ride home he thought himself lucky because he found a seat at 14th Street and he could doze in the packed car, in the midst of the sallow-faced men, and haggard women. There was always an incident; a woman shouting "go feel up your sister, you pig!" Once a man died beside him. There was a women he met most every morning on the same train and in the evening; he was too tired to even answer her smile. She became part of his poems and songs.

> I was looking at your beautiful hand
> Repeated saying goodnight
> My friend.

> Then I understand!
> I will remember tomorrow morning
> to put it on pad lika' other poem.

> I never had such lovely heart.
> This beauty of living art.
> I'm hesitated to speak the truth.
> I'm afraid I may harm your heart.

He developed insomnia and soon became fearful of the subway, particularly when crossing the bridge. He was convinced that it would collapse. In the evening he would sit at the kitchen table after the evening meal and stick the labels he had taken off the coats he had worked on during the day, into a book which was a record of his wages.

Sometimes, by the kitchen table he would stop and take out his pad and write his "poultry," or work on his inventions. When he stopped work at age 62, he took to painting and making collages; worked on his inventions which he patented and tried to market. He wrote lawyers and engineers. But he had difficulty explaining his ideas and concepts in English or Italian. Out of the designs for his inventions he began to draw elaborate abstract constructions on larger and larger sketch pads. He used soft pencils and charcoals; and one day used oils on wood. When the children were all out of the house, he began painting on the walls of the house; in the hallway leading up to the apartment he painted yellow daisies the color of sulphur and in their midsts he had painted 1927. He was 72 then and in the ten years of his life he painted murals on the sewing room walls, the kitchen and part of the living room walls.

He never went into the city anymore. He walked about the neighborhood talking to children, men and women, and avoided dogs He walked endlessly down to the bay where once he had swum, over to Bay 13th Street where he had lived as a young man not far from Petruzzella, and back to Bay 50th street where all the old homes built by Sicilian masons had been torn down to make room for brick houses built by Trump. Her returned to sit facing one of the walls, and, still wearing his sweat-stained fedora, contemplated the wall, his paint brush, trowel and rags beside him. Sometimes he would just sit there and cry; once he scrawled "Abbey Lane" on the living room wall; on another he painted three rounds of cheese.

Teresina worked, saying if she stayed home she would lose her senses. And Mike filled her old age with kindness. He did the shopping cleaning and cooking. He always let her find dinner prepared, the table set, with a napkin neatly folded at her place. But she worried about him: she thought he might be going crazy. He feared everything: abarking dog, the sound of a siren, drafts of cold air, the sound of his own heart, above all he feared the coming of a new depression. He opened small savings accounts all over Brooklyn, as far as he could walk—at the Dimes Savings, The Williamsburgh Bank, The Chase Manhattan, The First National. He grew angry with Teresina over the house. He wanted to sell it because "when the depression comes they'll take it away from you." His plan was to sell the house at a high price, divide the money into small accounts and live in the an apartment, needing nobody. Yet he still looked through the real estate properties for a farm that would be converted into a small chicken farm, "Where we could all live lika people in harmonious with the nature."

When he turned 76, in spite of his poor circulation and his fear of the subway, he went to the Columbus Day Italian celebration held in Columbus Circle. He had heard about it from his cousin Mimi. He said he had had enough of Italians being *disprezzati*— disparaged. "Everybody wants something, The Blacks, The Jews, The *Portoricani*, and the Italians stay here like a bunch of *fissa*—cuckold fools."

He came back from the celebration with an exhilarating that lasted for weeks. He had been politicized for the last time. If his neighbors told mafia had organized the whole show, he answered, "You can be as stupid as you want, but the crowd that was there was there because they was Italian and if there was racketeers too, they was Italian too. We didn't invent *dilinquenza*. I gave my blood to this country; I don't know what it gave to me."

The last time he voted, he voted for Nixon. He talked to Bennie about politics, he expressed fears of blacks and criminals. Bennie once tried to talk to him, to ask, why he, an old Anarchist, had ended up voting for Nixon, but he never had the heart to bring up the subject.

Teresina voted for Nixon on the counsel of her boss at the shop where she picked up most of her political ideas. The store-front shop where Teresina worked was regulated by the International Ladies Garment Workers Union which closed its eyes to long hours and low wages paid by these sub-contractors. Teresina worked for a sub-contractor who paid non-union wages and who often declared bankruptcy.

After being closed for a month or so he would reopen under a new name, and he would pay 10 cents on the dollar, of the 400 or 500 he owed Teresina. It was a huge profit. The Union was paid off and if anyone complained there were the bosses hoods who would make them understand that it was to the benefit of all to keep their mouth shut.

Teresina, one of the best workers, who taught a whole generation of women to make wedding gowns, was paid 10 cents on a dollar after two such "bankruptcies". When Bennie wanted to see a lawyer, she would have none of it. The union officials in New York said they would look into it; nothing was ever done. Now that Teresina is old, the owner of the store-front factory comes in winter to pick her up in his Cadillac to drive her the two blocks to the shop where, at 74, her eyes going bad, she still works, saying, "What am I to do alone in the house" In the last days of his life Mike would come and sit by her side as she worked, and talk to her and help her thread a needle which she could not manage anymore. At times he would just sit silently beside her.

One day in the summer of 1977 Mike paced the small flat they had moved to on 20th Avenue; his circulation was poor, he was often cold and roamed the rooms closing the windows even on the hottest days. With his sweat-stained Fedora hat firmly on his head, he would sit in a patch of sunlight in the front room and if he got up suddenly he would have to hold on to the chair as he said, *"Mi gira la testa."*

One Friday he had difficulty breathing, he grew cold and frightened and sat on the floor. Teresina called for an ambulance and because his second son, Julie, was a sergeant now in the New York Police Department, squadcars came and escorted him to the hospital. In the emergency room tubes were stuffed down his nose. Mike's eyes, always deep set, had sunken into his head and seemed alive with fear. He asked for the children and the grand children; then he angrily pulled the tubes out of his nose and shortly thereafter died. He was 82.

The funeral was one of the last reunions of the Don Baldassare and *lu zi* Giuliano family. There were few nephews or nieces, although there were dozens scattered throughout the country. The children of Wallace had disappeared soon after his death, as had the children of Angelo. Some said they lived in Florida. Suzie's children were in California. Mike's brother Luigi came down from the Bronx, but his children did not. Al came, and stayed the three-day wake. Joe, who once had climbed the Williamsburgh Bridge, came to the funeral parlor close to St. Finbar's church, stayed for a few minutes and left, pleading nervousness.

Teresina sat in one of the front seats, watching Mike laid out in the coffin, his dead hands clutching a rosary. She wailed from time to time, "What am I going to do now, all alone?" Angelina and Santa, both women she had known in Racalmuto, sat by her side.

Bennie came down from Vermont where he was living and when he entered the funeral parlor, Teresina pointed to him and to Mike, "*Vidi*, your son has come."

For two days they sat and stood around the body and talked about everything but Mike.

A cousin of *lu zi* Giuliano who was a postman said in a reverent whisper, "I love going to Vegas... you know they take you, they pay for everything, flight, room, food. the rooms are really great, the food terrific. And then the show with Sinatra! I tell you, that Sinatra is something, always will be. That's what I love; going to Vegas and listening to Sinatra."

He was a small dark man who once had been a promising welterweight; he was still in good shape at 52.

"Vegas, I can drop a bundle, but the trip is all paid for."

"What if you don't gamble?"

"They know. I mean if they know they don' t ask you back."

A florid, red-haired man stood by the coffin touching Mike's dead hands with his finger tips and then crossing himself. This was another cousin who still worked on the docks as a longshoreman.

Gambling was still a big thing with Sicilians in Brooklyn. They began to talk of money and its risks. the red-haired man said, "I coulda made a fortune if I wanted to put money out on the streets. But I' m not that kind 'a guy. When I lend out 5 dollars, I want 5 dollars back."

He too had been a boxer in his youth. His eyes were scarred and one ear was puffed slightly. "You' ve been back to Racalmauto"he said to Bennie, and before he could answer, he went on, "I' m guna retire soon. I'd like to go see it. I was born there, but I came here when I was five, but I remember my father—rest in peace—talking about the sun and the fruit and how nice it was living there. I'd like go see it."

The women spoke of their children.

"Bennie is a *professuri O Vermunti*."

"My daughta' is married is an account' *O Stat 'Isle*."

"My Sonny is a managa' of a pencil factoria *O Connicuta'*."

"Charlie is postman."

"My Sal is *divorziatu* two times. And now he regrets his first marriage. She was such a nice girl."

Bennie wanted to be a pall bearer and carry Mike's coffin out of the church along with his brother and cousins, as he had so often seen done in Racalmuto. The funeral director though, said it would not seem right. A little to the side six men waited to carry the remains.

They were paid union wages to do so. It was part of the "package".

The last time Bennie had seen his father he had come directly to ask him how was it that he had voted for Nixon. Now as he followed the coffin out of the church he remembered in the strange way one remembers scenes at a funeral, that he had forgotten to bring cannole. Once it had been his custom to bring at least six each time he The apartment Mike lived in was the upstairs of a house that once had meant so much to a family from Naples. Now it needed painting. The porch was covered with thick layers of lumpy paint. On the walls along the stairs leading up to the apartment, Mike had painted yellow daisies, using a two-inch brush for the leaves and a trowel for the stems. Woven in between the grass and the stems of daisies, he had written in a fine script "Abbey Lane". And Bennie remembered that it was more than fifteen years ago that Mike had pointed to Xavier Cugat who was wearing an obvious wig and the singer Abbey Lane prancing about on the television screen and he had said, "Look at the embalmed face of a pig! He is older than me and he is married to her'"

He had grown restless that evening and walked from room to room of the big house they lived in then, staring at each wall. Bennie had gone past the "Abbey Lane" when he looked up and saw his mother at the head of the stairs looking down at him, her biceps like loaves of bread, her corseted body a tree trunk. She smiled, "Well, at last you show ow your faen around here."

"I see Pop has been at it again. When did he do this?"

"That fantasy took him two weeks ago. Don't get paint on you. It's still wet."

On the wall of the narrow hallway that led to the living room he had put together a collage—an old photograph of himself, sheepishly grinning, set on top of a missile about to be launched, aimed at rolling mountains he had painted high up near the ceiling. Among those mountains he had carefully pasted the face of Christ cut out from the Sunday papers one Easter. In the foreground he had painted a river, on its bank he had pasted a picture of a group of Australian life guards launching a boat. In the skies above the mountains he had painted pink clouds in the midst of which he had glued pictures of his two boys.

Teresina who never appeared in these murals, shrugged her shoulders, "Eeh, what can you do? These things take him sometimes..."

Bennie found Mike sitting in Teresina's sewing room, on small folding stool, wearing his old sweat-stained hat with a broad brim popular in the 1950's. He was staring at the narrow wall. He did not acknowledge Bennie's arrival and he went on whistling softly through the gap of his missing teeth. After a while he muttered "I can't whistle no more. I lost my pocker, purposely mispronouncing pucker. It was his way of greeting Bennie.

The wall before Mike was painted black, splattered white and green. "How do you like my fire flies?" he asked and before Bennie could answer, Mike said, "Come on, let's go eat." As they left, Bennie noticed in the corner as if a signature, 1927.

"I brought some cannoli," Bennie said.

"What for? To spoil my stomach? Ruin what's left of my teeth."

At the dinner table Bennie watched him eating, cutting his steak angrily, ripping it apart, then chewing on one side of his mouth, staring sullenly at the wall, until he suddenly grimaced, exposing his almost toothless mouth, pausing, almost in tears, then swallowing, and once again attacking the steak before him, grimly. Bennie wanted to ask him about Nixon but just then his father seemed to be removing himself from the life around him. Teresina put a platter of eggplant before him. He knew she had spent the night before cutting the eggplant into thick slices like bread, mixing the minced meat with mint, making sandwiches of it, simmering the tomato sauce and then the long walk to a special store that made mozzarella from a recipe

197

brought from Battipaglia. Then, after working the store-front dress shop until four in the afternoon, coming home to have the eggplant bake in the oven until it was crisp, almost dry. She knew Bennie liked it that way. Bennie knew too, with his mother, after he had asked her, "Are you still working?" and she answered, "What am I goin' to do? Stay in the house? My senses would leave me," there was little else to say. She cooked for Bennie as an act of affection and he ate because he didn't want to be indifferent to that affection. But then, with the wine it tasted like hazel nuts and mint in his mouth.

"It seems to me," Bennie said, "we never celebrated birthdays in our house, did we?"

"Sure," Teresina said. "When you was born we were making a party for you brother Giuliano."

"No, I mean in the old country in Sicily. You never celebrated a birthday, did you?"

"They only celebrated the *burday* of the saints over there," Mike said, mispronouncing birthday.

"What is the word for it in Sicilian."

Mike grew annoyed.

"Burday."

"No, come on."

"*Compleanno*," Teresina said.

"No, that's Italian, I mean in Sicilian."

"One says that it's the day one completed his year."

"No, I tell you, the celebrating is always for the saints and then it is a feast. The man is worth nothing," Mike said.

When Teresina brought the fennel in a bowl of ice, which she knew her son also liked, Bennie asked, "Have you heard from Julie?"

"Who hears from anybody? In this life there is nothing. Nailed to these four walls, like two old owls."

Teresina said nothing; she rubbed some bread crumbs between her fingers. It was growing dark out.

Mike suddenly stood up, stared down at the plate before him with the remnants of cheese, took a swallow of wine, put on his hat and went into the living room. The wine had made Bennie drowsy.

He napped and when he woke Teresina was cleaning up in the kitchen. It was almost dark out. Mike was sitting on his small stool facing the wall and softly whistling to himself. He was looking with head tilted at a sketch he had made on the wall.

"Pop," Bennie said, "Pop, I'm going."

Mike stopped whistling, "You just got here. "Then in Sicilian, "What are you doing, come to kiss the four walls and leave? Stay, stay." He began to stammer, which made him angry and, almost in tears. he added, "Stay. Mamma will make us a cup a coffe."

As he walked behind his father's coffin, he realized his father that evening, was leaving him his memories of his early days in America He talked of his real estate work, the movie house he once owned of which Bennie knew nothing, and how he enjoyed walking on Fifth Ave, "with spates on my shoes and cane wit a silver handle on top. But the world its shrunk hasn't it...? Look how small things have become."

It did seem, as the light faded as they drank their coffee that evening, that the world was shrinking; the corners of the room had disappeared, the paintings on the walls were gone, only the evening blue-tinted squares of windows remained and the mass of wall, and Mike's shadow talking.

"You know you had another brother?"

"What do you mean?"

"You were twelve and your brother five or six."

Teresina sighed, "He was *srematuratu*— how d'ye say. I almost lost my life."

"He was in a hurry," he heard his father's voice say, "he was in a hurry."

"We gave that child to poverty," Teresina said.

"If he had lived who knows what he might have become,"Mike said.

"Pa, what happened in 1927? "

In the shadows Mike stopped moving. "Nothing, Bennie, nothing.It's no use stirring manure that stinks."

When they could no longer see each other, Bennie left. Mike kissed him good-bye, walked him to his car and waved, his hand held high, in that beckoning way people have from Sicily which seems to say come back, come back, until Bennie turned the corner.

The funeral cortege of limousines drove across the Verenzano bridge to Staten Island and into the cemetery. The grave had been dug, the mound of earth beside it covered with a tarpaulin; the priest gave a short prayer; everyone was given a carnation and told to lay it on the coffin resting on a cart just above the open grave. The union grave diggers were waiting at a polite distance for the cars to leave before they would lower the coffin into the open ground and bury Mike in his 'final resting place' in Staten Island.

In the small apartment among Mike's affairs Bennie found a dozen bank books the total sum, although not large, still astounded the children. Teresina was indifferent to the money. High up in the closet, where the things of the dead were kept, Bennie found his father's inventions, his poetry and books on Yoga and the Single Tax. In a rust-colored pamphlet entitled *Gottlieb's Diary of Invention*, in which Gottlieb warned him to "make all entires (sic) in this diary with ink. Do not erase. If you make a mistake, cross same out so that it is legible and may be read. Use this dairy for one invention only." On each page was stamped, "Remember, keepa record." There were intricate designs for radio aerials, for space ships, for space ship stations, for gathering sun's rays to be stored in batteries. Behind each design Mike had written, "These space traveler and taker energy from these. Beneath each sketch he wrote:

"Idea originated 1935, March 28 or Idea came in 1934 June first." In with these sketches was a NASA design of space settlements which were startlingly like Mike's 1935 designs. Behind another, Bennie read, "Dear Son, May you having chance to know some sinetist to work the enargy of the sun paowerful magnatic class ray from Sun liker reflacs to could running dinimo— produce electricity from house use and industrial. Keep to your self before disposal to somebody patten in your name. your father, good luck."

Behind still another designs, he found written, "I am lonely man in lonely country." Among his books were his poems and many of Robert Frost's which he had copied out and incorporated into his own.

With the burial of Marcu of Don Baldassare family in Staten Island surrounded by neat faceless tombstones with names such as Quinn, Murphy, Dole and Hofstetter, The spelling is left as found.

Bennie was left with the feeling that the flow of people which had begun in the hill top villages of Sicily, trickled down to the towns and cities, then moved off to join the stream of other people to America to its cities, and finally spread tumultuously across the land to settle, much like silt after the flood—had come to an end.

Those left now are old, mostly old women, hardly aware of the great migration and transformation of a people they had taken part in.

On muggy summer evenings Teresina sits alone on the porch of the house on 20th Avenue and looks out to the Sunday—empty streets. She remembers those youthful voices in the fading summer light, muffled by the giant fig tree on Papa Giuliano's aria and by the kindly time itself—voices, at times whispers now, that carried nonetheless from valley to valley, as they cried out with astonishment:

"There are the lights of Grotte."

"There's Naru."

"No, that's Agrigento."

And close by she could see the light of her own town of Racalmuto.

AVA GARDNER'S BROTHER-IN-LAW

In 1972 my aunt Pippina, the sole survivor of the Melluzzo family entered the Orsolini nursing home. Thereafter when I returned to Racalmuto I stayed with a distant cousin, Cettina, a loving woman who never married. She had much love to give and cared for the old who lived in her narrow street; bringing a meal to an aging woman, feeding the birds her left over bread and the cats that quietly squatted at her door.

During one of my earlier trips to Racalmuto I met Salvatore (Turiddru) Sinatra with whom I enjoyed walking in the *chiazza* whenever I returned.

When my aunt died in 1984 I returned to settled her affairs and I walked in the *chiazza* with Turiddru Sinatra as if our conversations had not been interrupted by an absence, on my part, of now a year, now two, at times as much as five.

Turiddru Sinatra was a wiry man then in his late fifties who still had the hungry look I first saw in him soon after the war. He spoke French, some English, and sarcastically called himself the *pique assiette* of the Western World. He had always lived with his mother who put him through three years of law school which he never finished, after he had given up on a teaching certificate within a year of obtaining it. For a while he was called, with some Sicilian irony, the lawyer Sinatra, up until he wrote to Frank Sinatra, that is, who Turiddru was convinced was a cousin. Frank Sinatra did not answer but he did send Turiddru packages which arrived regularly every three months for two years. It was the sort of thing a relative from America would do. It was understandable then, if, when Frank Sinatra married Ava Gardner he became known as *Lu Cugnatu di* Ava Gardner, Ava Gardner's brother-in-law.

I never knew how he discovered I had arrived in town, but two days into my stay Turiddru would be at my aunt's door hungry for conversation.

I remember our conversions as we walked in the *chiazza*, stopped for a coffee, standing at the Taibi bar, or later driving to eat by the sea. The last time we talked was the time I went to settle my aunt Pippina's affairs.

I remember our last talks when we spoke of things no one else spoke of in Racalmuto. Let me put it down as I still hear in my head. Turiddru greeted me:

Turiddru Ah, Mr. *L'Americanu*, once again among the shrewd and the crazy. What brings you here this time?

I I've come to settle the affairs of my aunt, Turi, who's old and has retired to the convent of the Sisters of Mercy. And I like to be here, to walk these old streets, to listen. I find it restful after America.

Turiddru Restful! With all these gossips, all the eyes of the town on you, so that half the time you're living looking over your shoulder and not for yourself? But let us speak of things that matter. Do you think Frank Sinatra likes Mary McCarthy?

I I really don't know if Sinatra reads anything.

Turiddru He must. You don't become a singer of genius unless you are well read. I once read he liked Erskine Caldwell. Do you think he likes Mary McCarthy?

I I don't think any body reads her anymore. What a strange pair. But it makes me think: now if Mary McCarthy had made half the money Sinatra did or had his renown.

Turiddru What do you mean?

I Well it's what America thinks important. Sinatra, who's just a singer after all, is overwhelmed with money and attention—even honors. Mary McCarthy, a writer, well if she make 1/100 of the money—and you don't even know who she is married to.

Turiddru But there is a harmony in all that. Sinatra brings sweetness and pleasure to millions. Speaks of a haunting yearning in all of us. McCarthy writes as if she has a burr up her, if you will excuse the expression, *cher amis*, *culo* if not somewhere else.

I It is a question of fairness. Sinatra is just a singer

Turiddru Eeh! First, if there were justice in the world we'd all have voices like Sinatra and then where would we be. There will always be injustice, if we are to have geniuses. Or let me put it another way—as long as there are geniuses in the world there will be injustices in the world.

I   Then Sinatra is not a just man?

Turiddru   What makes you say that?

I   You say he is a genius and genius produces injustice, which confirms then what many have said of him that he hurts people, hurts many people with his arrogance and tyranny.

Turiddru   Genius can hurt and it can soothe. It can destroy and comfort. When Frank sings "Oh Black Magic" there is the echo of yearning as old as Magna Grecia itself. Or when he sings (and here Turiddru began to sing softly to himself, his eyes half closed, in the middle of the *chiazza*) "You are the dearest things I know... are what you are." I'd give anything to hear Frank sing that at the Sands in Las Vegas. You know I am just a bit younger than Frank. If my parents had gone to America who knows. It would be nice to have people point to you and say, there goes Turidru Sinatra. But you need an audience and here everyone believes himself a genius and there is no audience. All men see themselves to be the best lovers—in competition with any one, we will, outlast anyone—we believe it so much it is a reality. Sicilian men will die to prove it. Men are competitive and women are possessive. This is our apple of discord.

But that Frank—all those girls of the chorus line, eeh, old blue eyes, eeh!

I   There you are Turi. That's the evil of genius then, eeh. to treat women like meat. Here at least that is avoided, a woman has a role and look how furiously they play the role. My distant cousin, a woman of eighty-seven; she cooks, she shops, she walks loaded with vegetables, meat and cheese, up the long stony hill and will not let me lift a finger to help. She washed my underwear, the other day, and in a huff said, "I see you have been washing your own underwear." With pride she lets me know only women know how to wash clothes. And my aunt, she begs a ride to come all the way from Grotte, ten Kilometers, to make my bed.

They fight for the right to serve, not us, just to serve. It gives meaning to their lives. The greatest joy my cousin had these past few days was to discover I like artichokes. "He likes artichokes," she said to a friend. She called another and I heard her shouting to the neighbors, while I napped, "My cousin from America, he likes artichokes."

Turiddru   Eeh! you're right. You've put your finger on the blight of Sicily. I was served by women since childhood. The first and only son of a hero of the first great war, killed on the field of honor at Caporetto. I was caressed, coddled, taken to bed with many girls as a child. I still feel their warm mouths on my chubby cold feet, the smell of bread on their breath. And how I was told I was beautiful that with my blue eyes andfair skin, I'd be a prince. It was the educationof a rooster. How couldI ever find all that love once I went out into world. Only Frank Sinatra could achieve it, find all that adulation in the real world. It is his true genius. He found an audience to serve and had one which sends back rivers of love. He found harmony.

Our difficulty, we men of Sicily, is that we havea great need and talent to serve, but no one to give it to and we are forced into a role by women,because of their needs, into the role of roosters.We can marry, sire children, even have mistresses,imagine ourselves the world's best lovers. But our poor woman are forced into a role by the way ofthe world. And we men are forced to live too much in our heads here because reality is not livable.But we must permit women to serve us.

I   A fine excuse for a system that serves you well.

Turiddru   Sure I am the example of a man well served. I would rather belong to Sinatra's happy America, where women don't serve men, where love is made freely. If we made love here more freely there would be less warfare, less violence, let me tell you. As it is the only way we can show affection, that we care for one another is by killing each other.

I   You speak of America like a priest speaks to a child about heaven. Turi, America too is in your head.

Turiddru   Excuse me, in many ways I am a fool, if not I would not be in my present condition—approaching sixty—my life a long complaining desire—but I know of no one who has died, gone to heaven and returned to tell me about its wonders. You on the contrary, go to America and return, many times. That is reality. And there are books. I read them. America has a language, it speaks to me.

Heaven has no language. America speaks to me in John O'hara, Melville, in Hemingway, Mary McCarthy. America is a reality, my friend.

I It is your America, Turi. American women do serve men you know. I've seen ardent feminists fight over men.

Turiddru Feudal vestiges, the nunneries play the same role as feminism here. Vestiges nothing but vestiges of a dying way of life.

I And you really believe American women freer, that they make love more freely and according to you then we should be happier, less violent?

Turiddru Where could there be more violence, less happiness, more emotional misery than here?

I Turi! There is more rape in Los Angles than in all of Sicily. More murder in Phoenix or Dallas than in Palermo. More women battered, not to speak of the violence we perpetrate on others; the Indian, the Asian, the Latin American. We have our need to be roosters. And it makes for a great deal of violence and not much happiness. God look at our alcoholism, our rate of divorce; In America you wake up at forty with two houses, two cars, two children and one wife and you start wondering if there is something wrong with you. And you start using women for...

Turiddru And why not the blacks, you left out the blacks and the buffalo, the very air you breath. You have the sense of the Christian martyr. These are the difficulties of a society in transition, the mixing of races, the turmoil of the emerging new way of life. Frank and his friends don't have a problem of violence.

I Sure their violence is against women. You don't think the use they make of the chorus line at Las Vegas is violence against women. The violence of men using their position, their power to dominate, humiliate, by forcing women to perform, sexually? If you went there do you think you'd have choice of the chorus line women; it would be the powerless meeting the powerless.

Turiddru The girls of the chorus don't have to go if they don't want to. They are free to choose.

I No they are not. They must chose the men with power. They would not chose you; you are powerless. The violence of Frank

Sinatra is institutionalized violence—power—telling women to dance *cu culu di fora*, to jump through sexual hoops. It is a subtle violence but nonetheless violence. It is not fair.

Turiddru   Life is unfair.

I   How comfortable. The lazy and the rich always say, "life is unfair". How comfortable, how comfortable for those who after a good meal, good wine to look out at the beggars of the world and say, "life is unfair". It is not enough to say life is unfair. What are you going to do about the unfairness?

Turiddru   Just being born is unfair. And we can't do anything about that, except to lead a full life as Frank does, the life most of us would lead if we had the power and the money Frank has. There are no new vices you know. What is wonderful about America is that vice which once were considered aristocratic are open to all. Look at John Kennedy from an Irish peasant family to the world of Frank Sinatra.

I   And what would you do if you had the power and the money of Frank Sinatra?

Turiddru   Ah! I would eat well, have my person taken care of, baths, coiffure. And I would have many women—see what are the possibilities of my sexual appetite. I'd permit myself to fall in love and marry and divorce and marry. Until I found my true love. And I'd tell people what songs to write, what films to make, who was to play in them. I would tell this one "you can be published" to the other "you cannot be published." I'd make careers and unmake them. In a word the same old vices; but they would be American. That is, the wealth and the women/men relationships would be in circulation. But as it is here where the wealth and women are just held onto and nothing grows. But most of all I would like to come home to an elegant apartment, filled with white furniture and a phone would ring as soon as I came home. I would like that.

I   I don't think you understand, Turi. We pay and have paid a high price for what you call growth. My aunt, whose affairs I've come to settle, has seen all her brothers and sisters go to America. Her life had been devoted to caring for them. They went and lived in buildings dank with the smell of urine. Three died of tuberculosis, one was killed in a steel mill accident. One died in the Great War, the women lived among the insults of immigrants who had preceded them by a few decades. My father who worked as a laborer had to admit that America was better, not that where he had come from was inferior—mind you— but he had to admit simply that America was better. Do you understand that subtlety?

Turiddru Of course, it is very Pirandellian. But all that suffering has made it possible for you to be what you are: an American. I remember you the first time you came from Paris in an automobile. We were living on wind and smoke here. It was a thing Frank Sinatra would have done, coming from Paris in a car as an American. All your relatives worked and suffered, so that you didn't have to live as I live. Here, the suffering simply goes on and on.

I You have your dignity.

Turiddru Bah! Dignity without power or money is humiliation.

I Power without dignity is brutality. And we are not any happier for it. You know. Look, I've seen men reach the age of forty, fifty, even sixty-nine and look around at their two cars, two houses and one wife and they soon begin to think they must consume women. We are not happier for our growth as you say.

Turiddru I know. You keep saying that. But, better to consume than to be consumed by these abstract furies.

I Consuming others leads to bad conscience.

Turiddru Only when you are not in harmony with your true nature. And it is a question of liberty too.

I But liberty without conscience is to put no limits on liberty. Where do you draw the line?

Turiddru I don't draw lines; lines appear. The wonder of America is that freedom of enterprise is translated to everything, commerce, religion, education, marriage and divorce. And you are right; we all want to consume and what greater logic than to enjoy people, in the free exchange of human commerce. What greater logic than to enjoy people. I would prefer to say, enjoy people, not to consume them.

I As you would enjoy a t.v. set, a new car. These are objects Turi. We are talking about human beings. And once you abstract people then you can do anything you want to them. What do you think Hitler was all about?

Turiddru Now don't you abstract. Of course, a t.v., a new car I would enjoy as an object. A woman I enjoy as a relationship to a human being who has the ability to love me, to hate me. She has the freedom to chose, to develop, to grow because of the joy or suffering of knowing me.

I Sure, grow, discover. And how could you with your Sicilian jealousy accommodate to having a woman who has been another man's. Who has been with another man? After all Ava Gardner had been married to Mickey Rooney before she married Frank Sinatra and here in Sicily if a man looks at another man's woman she is compromised in the spasm of a glance. You know as well as I do the word for widow in Sicilian is *cattiva*, evil.

Turiddru Oh this much touted Sicilian jealousy. First of all the word *cattiva*—might refer to the condition of widowhood of being alone—the evil of being alone. Look, I was captured in North Africa and I did the war tourism like so many in this town. I was sent to Yorkshire, Hull, and Darlington, in England. I've lived in Paris for a year; not under the best of conditions, but I've lived there just the same. I've seen other ways of living. And I can tell you—our jealousy here comes from our insecurities, our paura storica—from our historical fear.

Have you ever seen even those playful sails in summer rise out of the horizon and grow larger and larger. Imagine what it must have been like for centuries on this Island, crossroads of the Mediterranean World. Pirates, marauders, conquerors, men, insane men, storming our village and mounting our women. Racalmuto came into existence because people fled the coastal towns such as Agrigento which were constantly sacked by the insane of the world. Centuries of insecurities have been hoarded in the image of women. Roba wealth, stable wealth, land, houses and women, these are the two things which comfort the insecure; you save, you hoard, never take risks with money or women. So, if you touch the only thing giving a sense of security to men, you touch his vitals. And that is why the Sicilian is a great lover; his insecurities makes him imagine all kinds of images, producing jealousy and what is more flattering than a jealous lover.

I Turi, you'd be mince meat within a year in America.

Turiddru No. Jealousy is a great aphrodisiac. It is! And a form of violence, a self inflicting wound and a murderous feeling and it often leads to suicide or murder. Here it is most often murder.

I And in America it...

Turiddru No let me finish. Jealousy here is not real. It's just a way of controlling our women. Who would think of betraying even the most insupportable man when he is insanely jealous? So women find subtle ways of dominating.

I And in America jealousy leads to suicide. Look at Sinatra. They'd make mince meat of you in America. In no time, mince meat.

Turiddru Sinatra learned to accommodate. I would too.

I Look at Sinatra. At what price? He must have gone through his own season in hell with Ava Gardner.

Turiddru Sure. But what an experience eeh! Only a Sicilian can understand what he went through. It's consuming pride —a wound without healing. But I've fallen in the Sicilian abyss—abstraction. As if I am Sicily. Can't you see the consuming pride in all this?

I You exaggerate.

Turiddru Sicily is an exaggeration... has been for two thousand years. But we exaggerate because we abstract. I am incapable of talking, in all my suffering, about a relationship between a man and a woman, a man and a man, a woman and a priest, a child and a mother, without abstracting and turning it into an absolute. I knew a writer, Buonaviri, and in the morning I'd call him "what are you doing Giuseppe?' I'd ask. And without hesitating he answered, "I'm thinking of death" And you know why? Because we all aspire to be Gods and when we look around us and we see that we live like failed humans. We are, as the French say, ambitieux rates, worse we are des dieux rates—failed gods. Here too I'm abstracting. What I can't say in my own tongue is that I am an ambitieux rate. An ambitious failure.

I   It's the fault of the language, Turi.

Turiddru   What do you mean?

I   Italian sounds lovely. People like to hear it, it's melodious, limpid, and you say things just for the beauty of hearing it. The language makes you think you're important. It turned a fop like D'Annuzio into a hero. And listeners into sheep. I once heard Sara Ferratti, the actress, read the telephone book in Rome. She moved me, us to tears.

Turiddru   That may be so. It's the banality of our lives. But we have to live with it. Let me be more specific then. For years I wrote songs and sang as a young man without success. I followed the Pepi Boda show around Sicily—nothing. I wrote stories of my adventures around Sicily—a novel about Paris too. I took it with my own hands to and editor in Caltanissetta. "it is well done", I was told, "but this has been done so often, it will not sell". and I saw the greatest of stupidities being published—and my songs—I couldn't get a shepherd to sing them on Christmas eve—songs which I tore my heart out to write. I was left braying like a jackass, "Oh these successful writer like Sciascia". So I started painting, the metier of the solitary and the independent of those with pride and no power. But even that is frozen here. Guttuso and Bruno Caruso, great painters, but they are traditionalists, fine craftsmen of the line drawing, depth of perception, intelligent, committed, but the kind of talent needing years of study and practice, as old as Leonardo, the art of the elite and talented, *quoi*. In America art is open to everyone; a bucket of paint sprinkled on a canvas—*voila*! Jackson Pollack, Hans Hoffman. Even art has been opened to all in America. Oh Beatific America!

I   But how limiting. No boundaries. No boundaries in this school of bucket and sprinkle painting

Turiddru   Not to the artist.

I   I can't even call it a school of painting. In that painting there is no tie to the audience, who loves a story faces tell, and gestures. The abstract loses all that. It becomes like you; talk only a few can listen to it and everyone else is bored.

Turiddru   But the artist finds himself in his art with the hope others will find him in his work. If the artist has lost his audience, or if the audience has shrunk—so what. What is important is that now every man is capable of being an artist. Oh Beatific America where every man is capable of becoming a Frank Sinatra.

I Turi, how can you see so clearly about Sicily and yet be so muddled about America and yourself. You love America because you hate Sicily.

Turiddru I see myself too clearly there lies my difficulty. And you might like Sicily because you dislike America.

I That's not so. To love an America that does not exist is no solution. Why have you given up on your writing? And don't tell me it's your Sicilian pride. Have you tried other editors, other pleasures, satisfactions?

Turiddru That, no! I won't grovel before editors and journalists, because in this country if you are not taken by a friend, only the wife of the concierge will read you and it ends there. Everything thing here begins and ends with a friend, *L'amici*. Now I have no friends in court. No, let me be honest. If my work isn't startling enough to seize the first editor then it is not good enough.

Pleasures? Now I can only revel in the pleasures I find on other men's sorrows. I read only the bad reviews of films, of books, of tenors who were booed off the stage.

I Turi?

Turiddru Yes?

I Can I tell you something?

Turiddru Certainly.

I You won't be offended?

Turiddru I am beyond offense.

I I am simply wanting to understand.

Turiddru If I can contribute to human understanding, I am at your service.

I People here seem pigheaded and some are obsessed and call it pride. Why beat your head against the wall as they say at home. There are so many pleasures in life, things to give yourself to. Why didn't you marry. If I may speak clearly.... why didn't you? For most of us the family is a comfort; a good wife, the pleasures of raising a son, a daughter, the ability to love and be loved. We find our satisfaction where we can. I'm sorry if this sounds like a banality, but even banalities must be confronted as possibilities helping us to live. If you took away child bearing and all that surrounds it: courtship, love-making, birth, raising the child—most people would have little reason to live. You've missed out...

Turiddru   You've missed the point, *cher ami*. Let me put it this way, because I don't want to be abstract.

In Rome, many years ago, I met a young and beautiful woman who came with me to Sicily. She was from Finland, a head mistress of a kindergarten.

Every summer she came to Italy to be wicked. I fluttered around her like a bird, puffing up my chest, sticking out my bottom: I did a fandango. I bought her flowers, scarves and small blue earring. I dined her; I wined her; I nearly bankrupted my mother. We stayed in Mondello and one night while the lights of the automobiles descending from Mount Pellegrino stared down at us I made furious love to her. I was insane. the things I did were maddening, a pleasure as old and hysterical as life itself—all in telling her 'I love you' almost as a shield against the desire I had to kill her.

I   Good God! What for?

Turiddru   What for? I resented, I hated her freedom, her freedom as a woman capable of inexhaustible desire. I pummeled her with love. She mistook it for ardor. I left her in the early morning. The next day I met her in the piazza. She looked so common and ordinary to me.

I   Poor woman.

Turiddru   She smelled slightly of decay. What was all the fuss about? I asked myself. I turned and walked away without saying a word as if I had never known her.

I   The poor woman.

Turiddru   Far from that. And I tell you this because it is not an abstraction. But how could I tell her I felt disabused. The pleasure she had provoked in me had turned to the hatred of one who realized he had been dominated, subjugated to another will. What we call here being cuckold. I was ashamed and could not look her in the eye. Then too how could any woman come up to the images of woman I had been tediously weaving for ten years as I watched roosters proudly mount hens in the streets or Lana Turner come walking towards me in her soft sweater in the darkness of our sweat smelling cinema.

Is it true that Sinatra made it with Lana Turner?

I. I don't know. But it was a lot to lay on that poor woman.

Turiddru What do you mean? All I laid on her was myself.

I I mean abstractly. It's a way we have of speaking at home. To lay your troubles on to some one else. She made use of you too. Abstractly or otherwise.

Turiddru The abstractions certainly laid on to me over the years. I just had it with women. It was not time and it is not time to be living with them. There is a great divorce between men and women just now.

I Hasn't there always been. I once met a women whose father had molest...

Turiddru No, not more insanity. Maybe in time we can find a better arrangement; but right now we can only make each other sick. All the accoutrements of childbearing you speak of; love is sick, companionship is sick, friendship between men and women is sick and those who live ensemble are just pretending. The world is being Sicilianized.

I Come on. Quit bragging. Let me tell you I once knew...

Turiddru No, for us men here there is something else. There is the inability to give ourselves to someone else. We can't even give ourselves to God. Look how few men are truly Christian in this cuckold country— the churches in Sicily are filled with women but you'll find only a few frightened and defeated men there. How can Sicilian men believe in a religion whose founder is a cuckold, cuckold for having himself killed that way, for being made a fool. Because in Sicily death is the ultimate cuckoldry. It is the ultimate subjugation and why our pleasures come from other men's sorrows. And we grieve for other mens' successes.

I Goddamn it, Turi, if you understand, why don't you do something about it! What a waste of human intelligence.

Turiddru About what? Excuse me. I don't mean to be dull. Do you mean my relationship to women? That is not determined by me. For all our roosterism we men of Sicily are led by our noses by women. Let me tell you, with the woman from Finland I learned something. She made me feel a responsibility to play the role of the ardent Sicilian. What a responsibility! Thank God my organs were functioning *a merveille.* I learned then the role of ardent Sicilian did not suit me. I was a hypocrite, that is, I was not in harmony with the world. I was playing the role she wanted me to play.

I So she turned you into an abstraction and you didn't like it. But why the desire to kill?

Turiddru Because she made me aware of how much I needed women—that kind of woman—the eternal slut of inexhaustible desire who serves innumerable men and their desires. I learned the source of that great and sad Sicilian jealousy, at heart came from the realization that a woman is always calculated, controlled but capable of inexhaustible lust and I thought I could overwhelm that lust. And because of the primeval stupidity, how much of life, mens' lives, really was a failure; I wanted to kill her because she made me see what I would become in twenty years, because I saw myself as I am now.

I Turi, Turi.

Turiddru What?

I Why didn't you kill her?

Turiddru Because Frank Sinatra would never do a thing like that. And I am a sensitive soul which is a way of saying I am crazy in a different way. In any case, we rarely kill women here. Our insanity comes from other men. Our pleasure comes from seeing other men suffer and we are pleased that women can make us rage so we can go out and kill men. Why destroy the source of our pleasure.

(He points) See that girl passing, going to church of the Madonna of the Mount, wearing tight jeans like that? You would say something has changed; nothing has changed. We used to be controlled by the black skirt draped over the curve of a buttock— now it is the tight blue jeans in the shape of mandolin. And I feel a great sorrow for that girl. It is the only way she can survive.

I But Turi, what is it that you want now?

Turiddru Ohfff. I would like to have an apartment of my own with a phone and have it ring the moment I came home.

I   You ought to think of the things you really need.

Turiddru   Harmony with the world the way it really is and my nature. As Frank Sinatra has found. He would be as crazy as I am if he had not found harmony. Harmony! Harmony is a way of saying a state of grace and then I will be ready to die, to leave.

We have the gift of time—an impasto of life and death— time in which to find harmony, a state of grace. My state of grace would be to come home to an apartment and have my phone ring as soon as the door was closed behind me, not before or after, but as soon as I closed the door behind me. That would be nice.

I   Turi, you sound like a character out of a Pirandello play.

Turiddru   Where do you think Pirandello found his characters? Right here in the piazza, listening to the likes of me. Men who could not live their meager lives without imagining they were Gods in search of believers.

Let me tell you, in the face of all this imposing talk, do you know how I spend my days? In the morning I have a bowl of milk with a spot of coffee. My head is thick with reading I did the night before. I pick up the few lira my mother has left me on the table and I walk, avoiding the twenty-four imbeciles I must meet before I encounter one intelligent man. At noon I return to my mother's house and there I have a plate of escarole, bread and cheese. In winter, lentils and chicory. In the evening a bowl of milk and left over bread, after which I walk in the piazza hoping once again to find an intelligent man. Around ten o'clock I'm back in my room to read and wait for a song or a poem to come to me. In the morning my mother silently shuffles in the kitchen which smells of ancient decay. I rise to find the bowl of milk with a spot of coffee waiting for me and few lire on the table. How else could one lead such a life without imagining oneself a God, especially when I know I am related to Ava Gardner. So I sit and wait, knowing that time is a gentleman and forgives us everything.

***

When I went to the house on Cavour Street which had been Papa Giuliano's house from which all his children, including my mother had left for America, except Pina, and where I had spent my childhood, the house was empty, picked clean of all the cane bottom chairs once lining the room, the beds in the alcove, the armoire. The house had been pillaged by the neighbors and a priest who would never have touched a wet rag in the house while Pina lived there. Once it was known she had put herself away in the convent, the house was stripped clean. There were no relatives living in the town and only my mother was left in Brooklyn.

Up in the second floor where I once slept as a boy, there still was the reproduction of Christ tearing his chest apart to expose his bleeding heart, speckled with fly droppings. By the window was the trunk I used to stand on in order to see the Norman castle down by *La Baruna*. Inside the trunk I found pictures of marriages, confirmations, graduations, of men and women on the roofs of New York, in gardens in the suburbs of Argentina, one before a restaurant in Houston Texas.

One large picture was of my uncle in front of his grocery store in Brooklyn and in the foreground I recognized Ezra Lapidus, Iggy, who was killed in the Philippines in 1945. In the picture he is a boy of ten or so and he is holding a pineapple. Underneath the pictures, scattered about, were letters of the son Dominick killed in France in 1917. All his letters began "Beloved parents".

Now in Racalmuto 1996 no one remembers Ava Gardner's brother-in-law or Turiddru Sinatra. Some say he died somewhere in France or in Germany.

**AGMV
MARQUIS**
Québec, Canada
2000